D1760676

The Primary Science and Technology Encyclopedia

Unique in its field, *The Primary Science and Technology Encyclopedia* brings together in one indispensable reference volume over 250 entries covering a wide range of topics and ideas. The book provides clear descriptions, definitions and explanations of difficult scientific concepts, carefully chosen to reflect the needs of those involved in primary science education. In addition, this encyclopedia explains clearly how to teach scientific and technological ideas in a relevant and appropriate way. Extended entries are included on topics such as creativity, thinking skills and theories of learning and the book also provides insight into cross-curricular work, assessment and classroom organisation in the primary science classroom.

Compiled by authors with a wealth of experience in primary science and technology teaching, this book contains:

- Over 250 entries;
- Scientific definitions and pedagogical explanations;
- Extensive commentaries of current issues in primary science;
- A who's who of current and historical figures in the fields of science and science education;
- Annotated further reading lists.

This encyclopedia will be of interest to all teachers of 5 to 11-year-olds and anyone concerned with primary science and design and technology education.

Christopher Collier is Senior Lecturer in Primary Science at Bath Spa University and leads the BSU course for Primary Science Subject leaders.

Dan Davies is Head of Applied Research and Consultancy at Bath Spa University and founder of the Centre for Research in Early Scientific Learning.

Alan Howe has 16 years' experience of working with trainee teachers in primary science and is Co-Programme Leader for undergraduate Education Studies at Bath Spa University.

Kendra McMahon is Senior Lecturer in Primary Science at Bath Spa University and is science coordinator for the Primary and Early Years PGCE course at BSU.

The Primary Science and Technology Encyclopedia

Christopher Collier,
Dan Davies,
Alan Howe
and
Kendra McMahon

Illustrations by
Rebecca Digby

 Routledge
Taylor & Francis Group

LONDON AND NEW YORK

This first edition published 2011
by Routledge
2 Park Square, Milton Park, Abingdon, Oxon, OX14 4RN

Simultaneously published in the USA and Canada
by Routledge
270 Madison Avenue, New York, NY 10016

Routledge is an imprint of the Taylor & Francis Group, an informa business

© 2011 Christopher Collier, Dan Davies, Alan Howe and Kendra McMahon

Typeset in Garamand by
Exeter Premedia Services, Chennai, India
Printed and bound in Great Britain by
TJ International Ltd, Padstow, Cornwall

British Library Cataloguing in Publication Data
A catalogue record for this book is available from the British Library

Library of Congress Cataloging-in-Publication Data
The primary science and technology encyclopedia / by
Christopher Collier ... [et al.].
      p. cm.
Includes bibliographical references and index.
   1. Science—Study and teaching (Elementary)—Encyclopedias. 2.
Technology—Study and teaching (Elementary)—Encyclopedias. I. Collier,
Christopher
   LB1585.P744 2011
   372.3'503--dc22
                              2010031447

ISBN13: 978-0-415-47818-2 (hbk)
ISBN13: 978-0-415-47819-9 (pbk)
ISBN13: 978-0-203-83224-0 (ebk)

CC – to Becky, Eric and April
DD – to Sally, Philip and Jacob
KM – to Kevan, Jordan, Elliott and Lily
AH – to Alison, Holly, Caleb and Hattie

Contents

List of Illustrations

List of Entries

Introduction

This encyclopedia is written with primary school teachers in mind, both those in training and those in service, although it may also interest anyone concerned with primary science and technology. It may even appeal to a more general audience of those just wishing to discover more about the world of science and technology. It is a little different to a traditional encyclopedia – it does more than define the meaning of science concepts, it helps you, the teacher, to decide what children will need to know about a new scientific or technological idea and how they might learn about it in a relevant and appropriate way. Whilst we trust you will find it useful for your day-to-day teaching of science and technology, we also believe it will inform you about the thinking behind current approaches to learning and teaching.

There are four main types of entry. First, there are those that are intended to help the teacher to introduce and explain scientific concepts to primary school children. These entries cover all areas of science such as **electricity** (physical processes), **condensation** (material science) and **respiratory system** (life processes and living things). These entries also suggest classroom activities and, in some cases, where to find further information. Second, there are those entries which focus on aspects of science enquiry such as **exploration** and **fair test**. Here you will often find suggestions for ways in which science skills and processes can be introduced through appropriate contexts. Third, there are entries that are commentaries on aspects of teaching and learning in primary science that are general in nature, such as **contexts for science** and **risk assessment**. And lastly, there are those which deal with design and technology, such as **computer aided design** and **mechanism**. These entries are identified by the addition of '**D&T**' (design and technology) to their title. Not all of the entries fit neatly into these categories, but most of them do. There are five extended and boxed entries on topics which we thought warranted longer consideration. In addition to the main body of the encyclopedia, at the end we have included three lists – famous scientists, famous inventors and the authors' personal selection of influential people in primary science education.

How you use this encyclopedia will depend on the purpose to which you intend to put it. You may choose to dip into this encyclopedia by beginning with an entry that interests you, a voyage of discovery. For each entry you will find links made to other entries with words and phrases in bold type. Where you begin may not be where you end up! Alternatively you may have a specific topic which you need to research and it is our hope that our title entries will help you find what you need quickly. Finally, you could read it from cover to cover. Maybe this way you will unearth by chance some new nugget of information or something that is interesting to you. Whichever way you choose to use it, we hope it will help you to engage and inspire a new generation of scientists and technologists.

A

ABSORBENCY

A **property of materials**: solid materials will soak up liquids by varying degrees reflecting differences in their absorbent capacity. Gaps between the solid particles (see **particle theory**) of the material become occupied by liquid which is held in situ by forces of attraction. Enquiries into very absorbent materials (such as sponge) and non-absorbent materials (such as polythene) might start with the question 'Which material is best for mopping up spills?' Initially what is meant by 'best' would need to be discussed, possibly leading to the **investigation** focusing on the amount of spill soaked up by the materials being tested. Following this a range of paper samples could be examined closely to determine the factors or variables involved in the investigation (e.g. pattern, thickness, layers). Another investigation could explore the rate at which different liquids are absorbed: does a spillage of water, milk or tomato ketchup take the longest to clear up?

ACCELERATION

We usually think of acceleration as an increase in **speed**, though it is strictly defined as a change in **velocity**. It is measured in metres per second per second (m/s^2), so something accelerating at $1\ m/s^2$ would travel a metre in the first second, a further two metres in the second, a further three in the third, and so on. Like velocity, acceleration is a *vector* quantity; in other words it has direction as well as magnitude (size). This means that an object can be accelerating without changing its speed, if for example it is moving in a circle – in other words changing its direction. Acceleration can also be negative if an object is slowing down (decelerating). In the primary classroom it will probably be during investigations into forces that teachers introduce the correct terminology. For example, a car will 'speed up' (accelerate) as it rolls down a ramp and then 'slow down' (decelerate) as it travels across the floor. One of the common accelerations we experience in everyday life is that due to **gravity**; falling things tend to get faster. If there wasn't any **air resistance**, acceleration due to gravity would be the same for all falling bodies: a figure of about $9.8\ m/s^2$. So, after 10 seconds of falling, an object would have a speed of around $100\ m/s$; hailstones would crack pavements and kill people. Fortunately, because of air resistance, objects tend to reach a terminal velocity, at which point they stop accelerating.

ADAPTATION

Animals and **plants** are adapted to survive and thrive in specific environments. Children can look for adaptation in the behaviour or physical features of organisms by making careful **observations**. For

1

example, animals that live in cold climates are large and have a small surface area to volume ratio to ensure minimal heat loss (e.g. polar bear). They have thick layers of fat or fur for insulation. They have a white coat in winter for camouflage and may hibernate during the coldest months. A dandelion can survive in a meadow grazed by animals (or a lawn) because it has a short **stem** and grows close to the ground. It quickly grows a flower on a long stem, which then waves in the wind to release parachuted **seeds**. The seeds germinate (see **germination**) quickly to colonise pastures new.

AIR RESISTANCE

Air resistance is a type of **friction** between a moving object and the gas (usually air) it is moving through. At a microscopic level, it is caused by billions of tiny collisions of air particles (see **particle theory**) against the 'front' surface of the moving object – there are actually air particles hitting the object all over, but it's hitting the particles in front slightly harder as it's moving towards them. The air particles push back against the object, opposing its movement forward. Children often confuse air resistance with wind – they can feel the force of wind against their bodies even standing still and may assume that the wind just blows a bit harder if they start to run. However, air resistance pushes against moving objects even when there is no wind, as children can experience if they run holding a large sheet of cardboard in front of them in the gym (or the playground on a still day). The size of the **force** produced by air resistance depends on the surface area of the front of the object moving through it, the shape of the object (i.e. how streamlined it is) and how fast it is moving (the faster an object moves, the more air particles it will collide into). At very high **speeds**, air resistance can cause a huge increase in **temperature** as some of the **kinetic energy** of the moving object

is transferred to heat **energy**. This is what happens when lumps of rock called meteors enter the Earth's atmosphere; what we call 'shooting stars' are bursts of light from these meteors as they burn up. For things falling more slowly, such as parachutes and 'spinners' (sycamore seeds, etc.), air resistance can have a huge effect in slowing down objects with a large surface area relative to their weight. The maximum speed reached by a falling object is called its terminal **velocity**, which can vary hugely depending on the air resistance it experiences. Terminal velocity is reached when the upward force of air resistance balances the downward force of **weight** due to **gravity**. For example, skydivers can reach a terminal velocity of well over 100 kph, whereas when their parachutes open their terminal velocity slows to around 30 kph, making it much safer to land!

ALGAE

Algae (singular alga) are very simple plant-like living things. They are 'simple' because they do not have a **root**, **stem** or **leaf**, and 'plant-like' because they are green and therefore can photosynthesise (see **photosynthesis**). Seaweeds and the **micro-organisms** that make pondwater green are algae.

ALTERNATIVE FRAMEWORKS

Alternative frameworks are ideas that children have to explain phenomena that are different to the accepted scientific view. The term was coined by Ros Driver (Driver 1983) to acknowledge that what are sometimes called children's 'misconceptions' may actually be well thought-out and internally consistent personal theories about the world. If children are somehow innately motivated to make sense of the world around them, then it is not surprising that this process of theory generation occurs. This belief that children are developing

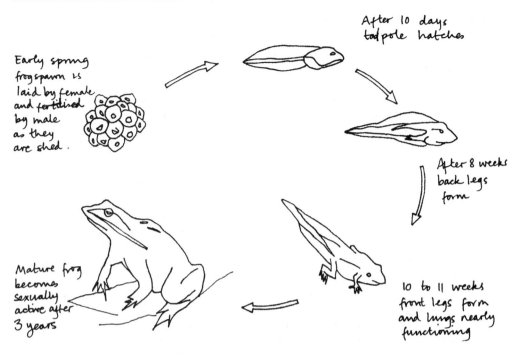

After 10 days
tadpole hatches

Early spring
frog spawn is
laid by female
and fertilised
by male
as they
are shed.

After 8 weeks
back legs
form

Mature frog
becomes
sexually
active after
3 years

10 to 11 weeks
front legs form
and lungs nearly
functioning

Figure A.1 The life cycle of a frog.

ideas about the world, even in the absence of being 'taught', is an important one. The ideas that children construct (see **constructivism** and **learning**) are not random or thoughtless, but are logical interpretations, based on the limited knowledge and experience the child has. Although not every child will construct the same ideas, there are some common patterns in alternative frameworks, and being aware of these is useful to teachers. The influential Nuffield SPACE Project (1989–98) identified many common alternative ideas that children hold. Examples of alternative frameworks would be that there is a universal 'down', rather than a gravitational force between objects, or that if something moves then it is alive (see **gravity** and **life processes**). Specific alternative ideas that might emerge as a consequence of these frameworks might include children drawing a ball dropped by a person at the South Pole as falling downwards on the page rather than

to the ground, or classifying a candle and a car as living things.

AMPHIBIAN

Member of the **animal** kingdom, e.g. frog. A cold-blooded **vertebrate**. Eggs are laid in water (e.g. frog spawn) and hatch into tadpoles (also called polliwogs). The tadpole metamorphoses to an adult by growing four legs and developing lungs which allow the amphibian to breathe on land (see Figure A.1). Most frogs need to keep their skin wet to aid this breathing while toads usually can tolerate drier conditions. Other examples include newts and salamanders. Amphibians in a pond or conservation area will be beneficial – they eat slugs, snails, small insects and their larvae. All amphibians should be treated with care, and it is illegal to disturb, kill, injure or catch the natterjack toad and the great crested newt or to have them in your possession; You must not sell, damage, destroy or obstruct their habitat – so if you find either species in your school pond take advice, e.g. from your local wildlife trust. It is legal to keep the tadpoles of a common frog in a tank in the classroom, but great care needs to be taken: if the tank is too warm or bright the tadpoles will perish. Taking tadpoles from ponds may upset the balance of the **ecosystem** you are trying to study. See http://froglife.org for advice.

ANALOGY

Analogy can be both a verb and a noun. In both cases it refers to the attempt to explain some difficult or unfamiliar concept by relating it to another more familiar example with which it shares some key features (contrast this with a **model**). For example, the flow of water through pipes is often used as an analogy for the flow of electricity through wires. In this case the common feature is the flow, contained within the outer casing of the pipe or wire. This analogy can help us to understand the concept of electrical **current**, which is defined as the rate of flow of charge from one place to another. However, any analogy has its limits, and it is important to recognise and highlight these to prevent it from being over-applied by children and potentially causing confusion. In the case of water and electricity, water can leak out of pipes or will flow when we open a tap, whilst electric current stays confined within the **conductor** from which the wire is made. Water is also stored in tanks, but it would be a mistake to apply this analogy to a **battery**, which is not a store of electricity. Therefore a better analogy to use in the primary classroom might be a loop of rope representing electric current in a circuit held loosely by a group of children standing in a ring, whilst one of them – the 'cell' – passes the rope through their hands to make it move around the circle. Analogy can be a useful teaching tool to help children understand some of the more abstract ideas in science, though as teachers we need to be careful to check that the example we are using as the analogy is familiar to the children, and that they are not confusing the analogy with the real thing. For example, we might use the ripples on a pond when we drop a stone into it as an analogy for the way **sound** waves travel from a source, decreasing in **loudness** as they spread out. Children might not have had the experience of watching ripples on a pond carefully, or might confuse the ripples with the sound waves travelling through water. Another problem with this analogy is that water forms 'transverse' waves (individual water particles move up and down as the wave travels through them) whereas sound waves are longitudinal (the particles of air – or other materials through which they pass – move backwards and forwards along the wave). So choose analogies carefully, and use them sparingly!

ANIMAL

A member of the **kingdom** *Animalia*. Animals come in many shapes and sizes from ants to zebras, zooplankton to blue whales. They are complex, multicellular organisms, and each cell usually has a nucleus but not a cell wall (this last feature distinguishes an animal from a **plant**). The kingdom is divided into two main groups – those with backbones (**vertebrates**) and those without backbones (**invertebrates**). Children may be familiar with **minibeasts** such as slugs, snails, worms, centipedes, spiders; these are all examples of invertebrates. Perhaps the strangest animals are the sponges and sea anemones which have one digestive opening (so it is a mouth and an anus). The largest single class of animals is insects. The vertebrate groups are: **fish, amphibians, reptiles, birds, mammals.** Children will be familiar with many animal groups but research has shown they sometimes don't think organisms such as birds, insects and worms are animals. They may confuse the term with 'mammal'. A main aim of primary science will be to give children a sense of the diversity of the animal kingdom, broadening their experiences from the familiar to the more exotic. This will involve children exploring (see **exploration**), examining and surveying local animal **populations**, encounters with pets, farm and **zoo** animals and perhaps looking after animals in the classroom, depending on local policy. The RSPCA offer useful advice on looking after animals and provide over 90 lesson plans, some with high quality photopacks, at rspca.org.uk.

ANNOTATED DRAWING

Annotated drawing is a means of children expressing their ideas and understandings about a concept (see **conceptual understanding**) and is a useful **elicitation** strategy (see Figure A.2 for an example). Often a visual representation communicates

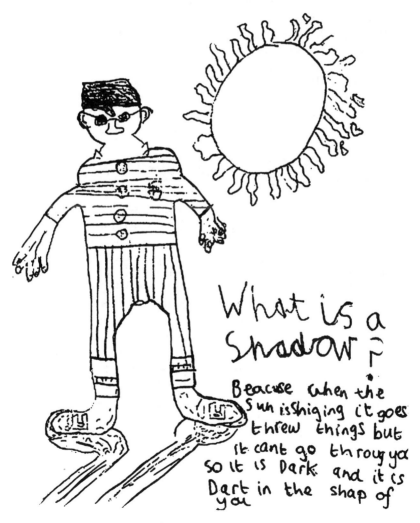

Figure A.2 Annotated drawing of a shadow.

an idea well. Annotating a drawing with labels or a few sentences to explain what it shows makes it even more helpful. This is not a formal 'diagram', but is a different way of representing the mental picture that a child holds. If a child's writing skills are limited, someone else can scribe their ideas on the drawing for them.

APPLICATION

Application is seen as the last stage of learning in the Constructivist Teaching Sequence (see **learning**) formalised in the 1980s as part of the Children's Learning in Science Project (CLIS) at the University of Leeds. In the application stage children use their new learning in different contexts in order to take ownership of it and to be secure in their understanding of it. This enables them to see the value of the new ideas so they are less likely to revert to previously useful ways of thinking. Opportunities for this may come through **cross-curricular** work. Technology provides many opportunities to apply ideas about materials, **electricity** and **sound**. Children can be presented with problems to solve using their new understanding, such as working out how to separate out rubbish for recycling using their knowledge of the **properties of materials**. Sometimes ideas developed in one science topic can be applied in another – a child might draw on their understanding in a topic on **light** to suggest using **transparent**, **translucent** and **opaque** materials to cover germinating seedlings to test the effect of different amounts of light on **germination**. A cross-curricular approach helps them to make connections between ideas rather than compartmentalise different aspects of their learning.

ARTEFACT (D&T)

An artefact is anything made or used by people. In primary design and technology an artefact may be the product of children's **designing** and making activity, such as a hat for a teddy, a computer simulation of an ideal bedroom or a model lighthouse. It may also be something made by other people which forms the focus of **evaluation**, such as a torch or a sandwich. Looking at an artefact can give us an insight into the culture of the designer and user and so has links with history. An artefact can also be an unwanted by-product of human activity, which in science can lead to misleading outcomes of experiments. For example, in science a magnifying tool might affect what is seen – a stray hair under a microscope might be interpreted as a spider leg. In the nineteenth century many scientists believed there were canals on Mars and it is thought that this may have been due to an optical illusion of connecting lines created by the poor quality telescopes (see **observation**).

ASSESSMENT

Assessment can be subdivided into formative assessment – assessment that 'informs' planning, teaching and **learning**, often called assessment for learning – and summative assessment that 'sums up' an individual's achievement at a point in time.

It is notable that Paul Black, who along with Wynne Harlen was one of the directors of the Nuffield SPACE Project and one of the authors of the influential Nuffield Primary Science SPACE books, went on to argue that a review of the research evidence showed how using assessment to provide children with feedback on their learning could raise achievement (Black and Wiliam 1998). This began a significant shift within primary education towards 'Assessment for Learning' (AfL) and away from 'assessment of learning'. Wynne Harlen, who has written extensively on assessment in primary science, argues that there are key elements of assessment that help learning: teachers finding out about children's ideas using 'rich' questions (see **elicitation**); encouraging discussion and dialogue (see **dialogic talk**); giving feedback that shows children how to make progress (see **progression**) and engaging children in self- and peer-assessment.

Summative assessment in primary science involves making judgements of attainment using external benchmarks and criteria such as (in England) the National Curriculum level descriptors or Assessing Pupil Progress (APP) statements. The evidence for these judgements may take the form of externally administered tests such as the science SAT tests for 11 year olds (discontinued in 2010), but can also be made by teachers. The purpose of making the judgement may be to inform children and their parents about individual achievement, but is also likely to inform monitoring of standards by schools, local authorities and other government bodies such as Ofsted.

ASSOCIATION FOR SCIENCE EDUCATION

The Association for Science Education (ASE) is the national professional association for primary and secondary teachers of science in the UK. It offers conferences and courses regionally and nationally and publishes a range of teaching resources and books. Members can get involved in local and regional networks of science educators. Nationally it also acts as a political lobby group and frequently advises the government on matters concerned with science education. The ASE is also the awarding body for **Chartered Science Teacher** (CSciTeach). The ASE website www.ase.org.uk has areas that are open to the public as well as to members.

ATTITUDES

Doing and learning science requires a set of scientific attitudes, such as curiosity and a willingness to question the world around us. Other important scientific attitudes include a respect for evidence and open-mindedness; scientists need to be open to changing their ideas. Children can find it hard to change their own ideas, and even when the evidence is apparently compelling, they may suggest alternative explanations (see **alternative frameworks**) that mean they can stick to their original idea. Taking an ethical approach to science is also important, particularly when studying living things, but also in considering the possible consequences of doing research for commercial organisations or research which may have an impact upon the environment. Examples of ethical issues in school might include considering how data on the mass or height of different children in a class should be collected and presented, or how a survey of a **habitat** is carried out with respect for the animals and plants that live there.

ATTRACTION

The word 'attraction' has at least two meanings in science. The first is biological and concerned with sexual **reproduction**. The second – possibly less interesting – meaning in the physical sciences refers to any **force** between two objects which tends to bring them towards each other. This could be gravitational (see **gravity**), in the case of our attraction towards the Earth. However, it is often thought of in relation to magnetism (see **magnetic materials**). Objects made of iron, steel, nickel or cobalt are attracted towards a magnet, whilst unlike poles (north and south) of two magnets are also attracted towards each other. Electrostatic forces can also attract, as in the case of a balloon, rubbed on a woolly or synthetic jumper, which can attract our hair or a thin stream of water flowing from a tap, which actually bends towards the balloon when we bring it close. This is because of the attraction of opposites – negatively charged **electrons**

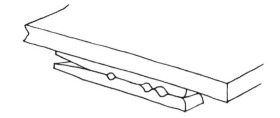

clothes peg glued on to hold the axle.

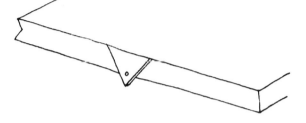

card triangle axle support

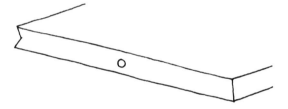

holes drilled directly through the chassis

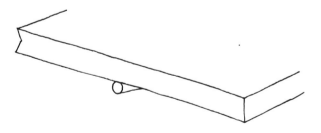

sawn off pieces of felt tip pen casing
glued onto the chassis.

Figure A.3 Four ways of fixing an axle to a chassis (adapted from DATA 1999).

rubbed on to the balloon attract the positively charged ends of the water molecules.

AXLE (D&T)

An axle is a rod on which one or more **wheels** can turn. If wheels are fitted tightly to the axle, the axle needs to be joined to a base (the chassis of a vehicle, for instance) so it can freely rotate. Alternatively, if the axle is fixed firmly to the base the wheels must be free to rotate. A Design and Technology Association helpsheet describes some of ways to achieve freedom of movement in the axle: by a clothes peg glued to the base with the axle fitted through the hole made by the two halves of the peg snapped together; by attaching a card triangle with a hole in it to the base; by drilling a hole directly through the base; or by attaching a short tube such as a short piece of a drinking straw to the base (Figure A.3; see DATA Helpsheet Unit 2C – DATA 1999).

B

BATTERY (CELL)

Strictly speaking, what we tend to call 'batteries' (cylindrical metal objects in 'D', 'C', 'AA' or 'AAA' sizes) are actually electrical cells. A battery is more than one of these cells (think of a battery of guns, or battery chickens). Each cell uses a chemical reaction to produce a **voltage**, or 'potential difference' of around 1.5 volts, which is then able to give electrons **energy** to flow as electrical **current** when connected in a **circuit**. Some of the more powerful batteries we can buy – such as those for old fashioned 4.5 V bicycle lamps, or the 12 V ones for smoke alarms – can really be called batteries since they contain a multiple number of 1.5 V cells. The details of the chemical reaction which produces the voltage differ between makes and types of cell, but all have the effect of driving **electrons** from a carbon rod in the centre (connected to the positive terminal) to the outer zinc casing, which acts as the negative terminal. When the battery is connected in the circuit, electrons are then repelled from the negative and attracted towards the positive terminals, creating the current (see Figure B.1). Once the chemical reaction in the battery is complete, it no longer has energy to drive electrons around the circuit and the battery is said to be 'flat'. Some types of battery are rechargeable, which means that the chemical reaction can be reversed.

These are not recommended for primary school use, since they have a very low internal **resistance**, which means that if they are accidentally 'short circuited' (the positive and negative terminals are connected directly together) a very high current can flow, heating up the battery to the point at which it bursts into flames!

BIODEGRADABILITY

Some materials will readily break down chemically into simpler materials when placed in the right environmental conditions (see **chemical changes to materials**). Living things that contribute to this process are called decomposers (e.g. fungi, bacteria, earthworms). Biodegradable materials will begin to decompose (**decay**) within a few days or weeks. However, non-biodegradable materials will remain unaffected. To explore the biodegradability of materials, items can be placed in sealed jars with a little soil (to test the idea that some children may have that, in nature, material is taken by an animal, washed or blown away). Over the space of a few weeks biodegradable materials will change but materials such as polystyrene chips will remain the same (and, in fact, will continue to do so for many years). This study of changing materials also provides many opportunities to focus on citizenship. Investigating a collection of packaging or 'clean'

11

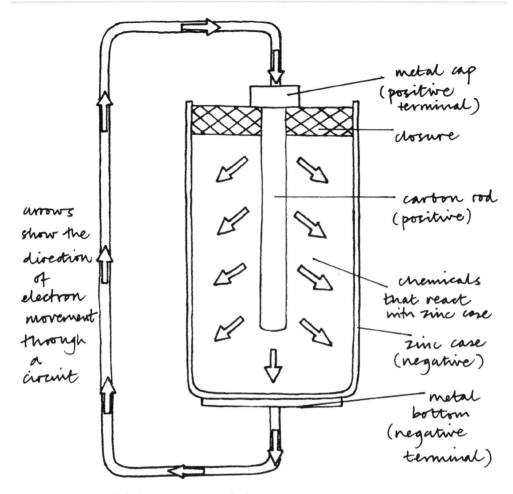

Figure B.1 Simplified cross-section of a battery.

waste products might encompass the life cycle of manufactured objects from 'raw materials' and lead naturally to the environmental impact caused by 'waste' materials. Concepts of biodegradability and 'recycling' can be introduced through an investigation of paper, which does degrade, and plastic, which does not. Collecting the class or school waste for one week could lead to a discussion on landfill sites, which in turn could be the impetus for a visit to a landfill, raising key questions about the huge volumes of waste that are buried at these type of sites each month. Who creates waste? How is waste treated at the landfill site? Is production of waste increasing and why? How can waste be minimised? How is compost made? Back in the classroom, setting up a compost bin or wormery provides a good practical context to take this further.

BIODIVERSITY

There are an estimated 100 million different types of **animal** and **plant** life on our planet. About 1.4 million are known and half of these are insects. It is exciting to think that there are plenty of species out there to be discovered by today's primary school children. There is also diversity within species – just look at the diversity of *Homo sapiens* in your school, road, town or country. Species are incredibly important because they are irreplaceable. This is a fundamental piece of knowledge needed to comprehend the fragility of some **ecosystems**. Biodiverse ecosystems are important to preserve for a variety of reasons. Rainforests, for example, harbour species that may be useful to us but are as yet unknown. Diverse populations tend to be better at surviving changes such as the introduction of a disease or pest, and a biologically diverse habitat also tends to be a more beautiful place. A local survey of plant and animal species would be an appropriate science **enquiry** activity. A class or school could conduct a local survey, pooling information on the number of species observed, and estimate **population** size. A further activity could be the development of school grounds to increase biodiversity – for example by the creation of a log pile, pond or wildflower meadow, or by putting up a bird feeder or nest box.

BIRD

Member of the **animal** kingdom. A warm-blooded **vertebrate**. Birds are characterised by being egg-laying and having feathers and wings, although not all birds can fly. The smallest bird is a bee hummingbird, the largest an ostrich. Feathers come in many shapes and sizes and have four main functions: they help the bird keep warm, help it fly, may help it communicate and finally help it to hide by camouflage. The RSPB (at www.rspb.org.uk) has produced a number of education resources. Each January it promotes the 'Big Schools' Bird Watch' which encourages children to record data on line. This data can then be accessed, which allows presentation and interpretation of real data.

BOILING

Initially as a liquid is heated, particles (see **particle theory**) will escape from its surface by the process of **evaporation**. As the liquid is heated further there comes a point at which evaporation takes place within the liquid itself and bubbles of gas form, rising to the liquid's surface. The **temperature** at which this happens is called the boiling point, which for pure water is 100 degrees Celsius. Once water reaches its boiling point, its temperature does not continue to rise any more. In observations of a pan of water being brought to the boil, the situation is slightly complicated by bubbles rising to the surface well before the water has reached its boiling point. These are dissolved bubbles of air coming out of solution as the water is heated and they are small. The big bubbles that rise to the surface when the water is actually boiling are not made of air but are water vapour. In common usage, boiling often just means 'very hot' rather than the more specific scientific definition. By measuring the temperature of a pan of water brought to the boil, it will be noted that the water can indeed be very hot but not necessarily boiling. An obvious context for the study of boiling is cookery (see **contexts for science**). Indeed, the Royal Society of Chemistry has teamed up with celebrity chef Heston Blumenthal to produce a set of resources for schools called *Kitchen Chemistry* (see www.rsc.org/education/teachers/). One activity begins by prompting children to discuss why salt is added to water when **cooking** vegetables (one reason being that it raises the boiling point of water so the vegetables cook faster), and leads on to **investigations** into the effect of salt on the vegetables' flavour.

BONDING

All materials are made of atoms. The nature of the bonds determines the **properties of materials** – e.g. **electrical conductivity**, **elasticity**, thermal insulation. There is an **attraction** between atoms caused by electrical forces, and it is these electrical forces of attraction that bond materials together. For example, the atoms of metals are joined together by metallic bonds in a way that makes metals good **conductors** of electricity. Each metal atom usually has one or two **electrons** attached to it very loosely, so that once bonded to another atom these 'free' electrons are able to move from one atom to the next. The movement of electrons becomes an electric **current** when a **voltage** is applied to the metal. Similarly, a heat source causes electrons to become excited and this is 'communicated' to others, thus allowing heat to be conducted through the material. Older primary school children can explore this explanation for the properties they observe through **models**. For example, the passage of electrons through a metal can be modelled by children (the atoms) passing balls (their electrons) from child to child in response to a stimulus such as a heat source. By contrast, all materials held together by covalent bonds (e.g. oil) are electrical **insulators** because atoms overlap in such a way that there are no free electrons. Another illustration of how bonds between particles affect the material's property is illustrated by diamond and graphite. Both of these materials are made of carbon, but one is very hard, sparkles and is clear (diamond) because the carbon atoms are joined together in strong tetrahedrons (three-sided pyramids), whereas the other (graphite) is soft, **opaque** and rather dull because its atoms are bonded together in sheets, the sheets being held together by weak bonding forces. Graphite also has a free electron, making it an electrical conductor too.

BONE – see **skeletal system**

BURNING

Burning, or combustion, is a familiar chemical reaction involving a fuel, oxygen and a high **temperature**. When a candle wick burns, some of the wax (a fuel made from atoms of hydrogen combined with atoms of carbon) becomes a liquid and melts (see **melting**). Some is drawn up the wick, evaporates (see **evaporation**) and becomes a gas. This gas combines (burns) with oxygen from the air to form carbon dioxide and water droplets (a **chemical change to materials** has occurred). The heat generated evaporates more wax and keeps the reaction going and a flame can be seen (see Figure B.2). In some situations the supply of oxygen is not great enough for all the fuel to be converted to carbon dioxide and water vapour (so-called incomplete combustion) and this typically results in smoke being formed from the sooty particles mixed with air.

One meaningful direction for teaching burning in the primary classroom is to study the process as a chemical reaction and apply this knowledge (see **application**) to being safe. Commonly candle wax is the fuel used in classroom studies because with simple precautions (see **risk assessment**) it can be observed safely by children. An understanding of what causes burning leads to an appreciation of how to be safe. Fuel, heat and oxygen make up the so-called triangle of fire; without one of these the fire cannot start or continue. A candle can be extinguished by being blown out because blowing the flame removes heat from it very rapidly. Equally a candle can be extinguished by depriving it of oxygen by snuffing it out. Slow-motion digital movies of a candle being extinguished make interesting viewing. Children can draw on their understanding to think of ways to be safe by grouping a range of

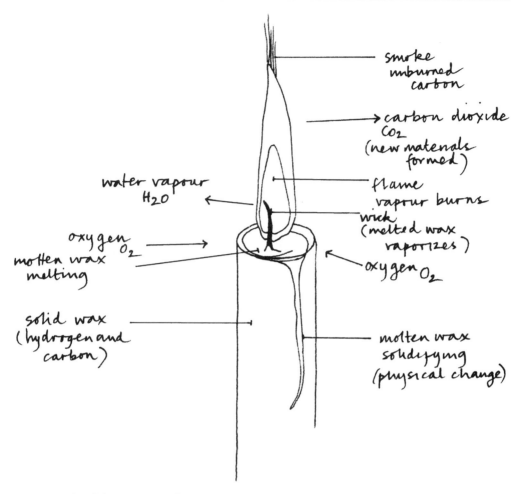

Figure B.2   A burning candle.

materials into those that burn easily and those which are relatively incombustible.

Children can be encouraged to study the flames produced by candles of different sizes and colours, and even scents (see **observation**). Do larger candles produce larger flames? Are more colourful flames made by colourful candles? The chemical reaction can be modelled (see **model**) through the medium of drama, children playing the role of par-

ticles of carbon, hydrogen and oxygen. At first carbon and hydrogen particles are firmly joined together, modelling solid wax. Heat causes them to melt so that carbon and hydrogen are in contact with each other but able to move relative to one another. Finally the bonds between the particles break down, and hydrogen joins with oxygen to form water vapour and carbon combines with oxygen to form carbon dioxide.

C

CAM (D&T)

A cam **mechanism** converts a rotary motion to a linear movement (see **crank** for this in reverse). The cam itself is an off-centre or specially shaped **wheel** that transmits its movement to a follower, which is the name for the arm that follows the movement of the cam. The follower may be attached to the cam by a split pin, or it may only rest on the cam, held in place by guides. Springs may push the follower against the cam or **gravity** may keep the follower in contact.

CARBON CYCLE

An understanding of the carbon cycle helps us to understand **climate change** more completely. Figure C.1 illustrates the terrestrial part of the cycle. Carbon in the air (as carbon dioxide) becomes incorporated into plants through the process of **photosynthesis**. This carbon passes through the **food chain**, and at each level the bodies of dead plants and animals are broken down by **micro-organisms** which release the carbon back into the atmosphere in the form of carbon dioxide. The carbon load in the atmosphere remains the same providing the amount released by **decay** is balanced by the amount taken up by new plant growth. However, deforestation upsets the balance, releasing carbon held in trees. Other man-made problems are changing the balance too. About 300 million years ago Britain occupied an area of the planet where plants died in an environment that inhibited their decay so that the carbon from them was preserved in the form of fossil fuels. The carbon remained trapped in **rocks** until very recently, when humankind's need for **energy** led to coal, oil and gas being extracted and burnt (see **burning**). This has released large quantities of carbon dioxide into the atmosphere. Many scientists believe that carbon dioxide (along with other greenhouse gases) traps the sun's energy on the surface of the Earth and its lower atmosphere, leading to **climate change**.

CELL (ELECTRICAL) – see **battery (cell)**

CHARGE (ELECTRICAL)

Charge can be thought of as the 'amount' of **electricity** in a particular place. It is measured in coulombs (C) after the French scientist Charles Augustin de Coulomb (1736–1806). Most of the tiny particles that make up the atoms and molecules in all the things around us carry an electric charge. Protons at the centre of atoms are positively charged, whilst the **electrons** that orbit around them are negatively charged. Since there are usually the same number of protons and electrons in any atom and their charges are equivalent they usually cancel each other out,

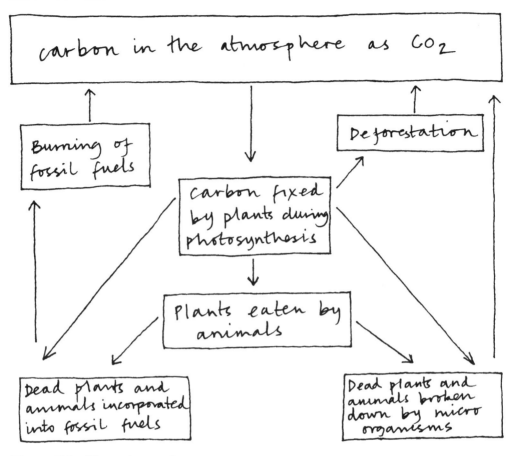

carbon in the atmosphere as CO_2

Burning of fossil fuels

carbon fixed by plants during photosynthesis

Deforestation

Plants eaten by animals

Dead plants and animals incorporated into fossil fuels

Dead plants and animals broken down by micro organisms

Figure C.1 The carbon cycle.

so the overall electrical charge is zero. However, when electrons move from one place to another – either through the chemical reaction in a **battery** or by being 'rubbed off' an insulating material (see **insulator**) – this causes a separation of charge. Wherever the electrons have gone to, they tend to outnumber the protons, so there is a net negative charge. Conversely, wherever the electrons have been removed from, the protons will be left in the majority so that area will have a net positive charge. This separation of charge creates an attractive force (see **attraction**) between the oppositely charged particles; the electrons are attracted to the positively charged protons, which can result

in the sparks or electric shocks we sometimes experience getting out of a car, lightning, or the flow of electric **current** around a **circuit**.

CHARTERED SCIENCE TEACHER

Chartered Science Teacher (CSciTeach) status is available to primary as well as secondary school teachers and to other science educators. It is a professional qualification which recognises the professional standing of an individual working in that field and carries a chartered designation in line with other awards, such as Chartered Accountant or Chartered Surveyor. The award is made under powers granted by the Privy Council. Chartered science teachers are required to be members of the **Association for Science Education** (ASE) and to have at least four years' experience in teaching science. Typically applicants are required to have a Master's level qualification in education and an honours degree with a minimum of 50 per cent science content, but it may be possible to demonstrate an equivalent level of expertise through other experience. The ASE is the awarding body for Chartered Science Teacher status.

CHEMICAL CHANGES TO MATERIALS

During chemical changes, new substances are produced. Such changes can be accelerated or caused by heat, and are usually permanent. In cookery, for example, a hard-boiled egg cannot be made soft again by cooling it, and dough baked in an oven and made into bread cannot be returned to flour and water. Neither can clay once it has been fired in a kiln be returned to its original state. During chemical changes, a chemical reaction takes place in which the particles involved undergo significant changes.

Two of the commonest processes that lead to chemical changes are **burning** and **corrosion**. In the example of a candle burning, new chemical bonds (see **bonding**) are formed between carbon atoms and oxygen atoms to make carbon dioxide molecules. The carbon atoms are firmly bound to the oxygen atoms inside the carbon dioxide molecules and cannot easily be separated. A new compound has been created. During a chemical change no new matter is created or destroyed. The same number of atoms exist but they have been rearranged – the mass has been conserved (see **conservation of matter**). When an iron nail corrodes, the iron reacts with oxygen in the air to create a coating of iron oxide or rust. **Decay** is another form of

permanent change often brought about by the actions of **micro-organisms**. If a material decays in this way it is biodegradable (see **biodegradability**).

A starting point for teaching chemical changes could involve presenting a particular material or object to children. Their ideas could be elicited about how it might change. Such items could be an ice cube or ice balloon, a puddle of water, a burning candle, chocolate, perfume, clay, an egg, a rubber band, sugar, a rock or a coin. Key questions to ask when eliciting children's understanding of chemical changes (as opposed to **physical changes to materials**) include: How can we change the material? Could you get the material to change back? Would any new materials be made?

From this starting point children's understanding can be developed through **cooking**, through studying materials that rust and through observation of objects being burnt (most obviously candles). Attention can be focused on the material that is being changed, what new products are formed and the process that produces these new products.

CHEMICAL PROPERTIES OF MATERIALS

A **property of materials** that is determined by the way a material reacts when in contact with another material. An example of a chemical property is reactivity, which is a measure of a material's inertness or resistance to change in any given reaction. Materials which are more reactive take part in chemical reactions more readily. **Corrosion** is a specific type of chemical reaction that can be studied in the primary school. Iron metal reacts readily with oxygen and water to form rust, whereas copper corrodes much more slowly. There are a number of factors which affect the rate of corrosion and these can be investigated (see **investigation**) in the primary classroom.

19

CHROMATOGRAPHY

Chromatography is a technique which enables complex **mixtures** of chemicals in solution to be separated. Solutes (such as sugar and salt) dissolved in the same solvent (such as water) are difficult to separate; however, it is possible to separate some mixtures of solutes into their components by paper chromatography (see Figure C.2). In the primary classroom, possibly the commonest investigation involving chromatography is to separate out the coloured dyes of felt-tipped pens (maybe as part of a 'forensic' test to determine who wrote the mystery note!). Put a spot of each pen's ink on blotting paper and drip water on to it. As the water spreads out it carries the inks different distances. It is possible to separate inks into constituent colours by chromatography because the solvent soaks through the filter or blotting paper and the coloured inks separate out as they travel at different rates across the paper. Dark blue, brown and black inks work particularly well, sometimes revealing a range of other colours.

CIRCUIT (ELECTRICAL)

An electrical circuit consists of a loop of conducting material (wire), a source of electrical **energy** (**battery**/cell) and usually some other type of electrical component which transfers the electrical energy into another form (e.g. a lamp, buzzer or motor). Electrical **current** requires a complete circuit to flow, since all the tiny particles (**electrons**) move in the same direction. This is something children struggle to grasp; even if they have made simple circuits with batteries, wires and bulbs it still doesn't seem to make sense that you need wires going to and from the battery. This confusion results

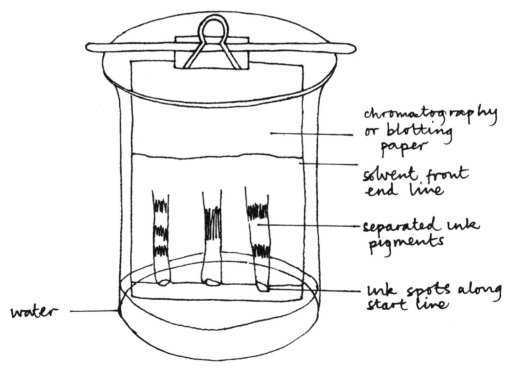

chromatography or blotting paper

solvent front end line

separated ink pigments

ink spots along start line

water

Figure C.2 Paper chromatography in action.

from a source-sink **model** which many people carry around in their heads. In this model, the battery/cell is the 'source' of electricity, which flows down the wire and gets 'used up' in the bulb/lamp, like water draining away through a sink. Such a model is reinforced by a superficial look at the electrical cables plugged into sockets around the home; there appears to be only one wire connecting each appliance to the source of **electricity** 'in the wall' (in fact within the cable usually there are two wires). If, however, we move to a more scientific view, in which the tiny 'bits of electricity' (electrons) are already in the wires and the bulb, before the battery makes them all start to move, it makes more sense that they need to keep flowing in a circular motion, since they don't get 'used up' themselves. Instead, the electrons merely pass on the energy from the battery to the bulb, like a series of coal trucks which then need to return to the 'depot' (battery) for refilling. Children can experience this kinaesthetically by 'becoming' an electrical circuit, using a loop of rope or a PE hoop which one child moves through his or her hands (the 'battery') whilst another can resist the flow by gripping it lightly (the 'bulb'). The two main types of circuit that children will encounter in the primary school are 'series' circuits in which the components are connected one by one sequentially, and 'parallel' circuits in which each component has its own pathway to the battery, enabling current to flow down several different 'arms' simultaneously (see **series and parallel circuits**).

CIRCULATORY SYSTEM

Living things need to transport nutrients, wastes and gases to and from every part of their body. In humans and higher **animals** this system consists of the heart, blood vessels (arteries and veins) and blood. It takes food and oxygen to cells and removes waste. The heart acts as a pump to move the blood through the vessels around the whole body and back. The system also plays a key role in defence against damage by carrying blood-clotting agents and white blood cells and antibodies which can attack disease-causing viruses and bacteria. The best way to start investigating this system is by finding a pulse in the wrist or neck, or a stethoscope can be used to locate a heartbeat. A count can be taken for 15 or 30 seconds then multiplied to get a 'beats per minute' figure (bpm). Children will be interested to find out how our pulse changes as we exercise, recover and rest. A pulse can vary quite a bit, with an average of 72 for an adult, 84 for a child and 140 for a newborn baby. It can easily increase to 140 bpm during exercise. The time taken for the heart rate to recover to 'normal' is an indication of fitness. Breathing rates (see **respiratory system**) too can vary – but these are more difficult to measure. This is partly due to the effect measuring a rate has on the breathing. Children may have limited experiences of pumps, and so referring to the heart as a pump may need explaining (see **exposition**) or modelling. A bicycle pump and a bucket of water can be used to demonstrate the principle. This can be followed up with a discussion – in what way is the heart similar to and different from the model?

CLASSIFYING AND IDENTIFYING

Children may be asked to identify something they are studying in science by matching the item with a name, or maybe to classify an object by putting it in a pre-existing category, or to create groups and categories themselves. This may be part of another enquiry – for example, sorting materials (see **sorting activities**) as **transparent**, **translucent** or **opaque** before testing how much light comes through them with a data logger – or an end in itself, such as recording the **biodiversity** within an area of land. Classifying and identifying can be the starting point for generating **hypotheses** and making creative links (see **creativity**) between aspects of phenomena. Decision trees (biological keys) are a useful tool for identifying living things; children can also construct their own using a branching database such as Flexitree.

CLASSROOM ORGANISATION

Practical (hands-on) activities providing first-hand experiences are an essential part of primary science. Organisation of **resources** and groups for these sort of activities (see **group work**) will be at the forefront of the primary school teacher's mind as he or she plans the next science lesson.

> *Resource organisation* How a particular science lesson might be taught is to a certain extent dictated by the resources (and space) that are available to the teacher. If there are sufficient resources available, it is possible for all children to be engaged in the same activity at the same time. If specialised equipment is needed and is only available in short supply, then the classroom may need to be organised as a carousel of activities with one group using the specialist kit. In some ways it is preferable to have children doing different activities linked together by one theme since this enables more interesting class discussions as children share their results and new understanding.

> *Group organisation* It may be the case that some scientific activities require constant adult support, possibly for health and safety reasons (see **risk assessment**) or to provide specific focused support for children to get the most out of the task. When this is the case, the other activities will need to be planned so children can work independently, or alternatively, well-prepared support staff can work alongside the group in need of support freeing up

the teacher to work with the remainder of the class. If the teacher is alone and working with a group, should the other activities in the class be science-based? The teacher will need to consider whether the science work of the focus group will distract other groups if their work is not scientific. Another consideration is the lost opportunity for the whole class to share their scientific experiences at the end of a lesson if only part of the class is engaged in science work.

CLIMATE CHANGE

Understanding the changes that are happening to our climate on a global scale is a way of helping children make sense of issues in the news such as renewable **energy** sources and **habitat** change (see **scientific literacy**). The scientific community is not entirely united as one on the causes of climate change but an overwhelming majority believe human activity is the explanation. The view is that the **burning** of fossil fuels from the time of the Industrial Revolution onwards is responsible for a rise in carbon dioxide concentrations in the Earth's atmosphere (see **carbon cycle**). Carbon dioxide is one of the greenhouse gases (along with others such as methane) that trap the sun's energy on the surface of the Earth and its lower atmosphere (acting like a greenhouse). An increase in its concentration is thought to be responsible for a global rise in **temperatures** and climate change.

Research by Palmer and Suggate (2005) has shown that younger primary school children understand that snow and ice will melt if warmed up (see **melting**) and that this will have an effect on animals that live in such habitats. The short-term impact on animals living in polar regions was described by children in terms such as: 'The penguin would have to go in the water.' Older primary children reveal a more general understanding of the dependence of living things on their particular habitat. This might be rather simplistically understood, animals being able simply to move on to another habitat. Some older children knew that the reason for the change in our climate is due to greenhouse gases or pollution, but there was a confusion between the greenhouse effect and the hole in the ozone layer. Other explanations for global warming given by children were that the sun is getting nearer to the Earth or that it was simply as a consequence of seasonal change (see **seasons**).

Teachers may want to engage children in a practical activity that **models** the greenhouse effect. The activity begins with children being set the challenge of raising the temperature of a beaker of water by as much as possible, using only the heat from the sun and a solar collector (this activity works best in full sunlight). Their solar collector may be a large plastic container such as an aquarium fitted with foil and possibly cling film and mirrors. Indeed an effective solar collector is made by simply inverting a plastic fish tank. The container's walls allow solar energy through them but they only allow some of the heat energy to escape. On a sunny day in the summer, expect temperatures in excess of 40 degrees Celsius to be reached. It is worth measuring **light** and temperature by using data loggers both inside and outside the collector. By logging light and temperature continuously, children will build up a detailed trace of data. Are they then able to tell a story from the graphs? For example, if the temperature rose steadily but then suddenly dropped at the same time as the light intensity fell, it might be that the sun was out initially but then went behind a cloud – or did the collector become shaded during the investigation?

The message 'think globally, act locally' can be supported in the classroom by children monitoring their use of energy. Once again, data loggers can monitor energy usage, for example by tracking classroom temperature over the course of a day. This in turn may lead on to a discussion about times during the day when the classroom thermostat could be turned down and energy saved. Other debates can focus on the types of lifestyle changes children would be prepared to consider to save energy. For example, would children be prepared to play on their games console for one hour less every day? Teachers should try to avoid 'doomsday' scenarios which may cause undue anxiety, but instead should focus on positive action that children can take to reduce their carbon footprint, such as walking to school, learning to cycle safely, switching off unneeded electric lights, and so on.

COGNITIVE ACCELERATION THROUGH SCIENCE EDUCATION (CASE)

The Cognitive Acceleration through Science Education Project began in secondary schools in the 1980s. Its aim was to raise children's level of thinking to cope with the demands of the science curriculum at that time. The CASE team, based at King's College London, designed an intervention programme of 30 activities that were taught throughout the academic year instead of a regular science lesson. It proved to be a success, with CASE pupils performing significantly better at examinations compared with the control group. Furthermore, there was evidence that the skills they acquired in science lessons were transferable, as it was found that the CASE pupils also scored better in English and mathematics exams. In the late 1990s the CASE team turned their attention to primary schools, which led to the publication of two intervention programmes. *Let's Think! A Programme for Developing Thinking in Five and Six Year Olds* (Adey *et al.* 2001) aimed to develop thinking skills using science and a wide range of other areas of learning as contexts. *Let's Think Through Science! Developing*

Thinking Skills with Seven and Eight Year Olds (Adey *et al.* 2003) aimed to develop thinking within the context of science alone. For more information on the theoretical foundations that underpin CASE and the ways of thinking that CASE develops, see **thinking skills**.

COLLOID

An activity that can be used to orientate or elicit children's understanding of **states of matter** is sorting a variety of substances into solids, liquids and gases. However, foams, gels and the like can complicate this as they are what are called colloids, which are two-phase '**mixtures**' of matter. Colloids have small droplets or particles dispersed within another different phase of matter. Unlike a solution, where the particles are completely dissolved, the particles of dispersed substance in a colloid are only suspended in the mixture. Examples of colloids include whipped cream, which is a gas dispersed in a liquid; jelly, a liquid dispersed in a solid; and pumice, a gas within a solid.

COLOUR – see **light**, **rainbow** and **reflection**

COMMUNICATING RESULTS – see **process skills**

COMPOSITE MATERIALS

When two or more materials are combined by **bonding** them together, they are known as composites. Usually the reason for doing this is to improve their properties, maybe by making them stronger. Layer composites, also known as laminates, are widely used to improve the toughness of materials by building up alternate layers of two or more materials. It is possible for children to 'manufacture' materials in the classroom to suit a particular purpose (see **manufactured materials**). For example, layering paper with sheets of lasagne will improve the rigidity of the paper and the brittleness of the lasagne, making a laminate suitable for a variety of purposes for which paper or lasagne alone would be unsuitable. Particle composites, as the name implies, are composites consisting of combined particles (e.g. concrete consists of gravel and sand with cement bonding the mixture together). Again, children can investigate the material properties of particle composites they have manufactured, possibly by binding Rice Krispies and cornflakes together with melted chocolate – what is the best ratio of Rice Krispies and cornflakes to chocolate so that the mixture holds together well?

COMPRESSIBILITY

A **property of materials**: the strength of a material is a measure of its ability to withstand deformation by **forces**. One of the ways to deform a material is by compressing it; compression is a squeezing force. (Other common ways to deform materials are by pulling forces – tension – and by twisting forces – torsion.) Testing materials' compressibility can be done in the primary classroom by a squeeze test, possibly as part of an investigation to discover which material would be suitable for Goldilocks' chair – is it too hard, too soft or just right?

COMPUTER AIDED DESIGN (D&T)

In the adult world, computer aided design (CAD) is used in a wide range of industries including car making, building, textiles, packaging and electronics. In the classroom it is increasingly likely children will have the skills to make use of software to help them in their own designing and making. Here are some examples:

- Painting software – to design greetings cards or t-shirts.
- Yenka Basic (free from www.crocodile-clips. com) – to design electrical **circuits** for toys, torches, etc.

- West Point Bridge designer (free from www.bridgecontest.usma.edu/) – to design bridges, of course!
- Flowol primary (free from www.flowol.com) – which mimics the control of toys and fairground rides to introduce children to computer aided control.

Other packages available will enable children to design packaging, vehicles, alien animals, etc. – with more products available each year. Teachers will need to evaluate the usefulness of any software. Ask yourself;

- Does the software enable children to achieve **learning objectives** more efficiently or effectively than other methods?
- Will all children be likely to see a value in it?
- Are all your children able to gain the necessary ICT skills to use it?

CAD software shouldn't be seen simply as a substitute for practical activities with actual materials and components. It is only after children have had experiences of working with materials, components and tools that computer simulations will make sense to them.

CONCEPT CARTOONS

Stuart Naylor and Brenda Keogh have developed various publications in which a central problem is posed in the form of a cartoon, and the responses of different children are shown in speech bubbles around it. For example, one shows a drawing of a tub of ice cream that has just been taken out of the freezer and has droplets of moisture on the outside of the tub. The speech bubbles contain the children's different suggestions about where the droplets have come from (see **condensation**). Concept cartoons are very useful starting points for discussions and debates, particularly with groups of children who are reluctant to express their own ideas or find it difficult to articulate them, as they can choose the idea that best matches their own. Concept cartoons can be used within teaching to elicit children's ideas but also to challenge and develop them (see **elicitation** and **testing an explanation**).

The websites www.azteachscience.org.uk and www.conceptcartoons.com have more information on using concept cartoons.

CONCEPT MAP

Concept mapping is a way of representing connections and relationships between different ideas. Key words are either given or generated by the children and are joined with arrows, each of which includes a phrase written along its line to explain how the words at either end are linked (Figure C.3). It is a way of eliciting or reviewing children's ideas, but also a way of helping children develop a deeper **conceptual understanding** and mental map of a topic area (see **elicitation** and **review**). The website www.azteachscience.org.uk explains one approach to developing concept maps.

CONCEPTUAL UNDERSTANDING

We can think of children's **learning** in science as being composed of three main elements: concepts (ideas about phenomena which link together into theories), skills (sometimes called 'procedural knowledge' – knowing how to go about scientific enquiry; see **process skills**) and **attitudes** (the essential dispositions such as curiosity and respect for evidence which are necessary prerequisites for children to make progress in science). Clearly the three areas are linked; children need scientific attitudes such as curiosity to want to explore their environment and skills to test their ideas systematically in order to develop their conceptual understanding. There has been a long-running

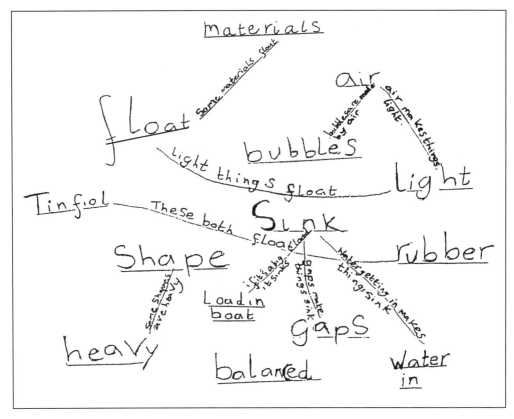

Figure C.3 Exploring ideas about floating and sinking using a concept map.

'process–content' debate in primary science over which element of children's learning should take precedence. Is it more important for children to develop scientific concepts (to 'know stuff') or for them to have the skills to investigate things scientifically – to be scientists? We believe both are equally important; it is no use developing the skills of enquiry if children don't have something interesting to enquire into, but equally, simply learning bits of scientific knowledge without any understanding of the evidence upon which they are based represents a very limited view of science. In some ways children's conceptual understanding is the 'hard stuff' – they may well hold many existing non-scientific ideas (**alternative frameworks**) and may struggle to develop a scientific understanding of 'big ideas' in science, such as a particle model of matter (see **particle theory**) or the notion of balanced **forces**. However, as teachers we need to persevere in finding as many different ways of helping children to access these important concepts as possible; through eliciting their existing ideas and helping them build upon them through discussion and **practical (hands-on) activities**. Often the most useful type of scientific enquiry here is to use '**illustrative activities**': for example, holding a ping-pong ball on a string against a vibrating tuning fork to illustrate the energy of **vibration** in sound waves.

CONCLUSION

Teachers may remember being asked to write a formal conclusion to investigative work in their own science education. For primary children a more appropriate title for the conclusion might be 'What we found out.' Conclusions could be spoken rather than written; perhaps they could be communicated to peers or parents at a 'science conference.' What matters is that the conclusion should be consistent with the outcomes of the **enquiry**, showing a respect for **evidence** and its limitations. This may include a summary of a pattern in the data, such as 'All the snail shells in our field are stripy.' It should also refer back to a **prediction** or initial idea: for example, 'I thought all the metals would be magnetic but they are not.' A conclusion may link specific findings to the concepts of the broader area of study: for example, 'It may be that there was only one species of snail in this habitat because there is only one kind of grass.' The conclusion may also indicate possibilities for further **investigation**: for example, 'We would like to see if there are different snails in the hedge.' Children can be encouraged to acknowledge the limitations of the enquiry and hence the conclusions as a key element of **scientific literacy**: for example, 'We found that only steel things were magnetic but there might be other materials we haven't tried that are magnetic.'

CONDENSATION

Condensation refers to the process of changing from a gas to a liquid, usually accompanied by cooling. Our everyday experience of condensation relates to water vapour. When we breathe on to a cool surface such as a mirror, or a tub of ice cream is left out of the fridge, tiny droplets of water start to appear (the mirror becomes 'misted'). We can explain it using a 'particle model' of matter (see **particle theory**).

Condensation happens because some of the invisible particles of water vapour present in the atmosphere – or in our breath – lose some of their **energy** on contact with the cool surface, so tend to collect there in larger and larger numbers until we can see the droplets they have formed. Children can find this explanation difficult to believe, preferring to attribute the appearance of water droplets on the outside of a tub of ice cream or glass of icy water to something that has 'leaked out.'

Condensation is also used as a noun; we use it to refer to the condensed water vapour on window panes on a cold morning. It doesn't have to occur on a solid surface; being able to 'see your breath' on a cold morning is because the water vapour is condensing in the cool air. In technical terms, condensation is a 'change of state' (when one state of matter – in this case gas – changes into another – liquid). It is a physical change (see **physical changes to materials**) since no alteration occurs to the substance itself. Water vapour is still H_2O, its particles are just moving a lot faster than they are in its liquid state. For this reason, condensation is also reversible – if we add energy by heating up the surface, the liquid will evaporate. In this way condensation can be seen as the reverse of **evaporation** or **boiling**, where in both cases liquids are changed into gases.

CONDUCTOR (ELECTRICAL)

An electrical conductor is any material that allows an electrical **current** to pass through it. The atoms in electrical conductors have so-called 'free **electrons**' which are less tightly bound within the atom than most electrons. They are thus free to drift through the material when given some **energy** to move by a **battery** or dynamo connected in an electrical **circuit**. Most electrical conductors are metals, therefore electrical wires are usually made out of copper or steel which also have the advantage of being relatively cheap and ductile (able to be drawn out into a thin wire without breaking). Some non-metals such as silicon have been called semi-conductors because they only conduct **electricity** under certain conditions. Semi-conductor devices like the transistor, which only allows current to pass when an electrical signal is received via a third connection, have led to the development of the entire electronics industry, upon which it could be argued that the whole of modern life depends.

CONIFER

A **plant** group. Typically trees that reproduce by making 'naked' seeds in cones (coniferous = cone-bearing). Examples include pine and spruce. The male cone releases pollen that is carried on the wind to the female cone (see **reproduction**). A **seed** develops, which drops out of the cone on to the ground. The seed germinates and a seedling grows into a mature plant. Children will be fascinated to find that female cones will respond to changes in humidity – they will open if kept in a dry place and will close when in a damp environment. This is an **adaptation** for **seed dispersal** – seeds will not be dispersed if the weather is too wet, which will cause seeds to rot.

CONSERVATION OF MATTER

Matter cannot be created or destroyed, but it can be rearranged in space and changed into different substances (see **chemical changes to materials** and **physical changes to materials**). At primary level, children can pour water or sand from one beaker to another and back again to confirm that the volume remains the same despite it changing its shape in vessels with different shapes. Similarly, a ball of clay can be reshaped then returned to its original spherical form. This may seem an obvious phenomenon to adults but can be difficult for children to comprehend. Children's thinking in this area can be improved by encouraging them to actively reflect on the results of the investigation and explaining them. Thinking about one's own thinking, or metacognition, supports children as they evaluate their investigations of this type (see **thinking skills**).

CONSTRUCTION KITS (D&T)

Children may be familiar with many construction kits from play at home, so teachers need to be alert to the different prior experiences children bring and be ready to support or challenge as appropriate. Although children can gain a great deal from unstructured open-ended play with construction kits, these can also be used within a design brief, such as to make something for a playground or a fairground. Construction kits may be used to experiment with different designs and to make prototypes that children then go on to build in more permanent materials (see **designing**). There is a wide range of kits available. Some kits lend themselves to making 'frame' structures, others to 'shell' structures. Other kits can help children to learn about different **mechanisms** and incorporate them into designs. As kits are quite expensive, there is unlikely to be enough of a single kit for a whole class to use at the same time, so the **lesson structure** will need to take this into account.

CONSTRUCTIVISM

Constructivist theories view learning (see **learning**) as a process in which an individual actively constructs ideas, rather than as a process of 'transmission' in which facts are poured into the mind of the learner. Versions of constructivism based on the work of Piaget emphasise the importance of interaction with the physical world and see young children as behaving like scientists – making and testing **hypotheses** about the environment: for example, 'This toy will fall to the floor if I drop it.' In this view of learning science, the **practical (hands-on) activities** become the most important element, and the teacher's role is to provide a rich environment for the child to explore. If we reflect on our own learning, few people would deny the power of handling objects, feeling and seeing something happen in giving us a depth of understanding. Interactionist theories such as this focus on the interaction 'between hand and mind.'

CONTEXTS FOR SCIENCE

There are numerous contexts for teaching science that make it a relevant experience for primary school children. Listed below by topic are some contexts or starting points for teaching a range of scientific phenomena.

Materials: links can be made to citizenship and sustainability by investigating packaging, with recycling being introduced. **Properties of materials** can be linked to technology projects by testing a range of materials and choosing the one that is most suitable for a design-and-make project (see **science and design and technology**). Changes to materials could be explored through **cooking**.

Sound: **sound** can be taught through studying musical instruments. Children could explore the way instruments make different sounds and they can make their own instruments, linking the work to design and technology. Alternatively, children can act out the role of a special effects technician by putting sound effects to their stories and poems.

Forces: the starting point for learning about **forces** might be a PE lesson. They might explore different ways of throwing a ball and discover that sometimes they push it and sometimes it is pulled. During a gymnastics lesson children can analyse their balances and movements in terms of forces. Other contexts for teaching forces include exploring playground apparatus and moving toys (including floating boats). Pushing and pulling modelling clay to make art sculptures enables children to study how forces can change the shape of objects.

Electricity: links can be made to technology work by getting children to explore a range of torches, then asking them to design and make their own for a particular purpose, e.g. a reading light or a security light (see **science and design and technology**). Aspects of 'education for sustainable development' could be taught by linking human consumption of **electricity** to the sources of **energy** used in its generation (wind power, fossil fuels, etc.).

Light: children might explore how **light** travels through some materials and not others by playing with shadow puppets. Lights are an integral part of many celebrations, both religious (e.g. Hanukkah) and secular (birthdays). The reflective properties of materials (see **reflection**) can be taught as children explore how to stay safe on the road. Issues of global inequality can be raised by looking at satellite images of the Earth at night: Which regions of the world have the most lights?

The Earth and beyond: it is difficult to imagine teaching this topic without referring to everyday contexts such as **day and night**, the apparent movement of the sun across the sky and the **shadows** that it forms, the **seasons** and the phases of the moon (see **phases, lunar**).

Humans as animals: there are obvious links between this science topic and personal health, hygiene, **drugs**, sex and relationships. A starting point

29

for a study of life cycles might be drawing comparisons between humans and other **animals**.

Plants: a good context for studying **plants** is food – farming, gardening and cooking. Younger children can explore plants by visiting a garden centre, then setting up their own in the classroom role-play area.

Living things in the environment: children can be taught about the natural environment by carrying out a 'green' audit of the school grounds. Links can be made to citizenship by children acting on the information they gather, maybe by considering how the grounds could be enhanced, putting together proposals for their improvement and presenting these to the school's governing body for their consideration.

CONTROL SYSTEM (D&T)

If we wish to switch something on or off at a distance, or regulate a mechanical movement such as a **lever** or gear (see **mechanism**), we will need to develop some kind of control system. Control systems are usually classified as either electrical (for example, a switch) or mechanical (for example, a handle or crank). Increasingly, the technological devices we use in our homes and workplaces are electronically controlled, using programs stored in microprocessors. Children can begin to simulate this process using control software such as *Flowol* which enables them to build sequences to sense incoming data such as **sound** or **light** levels and trigger lights or motors to start and stop. They can either use these sequences to control virtual situations within *Flowol* such as elevators or traffic lights, or can build their own models, complete with lights and motors, which can be controlled via an interface connected to the computer (see **computer aided design**). Such applications of ICT are popular with

some teachers but require considerable expertise, equipment and time for children to develop, test and refine their control sequences.

COOKING

Work with food can provide many opportunities for children to find out about how materials change. Baking biscuits and making jelly, porridge, ice lollies or chocolate cakes are guaranteed to motivate. Provided health and safety is kept in mind, with the risk of allergic reactions assessed and controlled (see **risk assessment**), such activities never fail to interest and allow for endless **questions** to be asked, answered and explored. The study of changes in materials provides an ideal opportunity for children to prepare and cook food. Take, for example, the possible learning opportunities presented by something as simple as making bread. Initially, flour and dried yeast, both solids which seem to behave like liquids as they 'flow' into the bowl, are mixed with liquid water to form dough, a material that behaves like a liquid in that, given time, it will flow into the spaces of a bread tin. Too much water and the dough is too sticky to knead; too little and it resists our attempts to squash it. After kneading, the yeast will feed off the flour and produce carbon dioxide, a gas, which leads to the dough rising. During baking, chemical changes (see **chemical changes to materials**) will occur in the risen dough that result in bread being made, a change that cannot be reversed. Bake the bread for too long and it will be dry and burnt.

Now that you have bread the next activity might be making toast. This can become an investigation in which there are lots of independent **variables** to explore. Try making toast on different time settings, with different breads or with bread that is fresh or stale. Encourage children to observe the changes closely with a hand lens or microscope (see **observation**). Create a 'colour chart' that relates time to colour change. Investigate how long before the butter will not melt on the toast. Do different spreads have different **melting** points (see **physical changes to materials**)?

Baking bread and making toast are just two examples among a myriad of opportunities that cooking presents when studying changes to materials. Another popular choice with children is making ice cream, which is an example from the kitchen of a change that can be reversed.

See also food technology.

CO-ORDINATOR, SCIENCE – see **subject leader, science**

CORNFLOUR

A suspension of cornflour in water behaves in a very odd way. It acts like a liquid until it is hit, at which point it behaves like a solid. As custard is primarily a type of cornflour mixture, it also exhibits this strange phenomenon. In technical language, the **mixture** is a fluid behaving in a non-Newtonian way so that the sudden application of a **force** leads to it thickening rapidly to the point where it is solid. Remove the force, and the cornflour mixture will dribble away. Exploring this in the classroom provides a fascinating context for investigating different **variables**. What happens when the ratio of cornflour to water is varied? Is the **temperature** of water a decisive factor?

CORROSION

When iron or steel corrodes it is said to rust. Rust is the name given to iron oxide. Quite apart from being unsightly, rust severely weakens the strength of steel. The chemical change (see **chemical changes to materials**) that causes iron and steel to rust involves the metal reacting with oxygen and water to form iron oxide and water. Unlike many other chemical changes which children might gain experience of in the primary classroom, corrosion happens at room temperature and the reaction takes place over a long period of time. A steel nail placed in a jar of water will corrode because oxygen is contained in the water in the form of dissolved air. That same nail suspended in humid air will also corrode because of the water vapour contained in the air. A walk around the school and playground or observation of an old bicycle could be the starting point for identifying materials that rust or corrode. A collection of materials, some coated with paint or galvanised and clean and some rusty, can be used to find out what happens when metals are left in air or water or oil. The coins chosen by one teacher for children to investigate rusting proved a poor choice, since these were made from or coated with metals which did not rust! Investigations might determine which metals will rust, what conditions are necessary for corrosion to occur, how long it takes for iron or steel to rust and how we can stop things rusting.

CRANK (D&T)

A crank is a rod attached to an **axle** that can be used to convert an up-and-down (or back-and-forth) movement to a circular motion (for the opposite of this – converting a rotary motion to a linear motion – see **cam**). In the example of a cyclist, the person's leg acts as the rod. It moves predominantly in an up-and-down motion on the pedal, turning the drive cog around. Children can explore everyday items such as the hand crank on a mechanical pencil sharpener before moving on to making their own. A simple crank **mechanism** is a rod attached off-centre to a wheel by a split pin. Attached to the wheel could be an axle around which string could be wound for raising and lowering objects.

Box 1   Creativity

Is science a creative activity and are scientists creative thinkers? The authors of this encyclopedia think the answer to this question is a definite 'yes', yet many people might not be so sure. There is much discussion about creativity in education at the moment, yet how often do we hear the minister for *this* or an expert in *that* begin to discuss creativity and then immediately start talking about the arts? Why does it matter that science might be thought of as concerned with correct facts and incontrovertible theories?

A useful definition of creativity is 'imaginative activity fashioned so as to produce outcomes that are both original and of value' (NACCCE 1999: 29). Science involves worthwhile purposeful activity that leads to original outcomes (ideas and explanations) that are certainly of value. To see science in any other way is to misunderstand the nature of science. Furthermore, a teacher who sees science as uncreative is likely to present science in a way that is, frankly, dull and tedious.

Research is very clear that everyone has the potential to be creative. It is claimed by Pfenninger (2001) that creativity is the high point of evolution. We must have an inclusive view of creativity so that, whether our young people are to become scientists or not, they must all have the opportunity to develop and express creativity during their education – and science clearly has an important part to play. So how do we teach *for* creativity in science? We can start by valuing children's questions as much as their answers.

Science is most exciting when it is 'cutting edge.' In this context this might mean exploring children's interests, challenging 'accepted ideas', realising that science is ever changing and there is plenty of room for original ideas (they may not be original to the world, or the teacher, but they may be to the child). Science, both in the 'real world' and in the child's world, can be thought of as a rough draft, not a final edition. There is room for debate and discussion everywhere. How shall we classify living things? (Is a mushroom a tree? Is a seaweed a plant?) Is there such a thing as a 'healthy' food? Is there life on other planets? Is there any point in recycling?

Another way to see creativity in science is to identify the factors that have been shown to encourage creativity. They include open-ended tasks, a non-threatening learning environment where ideas are accepted openly, opportunities to play with materials or ideas and a co-operative mood in the classroom (Howe 2004). Scientific enquiry activities lend themselves perfectly to such teaching. By carrying out investigations, children will have the opportunity to try out ideas, discuss, question, speculate, solve problems – in fact *be* creative.

Making connections between previously unconnected ideas is a central part of creative thinking. In science we try to make connections between what we already know and new experiences in order to develop a better understanding of the natural world. Really good theories unify different bits and pieces of knowledge. Insights can come through making good connections. The 1996 Nobel prizewinner for chemistry, Sir Harry Kroto, and his colleagues were working on a puzzle – why does the number 60 seem so important and common when examining the chemistry of carbon? Harry played around with models of shapes that carbon molecules could form. One shape was like a ball. He suddenly saw that the panels on a football create 60 vertices and that this could explain how and why carbon atoms join together in 60s – the shape is very stable. This discovery led to a whole new and important branch of 'nanotechnology.'

Science in the 'real' world is sometimes cross-disciplinary – this enables those connections and creative 'leaps' to be made. Sir Harry Kroto had an interest and skill in graphic design which may have helped in his work. Author and illustrator Beatrix Potter first produced botanic illustrations and wrote scientific papers before turning to children's books. The arts and sciences are alternative ways of seeing the world, but each on its own gives us only a partial view. In the classroom, science must at times be 'cross-curricular.' Through practical experiences and discussions, children can start to make connections – between swimming and forces, music and vibrations or cooking and chemical changes. We need to make the most of opportunities for 'connection-making' if we are to help children to become good scientists. When planning, teachers can look for and utilise potential links within science too: seed dispersal is a good context to discuss air resistance; the phases of the moon are a beautiful demonstration of the concepts of shadow and reflection.

There is a deeply emotional dimension to creativity. Most children feel good when they have the opportunity to be creative. Creativity is more than having fun or coming up with wacky ideas. It is purposeful and therefore can be immensely satisfying, or at times frustrating. The purpose may be to answer a question, solve a problem or communicate a new idea. The purpose may change during the process as new questions are raised, possibilities are imagined, hypotheses are tested and understanding is developed. This is creative science ... but what would uncreative science be like? It would be without clear purpose ('What is the point, Miss?'), without room for imagination ('Just follow this worksheet ...'), without time for play ('... I didn't ask you to play with those things ...') and without a useful outcome ('... just learn the answers'). In other words, uncreative science is boring science.

One problem with creative learning is that it is slow learning. It isn't an efficient use of time – we can't get so much 'covered.' But learning science shouldn't be about learning things at top speed before the test comes along. A decision needs to be made: do we want to encourage creative science which is arguably slow, unpredictable but enjoyable? Just as children need support from teachers to 'be creative', teachers need 'permission' and support from senior teachers, advisors and the government to take some risks. Creative teaching can be scary! The move away from SATs at the end of key stage two is a sign that teaching for creativity will be more possible, even required, in the future.

Creative teaching is a bit like life. If the conditions are difficult, only the fittest will survive. Similarly, there will be robust and resilient individuals who have adapted to be creative even in the most hostile of environments. If, however, optimal conditions for creative growth can be identified and maintained, creativity will flourish. This article has discussed some research that is showing that creativity can be supported in a number of ways. Harrington (1990) suggests that bringing together people, the physical environment and an understanding of the creative process will make a 'creative ecosystem' which will sustain creativity, just as a balanced natural ecosystem can sustain life. Science can be an integral part of that ecosystem.

References

Harrington, D.M. (1990) 'The ecology of human creativity: a psychological perspective', in M. Runco and R. Albert (eds) *Theories of Creativity*. London: Sage.

Howe, A. (2004) 'Science is creative', *Primary Science Review*, 81: 14–16.

National Advisory Committee on Creative and Cultural Education (NACCCE) (1999) *All Our Futures; Creativity, Culture and Education*. London: DfEE.

Pfenninger, K.H. (2001) 'The evolving brain', in K.H. Pfenninger and V.R. Shubik, *The Origins of Creativity*. Oxford: Oxford University Press.

CROSS-CURRICULAR

Primary teachers and early years' practitioners often make links between science and other learning areas within the **curriculum**. For example, there is a close relationship between science and technology (see **science and design and technology**). Although it would be a mistake to see the two as synonymous – broadly, science generates knowledge whilst technology solves problems – we can link them in different ways. For example, science can take the lead when investigating simple **circuits**, and designing a torch, a 'steady hand tester' or an electric quiz board can be seen as the **application** of that scientific knowledge in a technology activity. Alternatively, technology can take the lead, for example in solving the problem of keeping teddy dry in a rainstorm, whilst testing different materials for their **waterproofness** can bring a scientific dimension to this design activity. Of course, science also has close links with mathematics, for example in the **measurement**, recording, graphing and interpretation of data from a science **investigation**. Likewise, the special kinds of words used to describe and explain scientific phenomena (see **vocabulary, scientific**), together with genres of writing such as report, instructional text and explanation make many links with language and literacy. Natural links with music arise when investigating sources of **sound**, **pitch** and **loudness/volume**, whilst the topic of **light** and colour lends itself well to art and design, as well as exploring the symbolic role of light in different world faiths (see **contexts for science**).

CRYSTAL

Salt and sugar are everyday examples of crystals. A crystal is a substance with an organised structure such that the atoms or molecules of the material are joined together in a definite, regular pattern. It can be difficult to see crystals clearly without the aid of a microscope but good examples that can be seen unaided are the **rock**-forming minerals in some igneous rocks formed by the crystallisation of magma. For example, granite has in it three principal mineral crystals (quartz, feldspar and mica) which are large enough for children to see quite clearly. Another way that crystals are formed is by them precipitating out of a solution. For instance, when a salt solution evaporates, small crystals of salt will form and with the aid of a magnifier these can be seen to be cubic. Children can experiment with salt and sugar solutions, possibly growing the crystals up string. Slower **evaporation** produces larger crystals. Alternatively there are a variety of crystal-growing kits available commercially, providing many further possibilities for experimentation.

CURRENT

Electrical current is the flow of tiny charged particles (**electrons**) through conducting materials (usually metals) around a circuit. It is sometimes tempting to use the **analogy** of flowing water through pipes to understand this movement that we can't see. However, there are weaknesses in this analogy, since if we cut a wire the **electricity** doesn't leak out as water would from a cut pipe. Current is measured in amperes (amps or A for short), named after the French scientist André Marie Ampère (1775–1836), and can be measured using an ammeter, though the brightness of a lamp in a circuit can be used as a useful proxy in primary classrooms. A common misconception is that electrical current in a simple circuit flows out of the **battery** and gets 'used up' in the various components such as lamps or motors. To test this idea out, try placing an ammeter at different points in the circuit – the current is always the same! Alternatively two identical bulbs placed in series (see **series and parallel circuits**) will be as bright as each other – there isn't one very bright bulb consuming the current so that the other bulb is dim. This is because the electrons whose flow we measure as current are already present in the wire before the battery is connected; all the battery does is provide the energy to get them all moving around the circuit. They carry this energy to the various components, but don't get used up themselves. Only two things affect the current in a simple circuit: the **voltage** ('push') that the battery gives to the electrons and the **resistance** to flow in the wires and other components. The greater the voltage (or the lower the resistance) the greater the current. We usually think of current as flowing 'downhill' from the positive to the negative, and this is how it is usually represented in circuit diagrams. However, with the discovery that the moving particles (electrons) are actually *negatively* charged, we need to recognise that this 'conventional' representation of current is incorrect – electricity actually flows from negative to positive!

CURRICULUM (STATUTORY)

The current (October 2010) statutory curriculum for primary science education in England is the National Curriculum (DfEE/QCA 1999). This breaks the primary-age phase into two Key Stages; Key Stage 1 from age 5 to 7 (Years 1 and 2) and Key Stage 2 from age 7 to 11 (Years 3 to 6). In both Key Stages the Programme of Study (PoS – what teachers are required to cover) is divided into four areas:

- Sc1: Scientific **enquiry** – the procedural elements of scientific learning including ideas and **evidence** and investigative skills;
- Sc2: Life processes and living things, including the 'strands' of life processes, humans and other **animals**, green **plants**, variation and classification (see **classifying and identifying**), and living things in their environment;
- Sc3: Materials and their properties, including grouping and classifying materials (see **classifying and identifying**), changing materials (see **chemical changes to materials** and **physical changes to materials**), separating **mixtures** of materials;
- Sc4: Physical processes, including **electricity**, **forces** and motion, **light** and **sound**, and (in Key Stage 2 only) the Earth and beyond.

Sc2, 3 and 4 together constitute the conceptual knowledge to be taught across each Key Stage. Each area of the PoS has a corresponding Attainment Target (AT) which consists of criteria by which children should be assessed, set out as level descriptors for levels 1 to 5. Level 2 is taken as the median attainment at the end of Key Stage 1 (age 7), whilst level 4 is the median attainment at the end of Key Stage 2 (age 11). Up until 2009, children were required to sit Statutory Attainment Tests (SATS) in science during Year 6, but from 2010 onwards level judgements in science are to be arrived at by teacher **assessment**, attaching a weighting of 50 per cent to AT1 in Key Stage 1 and 40 per cent to AT1 in Key Stage 2, with the other three attainment targets sharing the remaining weighting.

CUTTING AND SHAPING MATERIALS (D&T)

The best way of cutting and shaping a material to make an **artefact** will depend on the nature of the material. Scissors are familiar cutting tools that are suitable for paper, thin card, some fabrics and threads and materials such as plastic straws, but young children will need plenty of experience cutting a range of materials to become proficient scissor users. More resistant materials will require specialist tools. Snips can be used for cutting a range of materials such as plastic sheets and even thin dowelling (wood cylinders) and older children can use small craft knives with appropriate supervision (see **materials, mouldable**; **materials, resistant**; **materials, sheet**). Primary-age children can be taught to use small saws to cut wood safely. Although this can be a source of anxiety for teachers the small hacksaws generally available in schools will not easily damage fingers, though it is a good idea for the children to wear goggles to protect their eyes from sawdust and from other children wielding sticks of wood (see **risk assessment**). Using a bench hook – a wooden block that hooks over the edge of a table – helps to protect the table and gives the saw a straight line to cut along. The bench hook can be clamped to the table with a G-clamp to stop it from moving around.

Files and sandpaper can be used to shape and smooth a range of resistant materials. Holes can be made using a single hole punch or, for a more resistant material, a drill. Again, using a G-clamp to fix the material in place helps to protect fingers and surfaces from drills, but young children can be taught to use them safely. Mouldable materials can be shaped in a variety of ways, some permanent, some not.

D

DAY AND NIGHT

The fact that we spend roughly half our time in daylight and the other half in darkness governs many of our bodily rhythms and seems such a basic phenomenon that it is perhaps surprising that it took until the seventeenth century for us to develop an adequate explanation for it, via Copernicus' model of a sun-centred universe and Galileo's telescope observations which appeared to support this idea. Maybe it is because we do not feel ourselves to be moving, since everything about us moves at the same rate. It is certainly hard to envisage the Earth spinning on its axis every 24 hours, so that someone standing on the equator would be travelling at over 1,000 miles per hour! No wonder that young children develop explanations for day and night based on their own needs – 'night happens because we need to go to sleep' – or the apparent movement of the sun – 'it goes round to the other side of the world' (see **alternative frameworks**). To **model** this process for children we need to get them used to the idea of a rotating Earth, perhaps by spinning themselves on a swivel chair whilst another child holds a large torch representing the sun (see Figure D.1). Once they realise that the light from the torch appears to move across their field of view even though the other child is standing still, it can help them to understand that it's us that moves, not the sun.

DECAY

There are plenty of ways that children can study the decay of materials providing simple health and safety precautions are followed (see **risk assessment**). Over time the decay of substances such as milk, bread, cheese, yoghurt or apple, carefully sealed in dishes or bags, can be closely observed (see **fungi**). Looking at leaves in autumn or objects buried outside can be used to introduce the concept of **biodegradability**. A record of the changes can be kept by drawing or photographing the changes while keeping a careful note of the time that has elapsed. It's even possible for children to make their own time-lapse films. A range of **questions** can be addressed during these observations. What changes can be seen? Do different materials decay differently? Do all materials decay? Do things go rotten faster if they are wet, hot or buried? How can we keep things fresh longer? What is causing the decay?

DESIGNING (D&T)

Designing is a complex and creative process that can happen before and during the making processes in design and technology. Designing begins with identifying a need, want or opportunity. This can involve children exploring existing products (e.g. bags or pizzas) and situations (the use made of a school library, the way children get to school) by carrying out research through

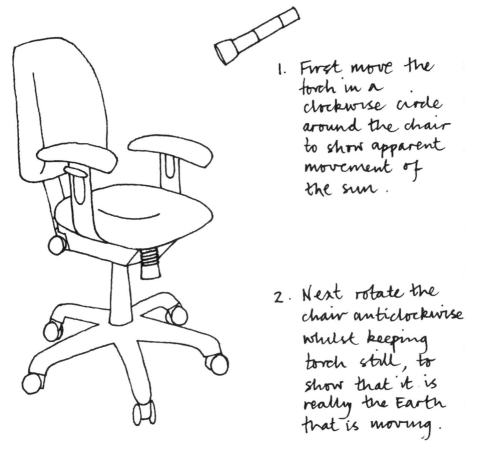

1. First move the torch in a clockwise circle around the chair to show apparent movement of the sun.

2. Next rotate the chair anticlockwise whilst keeping torch still, to show that it is really the Earth that is moving.

Figure D.1 Modelling day and night.

observation, surveying, interviewing, tasting, testing, etc. The next stage in the design process is likely to be the generation of ideas or solutions – it is good practice to discuss and develop a number of ideas before settling on one. The ability to imagine more than one solution is a difficult but worthwhile skill to develop. There are a number of techniques that can be used to generate ideas. 'SCAMPER' is a mnemonic for seven techniques. We need to begin by selecting an everyday object, e.g. a ballpoint pen:

Substitute your object with something else.

For example: use a nail and some paint.

Combine: what could you combine with your object to make something useful?

For example: attach a spoon to your pen so you can eat breakfast while doing the crossword puzzle!

Adapt: how could you change your object to make something new?

For example: the ink could glow in the dark for night reading.

Magnify or '**m**inify' an aspect: what aspect could you 'blow up' or shrink to make something new?

For example: you could shrink the pen to a size that will slot into a mobile phone.

Put some part of it to other use.

For example: use a ballpoint pen without the ink cartridge for a straw.

Eliminate some part of it.

For example: dispose of the nib to write with ink blots.

Reverse or replace some part of it.

For example: put an eraser instead of the ink in the tube.

Try to SCAMPER with these objects: plastic cup, sticky tape, paper clip, pad of paper.

(With acknowledgement to Kevin Byron and The Children's Museum of Indianapolis, 1999.)

Another way of encouraging the development of ideas is to carry out role play – children can imagine what it might be like to be in an unfamiliar situation (e.g. having to look after a baby, being unable to open doors) that might require a design solution.

The next stage in the design process is to develop some of the ideas into design drawings, **models** or prototypes. These can then be tested, evaluated and improved. This is often where a design process will stop in classroom D&T. The next stage – going into production – might be reached if the project has a real purpose, such as designing the school's Christmas card or cooking a pizza supper for parents.

Designing doesn't always have to be done on paper – young children will design and make concurrently. They will gain a great deal from experimenting with materials or construction kits which can easily be rearranged or reassembled. There is no need always to record ideas on paper. If plans and diagrams are required, then children will need to be progressively taught how to make useful design drawings – these are different from illustrations and may contain information such as required quantities or sizes of materials, sequences of events, views from different angles. Photos of the stages along the way would be a valuable record of the design process.

DEVELOPING SYSTEMS

According to the AKSIS Project, making artefacts or designing a system to solve a problem is a form of scientific **enquiry** (Goldsworthy *et al.* 2000). For example, children could devise a way of growing a plant with a long, twisted stem, or set up an organic garden with plants chosen to deter pests from other plants. This approach has overlaps with design and technology (see **science and design and technology**); sometimes by applying our understanding in a problem-solving context the limits of the understanding are pushed, and the process might stimulate further exploration and lead to **fair testing**.

Box 2   Dialogic talk

Talk for learning has become a focus across the curriculum, and the concept of dialogic talk has a particular relevance for teaching science because it helps to focus on how teachers can work with children's ideas and scientific ideas together. In science education there is a tension between wanting children to 'find out for themselves' and also to learn 'the right ideas', and the concept of dialogic talk helps to address this dilemma.

It helps to understand dialogic talk by thinking about what it isn't. It is different from authoritative talk, in which children's ideas are only accepted if they are in line with the scientific message (Mortimer and Scott 2003). This is talk focused on transmitting information. Children's comments can seem irrelevant, wrong or perhaps bizarre, and teachers often respond by ignoring or dismissing these ideas, focusing attention on answers that are in line with the point they want made. While this kind of interaction can help to establish clearly what the teacher sees as the right answer and might be useful for a brisk recap of information, it does not help in supporting new learning and deep understanding. It also conveys the hidden message that the teacher has all the answers. Authoritative talk is often made up of 'IRE triads'; the teacher initiates (I) with a question, the child responds (R), and the teacher evaluates (E) their answer.

In dialogic teaching children's ideas are seen as the starting points for building talk that explores different points of view and different meanings in order to reach a new shared understanding. Instead of evaluating a child's response to a question – for example, by answering, 'Yes, that's right' – and moving on, teachers can use children's ideas as starting points for further discussion: 'What makes you say that? Can you give me an example? What do you mean by …? Would anyone else like to add to that?' This helps to develop an extended discussion in which children's ideas are explored and then different contributions are linked, or 'chained' together to build up ideas.

Robin Alexander (Alexander 2008) uses the term 'dialogic' to express a 'genuinely reciprocal' process of communication between teacher and pupil in which ideas are developed cumulatively over sustained sequences of interactions. Using dialogic talk as part of teaching can support children, both in coming to understand the scientific view and in having their own viewpoints valued. Alexander characterises such dialogic teaching as:

- *Collective*: Teachers and children address learning tasks together, whether as a group or a class.
- *Reciprocal*: Teachers and children listen to each other, share ideas and consider alternative viewpoints.
- *Supportive*: Children articulate their ideas freely, without fear of embarrassment over 'wrong' answers, and they help each other to reach common understandings.
- *Cumulative*: Teachers and children build on their own and each other's ideas and chain them into coherent lines of thinking and enquiry.
- *Purposeful*: Teachers plan and steer classroom talk with specific educational goals in view.

Other indicators of dialogic talk would be that children, as well as teachers, initiate interactions by asking questions and making suggestions, and that children listen to each other and are actively involved when they are not speaking. Learning has emotional and social dimensions as well as the cognitive elements. If the classroom provides a safe environment in which children can express their views without fear of ridicule or of them being ignored, then the teacher is more likely to be successful in eliciting their ideas and in finding out whether understanding is shared. If children are secure, they take responsibility for checking their own understanding by asking the teacher questions – 'Do you mean that …?' – or they contribute: 'Oh yes, that's like …' Children can help to explain new ideas to each other – 'You know, it's like when …' – by accessing their shared culture in a way that teachers cannot.

The work of Mortimer and Scott (2003) also helps to explain how teaching can go beyond being 'interactive' to become 'dialogic.' In their model, interactivity refers merely to the extent of pupils' participation in the talk, and whether it can be characterised as 'dialogic' or 'authoritative' depends on whether the pupils' ideas are genuinely part of the discussion or whether the teacher's ideas or scientific ideas are dominating: 'either the teacher hears what the student has to say from the student's point of view, or the teacher hears what the student has to say only from the science point of view' (Mortimer and Scott 2003: 33). In their research they characterise the talk of episodes within science lessons on two dimensions, interactive–non-interactive and dialogic–authoritative, and propose four classes of 'communicative approach' as summarised below.

	INTERACTIVE	NON-INTERACTIVE
DIALOGIC	**A** Interactive/ dialogic	**B** Non-interactive/ dialogic
AUTHORITATIVE	**C** Interactive/ authoritative	**D** Non-interactive/ authoritative

Interactive/dialogic (ID) Teacher and students consider a range of ideas and viewpoints.

Interactive/authoritative (IA) The teacher focuses on the scientific point of view and leads students through a series of questions and answers aimed at reaching it.

Non-interactive/dialogic (ND) The teacher presents and considers different points of view.

Non-interactive/authoritative (NA) The teacher presents one specific point of view – that of school science.

(Mortimer and Scott 2003: 35)

The different classes of communicative approach have different teaching purposes. Mortimer and Scott (2003) suggest that good science teaching may involve cycles of talk in which there is a focus on exploring the children's ideas, then developing their ideas by relating them to the scientific ideas, followed by more authoritative summaries of the scientific point of view, then cycling back to a focus on the children's ideas. This idea has been developed into a recommendation that teachers maintain cycles of dialogic episodes for 'opening up' discussion of children's ideas and authoritative episodes for 'closing down' the dialogue and 'maintaining the scientific story' (Scott and Ametller 2007). Like Alexander, they see different kinds of talk as having different purposes, and share the view that there is a need for more dialogic talk in education.

Sociocultural perspectives on learning and teaching have led authors to use the term 'dialogic' in somewhat different ways, drawing on theorists Vygotsky and Bakhtin to try and make sense of the dynamic, two-way processes of talk and to apply this to the classroom context. Vygotskian interpretations of the word 'dialogic' tend to focus on the role of talk in scaffolding children's learning to an end point in which the children and the teacher have a shared meaning. For example, children may have the idea that a sponge is not a solid because it can be squashed. Hands-on experience alone would not address this alternative framework; talk would be needed to explain the particular scientific meaning of solid and to relate this back to the children's experiences and ideas. Bakhtinian versions of 'dialogic' focus more on how people will inevitably have differences – perhaps subtle differences of nuance – in what they understand of a situation. Suppose the teacher says that the class will be learning about flowers; the word 'flower' will conjure up different mental images and associated contexts, such as cut flowers like roses, daisies growing on the playing field, or daffodils in a pot for Mother's Day. By contrast, a scientific definition of flowers would include catkins, grass flowers and horse chestnut spires. How would these different meanings of 'flower' relate to the cross-section of a 'standard flower' (often a buttercup) that is sometimes presented as the only possible structure? The differences between meanings are valuable as a starting point for generating new ideas and questions, perhaps about where and how different kinds of flowers grow, or whether they all have stamens.

To resolve the tension between supporting open-ended development of ideas and introducing children to an existing body of knowledge, Alexander (2008) makes a distinction between dialogic talk that is 'discussion' – which is open-ended and involves shared problem-solving – and dialogic talk that is a 'scaffolded dialogue' in which the teacher has some specific aims for learning: 'structured, cumulative questioning and discussion which guide and prompt, reduce choices, minimise risk and error, and expedite "handover" of concepts and principles' (Alexander 2004: 23).

In dialogic talk primary teachers need to pay attention not only to the conceptual content of children's ideas, but also to the cultural contexts and personal experiences that make them meaningful and relevant. This is entirely consistent with a sociocultural approach to science education that sees children's learning within a broader social context. Rupert Wegerif argues that 'dialogicality' is itself the endpoint of education (Wegerif 2006). In practice this would link creativity with 'playful' dialogic talk, a dimension that is missing from an account of a dialogic education that focuses only on reasoning (Wegerif 2005). Taking a global view, Alexander (2008) sees a dialogic approach to education as vital for the future. If children are to be politically empowered through dialogic teaching, then developing dialogic talk in science is not only about helping children to come to understand scientific ideas but about experiencing the science process of developing new ideas for themselves and seeing ideas as open to change.

References

Alexander, R. (2004) *Towards Dialogic Teaching: Rethinking Classroom Talk*. Cambridge: Dialogos.

Alexander, R. (2008) *Towards Dialogic Teaching: Rethinking Classroom Talk*. fourth edition, Cambridge: Dialogos.

Mortimer, E. and Scott, P. (2003) *Making Meaning in Secondary Science Lessons*. Maidenhead: Open University Press.

Scott, P. and Ametller, J. (2007) 'Teaching science in a meaningful way: striking a balance between "opening up" and "closing down" classroom talk', *School Science Review*, 88 (324): 77–83.

Wegerif, R. (2005) 'Reason and creativity in classroom dialogues', *Language and Education*, 19 (3): 223–38.

Wegerif, R. (2006) 'Dialogic education: what is it and why do we need it?' *Education Review*, 19 (2): 58–67.

DIET

A diet is simply what an organism eats. We tend to use the term to mean a restricted intake of some sort – to 'be on a diet' – and this may confuse children. The human diet is an omnivorous one – we eat pretty much anything, unlike grazing animals (herbivores) or meat eaters (carnivores). In our diet, carbohydrates (grains, bread, rice, potatoes, pasta, sugar) are the main source of **energy**, proteins (in pulses such as beans, and in meat, fish, milk) are the main building material of the body and are mainly used for **growth** and repair. Fats (oils, butter) are also a source of energy, but certain fats are needed in small quantities for specific purposes such as insulating nerve cells. Vitamins and minerals have a number of specific functions: for example, vitamin C has a role in strengthening skin, and the mineral iron plays an important role in red blood cells in transporting oxygen. Water is essential as a medium in which all the chemical processes of the body take place and is one of the main constituents of the human body. (Some estimates suggest we are about 70 per cent water!) There are a number of ways of explaining what makes a healthy diet, all of which express current ideas about what constitutes an appropriate quantity of food and balance of food groups to maintain our bodies' systems and processes. It is important to note that we should avoid referring to 'unhealthy' foods as such. One explanatory approach is to think of a 'food pyramid' where the base represents food we can eat most of and the top represents foods we should eat little of. Grains and vegetables are at the base, with sugars and fats at the top. Another approach is to divide a plate into a 'pie chart' showing the relative proportions of food groups of a 'healthy' diet. This is known as the 'eatwell plate' – see www.food.gov.uk. Children will need to understand that we all make choices about food, and we can make choices that are likely to have a detrimental effect on our health.

DIFFERENTIATION

Differentiation is the practice of catering for the differing learning needs of the children in the classroom. Children may bring a wide range of scientific experience with them to school, may hold a number of different preconceptions about each scientific topic, and may have different preferences for learning style, or particular physical, emotional or cognitive difficulties in accessing the science curriculum. Most teachers tend to differentiate scientific learning by task, outcome or support. For example, an investigation can be varied in difficulty by the choice of independent **variable**. A categoric variable, such as bouncing a ball on different surfaces, is probably easier to conceptualise than a continuous variable such as the height from which it is dropped (with its associated effect upon the speed at which the ball hits the floor), and the results will be accordingly easier to interpret. So different science attainment groups within the class could be given different investigations, or variations on the same investigation which make different cognitive demands (see **group work**). Many scientific activities, such as exploring the properties of magnets (see **magnetic materials**), can be sufficiently open to enable access for all learners, whilst those attaining at a higher level might be expected to produce findings or explanations which are more sophisticated and scientifically accurate. When differentiating by support, a teacher or additional adult might work with a lower attaining group to help read instructions or guide them through an enquiry activity, whilst other groups might be expected to work more independently (see **classroom organisation**).

DIGESTIVE SYSTEM

This system of organs and tissues includes the mouth, teeth, stomach, intestines, liver and anus. The digestive tract from mouth to anus can actually be thought of as being 'outside' the body, and its purpose is to break food down into molecules so it is small enough to pass through the walls of the intestine and into the bloodstream. The digestive system first breaks down food mechanically in the mouth, and different **teeth** have particular roles in doing this. At various points in the digestive tract, chemicals known as enzymes are released and these help break down particular kinds of food. Any undigested food is what forms the faeces (aka 'poo' – there is a lovely non-fiction book for older children, *Poo* by Nicola Davies, which contains many fascinating facts on the topic; Davies 2004). With primary teaching it is not appropriate to teach about the internal processes of digestion. There are a number of activities possible around the topic of 'teeth' which can build on children's prior knowledge. Children will also know about 'tummy aches'; **questions** can be starting points for learning, such as: Where is our tummy? What gives us a tummy ache? How do we avoid tummy aches?

DINOSAUR – see **reptile**

DISSOLVING

If a substance can totally mix with a liquid we call this dissolving. One liquid can dissolve in another liquid or a solid can dissolve in a liquid. A solution, a completely uniform **mixture**, is formed. The solvent is the liquid that does the dissolving; the solute is the solid that gets dissolved; and the solution is the mixture of the two. Something that dissolves in a solvent is described as soluble whereas those materials that do not dissolve are called insoluble. Salt and sugar are examples of materials commonly studied in the primary classroom that are soluble in water. There is a limit to the amount of solute that can be dissolved in a given volume of solvent. The solution eventually reaches a point where no more solid can dissolve. This is called a saturated solution. The saturation limit depends on the solvent and solute concerned and also on the **temperature**. Usually, as the temperature is increased, the mass of solute that can dissolve also increases. Dissolving is a reversible change making it possible to retrieve solid salt **crystals** from a saltwater solution by **evaporation** of the water.

Dissolving and **melting** are frequently confused.

- Dissolving can happen without heat, whereas heat is needed for melting to take place.
- Dissolving requires two or more substances, melting only one.
- Dissolving involves substances mixing; in melting the substance remains pure.
- Dissolving cannot be reversed by cooling whereas melting can.
- Dissolving involves two different kinds of particles mixing whereas melting involves the rearrangement of one kind of particle.

Fruitful lines of enquiry for children might begin with a **concept cartoon** about getting sugar to dissolve in tea which may in turn lead to **questions** about the size of sugar granules, the temperature of tea and the amount of tea/sugar. Investigation of what happens when sugar, jelly, paint or baking powder are dissolved in small amounts of water encourages **prediction** and **hypothesis** about what will happen: where the substance has gone, whether we could show it is still in the water (for example a taste test), how we could make it dissolve more quickly, whether it can be retrieved. Other insoluble powders or grains such as flour, sand or talc can also be tested to encourage further questioning and thinking.

DNA

Standing for deoxyribose nucleic acid, this is more use in a pub quiz than in a lesson, although children might have heard of 'DNA tests' by later Key Stage 2 and may know it is a way of identifying people, as

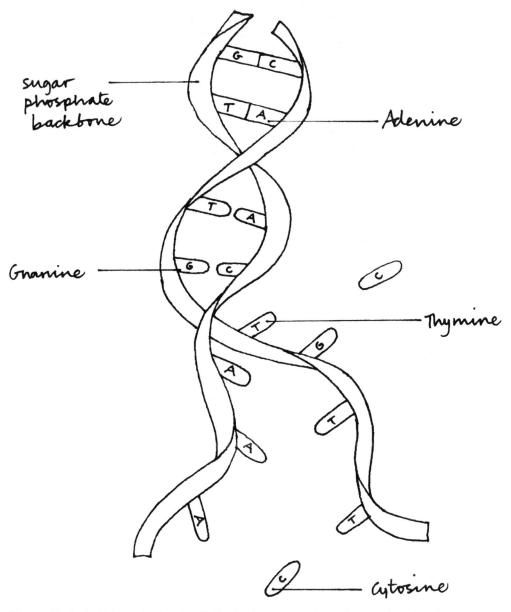

Figure D.2 DNA unzipping itself. Each nitrogenous base forms a bond with only one other base – guanine to cytosine, adenine to thymine.

DNA is almost unique to each individual. Identical twins will have the same DNA. Figure D.2 shows a DNA molecule 'unzipping', which enables it to make a copy of itself – this is the basis for **reproduction** and how information encoded in our genes is passed from generation to generation.

DRUGS

Although we use the terms 'drugs' to mean illegal drugs in everyday conversation, medicines are drugs, though not all drugs are medicines. Different drugs act at different sites in the body: for example, alcohol affects how messages are transmitted

45

between brain cells. Some drugs, which may or may not be used as medicines, affect the **nervous system** and may reduce feeling pain, slow down mental activity or lead to hallucinations. Smoking cigarettes has a stimulant effect, increasing alertness, but the nicotine in tobacco is also addictive so that smokers may need to continue to smoke to feel 'normal.' Regular smoking leads to a build-up of tar on the lungs, reducing the area available for oxygen and carbon dioxide to be exchanged (see **respiratory system**). Carbon monoxide in the smoke goes into the blood and prevents red blood cells from carrying oxygen as efficiently. It also increases the build-up of fat in arteries, which increases the risk of a heart attack. The effect of alcohol, as with many drugs, depends on the 'dose' – on how much is taken. It has a number of effects – it causes blood vessels to expand, leading to flushed cheeks, and this effect might be helpful in preventing heart disease (see **circulatory system**). It also causes excessive passing of urine, leading to dehydration (see **excretory system**).

Brain function is affected, and at low intakes this leads to a feeling of disinhibition which is often experienced as being pleasant, but as the levels of alcohol in the blood get higher mental function is increasingly affected, and can lead to risk-taking behaviour, impairment of co-ordination affecting speech and movement, and also judgement. High levels of alcohol intake also lead to liver damage. Dependency on alcohol is a serious condition and there may be unhappy consequences for the individual and their families. Children need to know about drugs before they leave primary school. They need to understand that some drugs are beneficial, some are harmful and some are illegal to possess or use. Schools should have a drugs education policy and teaching should be informed by it. Teaching will be in the context of personal social and health education (PSHE). The definitive guidance is currently the 2004 publication *Drugs: Guidance for Schools* published by the DfES (DfES 2004). Further guidance can be sought from www.drugeducationforum.com.

E

ECHO

When we hear an echo, we are listening to a reflection of a **sound**. If we shout, we hear the sound of our voice. That sound also travels away from us. If it hits a suitably hard surface, like a rock cliff or stone wall, it will bounce back towards us and we hear the same sound again. The time between the two sounds will depend on how far away the hard surface is. If the shout comes off different surfaces at different distances, for example in a large rectangular hall, we might well hear more than one echo. This can be modelled using a 'slinky' spring pulled between two children (see **model**). One child pushes the spring in towards the other child sending a 'sound wave' down the spring. The wave will reach the other child then bounce back towards the 'sender.' It is a myth that a duck's quack doesn't echo, although it would be interesting to try to prove it!

ECLIPSE

There are two types of eclipse visible at various times from various points on the Earth's surface. The more common of the two is a lunar eclipse, which occurs when the **moon** passes through the Earth's shadow. As the Earth is larger than the moon this can take an hour or so, moving from a partial eclipse to a total eclipse and back to partial again. Since a lunar eclipse only occurs when the moon is on the opposite side of the Earth

from the sun it can only happen during a full moon (see **phases**, **lunar**). All parts of the Earth facing away from the sun (i.e. in darkness) can see the eclipse simultaneously. Sometimes the moon appears to be a reddish colour during a lunar eclipse because of the sun's light that has refracted (bent) around the Earth through the atmosphere – the same reason that a sunset appears red.

The other kind of eclipse – a solar eclipse – is much rarer. This happens when the moon passes between the sun and the Earth (always at new moon) and casts a **shadow** on the Earth's surface. Because the moon is comparatively small and only just overlaps the sun, its shadow is only a few hundred miles across and the period of totality is relatively short – typically a few minutes. The shadow travels quite rapidly across the Earth's surface, however, so people in several different countries may see the eclipse at slightly different times. The last total solar eclipse visible from the UK mainland was on 11 August 1999; all parts of the country enjoyed a partial eclipse whilst only west Cornwall experienced totality, unfortunately under thick cloud. Sadly, for those of us who missed it, there won't be another total solar eclipse visible from the UK until 2090!

ECOLOGY

A branch of science that includes the study of global processes, the study of **habitats** large and small, and the individual interaction between organisms such as those between predators and prey or insects and flowering plants. Key ecological concepts include **adaptation, biodiversity, interdependence, populations** and **sustainability**.

ECOSYSTEM

A community of **plants**, **animals** and other organisms plus the environment that supplies them with water, air and other elements they need for life. Ecosystems can be studies on very different scales, from a slice of mouldy bread, to a single tree, to a forest, to the Pacific Ocean. Within an ecosystem the living things will interact with each other and with the physical environment. The interactions between living things can be described with **food chains** or food webs.

ELASTICITY

A **property of materials**. When a **force** is applied to a material it will deform in one of two ways: elastically or plastically. An elastic material (e.g. an elastic band) will return to its original shape and size after the force has been removed whereas a plastic material will remain permanently deformed after the force is removed (e.g. Plasticine; see **plasticity**). Some materials are only elastic up to a point, beyond which increasing the force will lead to permanent change, e.g. a steel spring. A related but different property is flexibility, which is a measurement of the ease with which an object deforms. It is more difficult to stretch very thick elastic bands compared with thin ones. However, each band is still made from an elastic material as they will both return to their original shape when no longer pulled. Older primary school children can develop a 'pull test' to determine which materials are elastic and their degree of elasticity. They could apply this knowledge when choosing suitable

materials for a design and technology project, e.g. which material is best for driving a hand-wound paper aeroplane propeller.

ELECTRICAL CONDUCTIVITY

Electrical conductivity is a measure of the **resistance** a material provides to the flow of electricity. Materials such as metal are called electrical **conductors** because they offer very little resistance to this flow. In the case of metals, they make very good conductors because individual atoms of metal are bonded together in such a way as to allow **electrons** to move freely from atom to atom. Conversely, electrical insulators (e.g. wood, plastics and air) don't have this structure so offer a high level of resistance to the flow of electricity. Between the two extremes lie semiconductors, whose resistance can vary with heat which makes them useful in such devices as fire alarms: as the semiconducting material heats up it becomes more conductive, creating a circuit for an alarm bell. Primary school children can investigate the electrical conductivity of a range of materials by simply using an electrical test circuit (see **properties of materials**).

ELECTRICAL ENERGY

Electrical **current** can carry **energy** from one place to another; by definition this is in the form of electrical energy. In a simple circuit, each **electron** transfers some energy from the **battery** – which converts chemical into electrical energy – to a component such as a lamp; which then transforms this electrical energy into **light** and heat. It is useful to distinguish between electrical energy and **electricity** (the flow of electrons), since it is the energy that gets 'used' (transformed into another type) not the electricity itself. This is why electricity doesn't get 'used up' in a simple **circuit**, and why we don't really pay for 'electricity' in our electricity bills. After all, we send just the same number of electrons back to the power station as we received (actually they just jiggle backwards and forwards in our wires)! Whether the power station transfers energy from fossil fuels (see **carbon cycle**), wind or nuclear sources, it will probably use some sort of dynamo to set up an alternating current in the power lines, using electrons which are already there. What we are paying for is the energy that electricity carries, measured – as are other forms of energy – in joules (J), named after the British scientist James Joule (1818–89).

ELECTRICITY

Electricity is a phenomenon caused by the movement of tiny charged particles (**electrons**) from place to place. Electricity can be *static*, where the electrons concerned have been moved to or from insulating materials, such as rubber, plastic or textiles. This results in an electrical charge building up on the surface of a material (e.g. a balloon), which is not able to move but can exert electrostatic **forces** on other charges. So, for example, an electrically charged plastic comb can attract small pieces of tissue paper, even though both are insulators (see **attraction**). The other, more useful, type of electricity which forms a major topic of study in the primary years is *current* electricity, where the electrons are free to flow along conducting materials (usually metals such as copper). They require a source of **energy** – such as a **battery** or power station – and a complete **circuit** around which they can flow. This flow of electricity, called **current**, can then carry energy to a variety of appliances such as lamps, motors, buzzers, computers, etc. Research by the SPACE Project (Osborne *et al.* 1991) indicates that children associate electricity with something that travels very fast and is very hot. They may not necessarily make the links between battery and mains electricity, so it is worth showing them appliances that can be run from either source. The principal differences between battery electricity and mains electricity are first that the latter is much more powerful – so more dangerous – and second that mains cables carry 'alternating current' that switches direction fifty times per second, whilst batteries cause electricity to flow in one direction around a circuit (see **risk assessment**).

ELECTRON

An electron is a tiny elementary particle which scientists believe forms part of every atom of every material in the universe. Different atoms have different numbers of electrons (hydrogen has one, helium has two, etc.) which are thought to move around a central nucleus – though according to Heisenberg's Uncertainty Principle we can never be exactly sure where they are until we try to measure them! The main relevance of the idea of electrons to primary science is that they are believed to carry an electrical **charge**, and their movement through conducting materials (see **conductor**) such as copper is what we experience as an electrical **current**. Until the work of the British physicist J.J. Thompson (1856–1940) it was widely believed that an electrical current flowed from positive to negative, so Thompson's 1897 discovery of the *negatively* charged electron which moved in the opposite direction came as a great surprise. As an interesting 'how science works' footnote, it was subsequently found that Thompson had formed such a strong belief in the answer he was expecting that he suppressed data which didn't seem to fit his predictions.

ELICITATION

Elicitation is a process of clarifying and finding out children's existing ideas. It is the second phase in the Constructivist

Teaching Sequence formalised in the 1980s as part of the Children's Learning in Science Project (CLIS) at the University of Leeds, and follows on from **orientation** in this model (see **learning**). For the teacher this means gaining an insight into the child's current understanding of the concept(s), which can inform their teaching (see **conceptual understanding**). For the child, it is a process of becoming aware of their own ideas (of making them tangible or 'structuring' them); this is the start of developing and possibly changing their ideas. They may begin to be aware that other children have somewhat different ideas or that they cannot explain something to their own satisfaction. Recording these ideas may be part of the process of clarifying them, and may be useful for both teacher and children to reflect on later. Different topic areas lend themselves to different ways of finding out and recording children's existing ideas; these are known in science education as 'elicitation strategies.' These include: observing a child, talking with a child, sorting a collection (see **sorting activities**), making an annotated drawing, completing **floor books**, making a **concept map** and using **concept cartoons**. In practice there is not always a clear distinction between elicitation of ideas and **restructuring** them.

Eliciting children's ideas is important at the start of a topic or unit of work as it can then inform medium-term planning for the class as a whole and identify groups or individuals who may need additional support or extension. However, it is not only for the start of the topic; it is important that teachers continue to provide children with opportunities to express their developing knowledge, so elicitation strategies can be used at any point as part of assessment for learning. If elicitation is seen as a collaborative rather than solely individual activity, a variety of ideas and views are made available on the 'social plane' of the classroom for children to consider (see **sociocultural perspective**). The process of elicitation can be seen as creating a shared pool of different ideas and experiences, providing a rich starting point for everyone to learn from. Owning a range of ideas as a class might enable those ideas to be examined more critically; it is not a person being examined, it is the idea.

ENERGY

Understanding the concept of energy is important to studies of biological, material or physical systems; it is a unifying concept that links many areas of science together. When change occurs in a system, it is energy that enables that change to happen. There are different forms of energy: **light**, thermal, **sound**, kinetic (movement; see **kinetic energy**), electrical (see **electrical energy**) and potential forms of energy (stored in a system providing the potential for change) such as chemical or gravitational-potential energy (see **gravity**). Energy is conserved; it is not created or destroyed during change but its form might be changed. Take, for example, a rocket being launched into the sky on Bonfire Night. Energy stored in the firework as chemical energy is changed to kinetic, thermal and sound energy as it whooshes upwards. Then the stored energy is changed to thermal, light and sound energy as the rocket explodes. Energy and **forces** can be easily confused: although they are related they are separate concepts. A force is a way of transferring energy, but pushes and pulls are not forms of energy themselves. In the example of the rocket, there is a push upwards acting on the rocket, known as thrust, which is in reaction to the flow of gases (formed by **chemical changes to materials** in the rocket) pushed downwards.

ENQUIRY, SCIENTIFIC

A scientific enquiry will involve using scientific **process skills** to develop understanding of the natural world. Although, as the AKSIS Project (Goldsworthy *et al.* 2000) found out, it is often equated with a **fair test**, scientific enquiry can take many different forms: **exploration**, **classifying and identifying**, **pattern-seeking enquiry**, **developing systems**, investigating models (see **model**).

EVALUATION (D&T)

Evaluation is an important skill in relation to design and technology (see also **designing**). Children should learn to carry out evaluation systematically to bring about improvements in processes and outcomes. To achieve this, the teacher will need to provide support in the opportunities and encouragement to think critically (but not negatively). Support can take the form of key questions to guide the evaluative process. **Questions** can focus on the process and the outcome:

Process: What stages did the design go through?

What materials were used to make the outcome?

What tools and techniques were used to create it?

What was difficult about the project?

What was enjoyable about the project?

What should you remember for next time?

Outcome: What need does the outcome meet?

Who would want to use the object?

What does the user think of the object?

How could you test the object?

Older children might also be asked:

Process: What helped you achieve success?

What difficulties did you need to overcome?

What can you say about designing, making and being creative?

Outcome: What effect will the object have on the environment?

What effect will the outcome have on people's lives?

Does the object discriminate?

EVALUATION (SCIENCE)

One of the **process skills**. When children are asked to evaluate during scientific enquiry, they may be considering evaluating their own performance on a task in a generic way, for example the extent to which they co-operated as a group, or whether they finished on time. However, a more science-specific interpretation of evaluation is about the quality of evidence a scientific enquiry has produced. This might include the extent to which they could control different **variables**; for example, in a test to find out which trainers have the best grip, did they take into account the area of the tread? In a survey (see **pattern-seeking enquiry**) of how many spots there are on a ladybird, they might reflect on whether the sample was representative of the **population** being studied, or whether it was large enough to generalise from. Other aspects that can be evaluated are the precision of **measurements** or their reliability; could the test be repeated and get the same results? The ability to evaluate the quality of the evidence that is used to justify claims is an important element of **scientific literacy**.

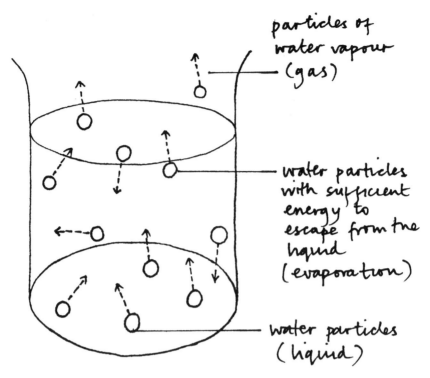

particles of
water vapour
(gas)

water particles
with sufficient
energy to
escape from the
liquid
(evaporation)

water particles
(liquid)

Figure E.1 Particles of water evaporating from the surface of the liquid, forming water vapour (gas).

EVAPORATION

Evaporation is a change of **state of matter** from liquid to gas which can be explained by **particle theory**. In their liquid state, particles are able to move about relative to each other so that at the surface of water some particles may be moving fast enough to escape from it, changing state to a gas as they do (see Figure E.1). If the liquid is heated up the particles will move faster so more will escape and the rate of evaporation increases. If those particles that have escaped are transported away from above the surface of the liquid (by wind, for instance) so that they cannot rejoin the liquid, then the process will accelerate. The process can be observed by looking carefully at warm water lit from the front. Water begins to rise from the liquid in the form of minute water droplets, these eventually disappearing as the droplets change into water vapour. Even on cold days puddles will seem to 'steam' as they are warmed by the sun.

Primary teachers can uncover children's understanding of evaporation and **condensation** (the reverse process) by getting them to monitor the change of water level in a large container over an extended period of time (see **elicitation**). Research by the SPACE team (Russell and Watt 1990) discovered that many younger children use non-technical terms such as 'dried up' to describe the process they witness. Older primary school children use 'evaporated' much more frequently as a way to explain their **observations**. However, for all ages of children, a great majority could not explain the change they describe in terms of water as a substance having different states. Only a minority of children understood water could undergo a transformation from liquid to gas. Possibly the reason for believing the water ceases to exist arises from the common usage of the word 'evaporate' to indicate that something no longer exists. It is difficult for children to grasp that the water is still present in the air, so alternative explanations such as the liquid has seeped away will be given to explain what has happened. This idea can be challenged, of course, because as the level of liquid falls no water will be seen pooling underneath the vessel.

Our sense of smell can be used to detect evaporated molecules. Perfumes and air fresheners work because certain 'smelly' molecules evaporate easily from the liquid (they are said to be *volatile*). Our nose then senses these molecules as we breathe them in.

One way to investigate evaporation further is by raising questions with children about how clothes dry. Do clothes washed in warm water dry quicker than those washed in cold? Does the colour of the clothing affect the rate of drying? It may be the case that these questions can be directly tested if the class's art shirts are in need of a clean (see **contexts for science**). Another direct experience for children to reflect on is what happens when they sweat. In this instance particles evaporate from sweat and as they do so **energy** is transferred from the liquid to the vapour so that the sweat feels cooler as a result – all very helpful on a hot summer's day.

EVIDENCE

Historically, a key point in the development of scientific thinking was a philosophical shift from seeing the validity of ideas in terms of their logic to requiring evidence to support those ideas. This was the movement from the Rational approach of the Greek philosophers to the empirical science of the Renaissance. Modern science is about the relationship between ideas and evidence, so debates about what counts as scientific 'truth' are often debates about the strength of the evidence (see **evaluation**). A contemporary example is about the extent to which human activity is responsible for **climate change**. Evidence may come in the form of a single description of an observed phenomenon, numerical data from a test with controlled variables (a **fair test**) or survey responses from a large population (see **pattern-seeking enquiry**). What matters is that the claim being made is consistent with the evidence. Young children may find it difficult to accept evidence that contradicts what they believe to be true (as may adults!), so an important aim for science education is to develop children's capacity to change their own ideas. They also need to develop their enquiry-planning skills to gather appropriate data for a question and a readiness to interpret evidence critically. This helps children to develop an understanding of the **tentative nature of science**; the ideas we have at the moment seem to fit the evidence, but we may produce more evidence that doesn't fit that picture and then the ideas will have to change. This is the Karl Popper principle of 'falsifiability.' A **cross-curricular** link can be made with history and sources of historical evidence which children can analyse as 'detectives.'

EXCRETION

The process of getting rid of waste, carried out by all living things. See **excretory system**.

EXCRETORY SYSTEM

Every living thing produces waste products which are potentially harmful to it if not removed. In humans, the skin, kidneys, liver and bladder are parts of our excretory system. The function of this system is to remove certain unwanted or waste products from the body. Waste can

53

be in the form of gases (e.g. carbon dioxide), liquids (e.g. urine) and solids (e.g. faeces – although a strict definition would not include 'poo' as it is not a product of metabolism; see **digestive system**). **Plants** excrete through pores called stoma. The system also regulates the amount of water in the body.

EXERCISE

Exercise keeps humans healthy. It maintains and builds muscle strength, including the heart muscle (see **circulatory system**) and muscles around the lungs, and maintains the range of movement of various joints. Aerobic exercises involve increasing heart rate and breathing rate (see **respiratory system**) over an extended period. (A quick sprint is not 'aerobic' but 'anaerobic' – without increased oxygen uptake.) It is really important for children and adults to 'warm up' before exercising. A warm-up prepares us physically and mentally, gradually increasing heart rate and preparing muscles for intense activity. The topic is an ideal way to combine physical education with science as children can observe changes in the body as a result of exercise, monitor their heart rate and breathing rate and keep a record of performance (see **cross-curricular**). It may also provide a motivating context for learning about other processes and systems – some children may find fascination in the training of footballers, or comparing the exercise regimes of Olympic athletes from different sports.

EXPLORATION

Exploratory activities involve handling or playing with objects or a collection, e.g. a tank of water and a collection of toys, or various magnets and different materials. For young children this exploration may be an end in itself; for older children it may be used to engage their interest in a new topic, allow them to play with new resources or stimulate their raising of questions. Exploration involves **observation** (which includes all the senses), possibly using particular equipment to record the observations or to take **measurements**, but in an open-ended way rather than to test a particular **hypothesis**. Teacher interventions to support further exploration might include taking part and demonstrating curiosity, or asking questions such as 'What have you noticed here?' and 'I wonder what would happen if …'

EXPOSITION (EXPLANATION)

As well as finding things out for themselves and expressing their own scientific ideas, children also occasionally need their teacher to explain things to them. This process of exposition – direct teaching of a concept – is perhaps an underrated pedagogical skill, since the learning theories (see **learning**) upon which most primary science education is built tend to emphasise open-ended questioning (see **questions**) rather than 'telling children the answer.' However, exposition can be particularly useful at the end of a lesson during a plenary discussion, in which children are reporting back on their findings from **practical (hands-on) activities** and a skilled teacher can bring out the key learning objectives by summarising 'what we know' about the phenomenon under investigation. Effective exposition often relies on practical demonstration, since being able to give an authoritative commentary on what is happening when, for example, a ping-pong ball bounces off a vibrating tuning fork can help children build their own conceptual **model** of the situation. Exposition also frequently draws upon **analogy**: for example, explaining how a battery drives electric current around a circuit by comparing it with a bicycle chain being pulled around by the pedals.

Of course, there is always the danger that an expository style of teaching can become mere 'transmission' of information which may not add to children's understanding, so it is important to combine explanation with frequent questioning to check on the messages being received and to adjust the level accordingly.

EYE

We see things because **light** coming from them (either because they are **light sources** or because they reflect it) enters our eyes and is detected by light-sensitive cells at the back of the eye (the retina). The small holes through which the light passes are called pupils and contain lenses to focus the light on the retina to form an image. Because the various light rays from different parts of our field of vision have to cross over each other in order to pass through the pupil, this image is upside-down and back-to-front. The electrical signal sent along our optic nerves (see **nervous system**) from the cells in the retina is interpreted by a special part of our brain (the visual cortex) which corrects the image for us. In a famous experiment conducted by George Stratton in 1896, people who wore inverting glasses for a few days found that their brain eventually turned the images the right way up, then when they took the glasses off they saw everything upside-down. Children's ideas about seeing tend to parallel those of some Greek philosophers, who thought that in order to see something, we had to send a beam of light from our eyes to illuminate it. This **alternative framework** is reinforced by the other misconception that cats' eyes 'glow' in the dark, and could be challenged using a dark-box – first nothing can be seen in the box because it is dark, then when a source of light is shone, an object becomes visible. It took the tenth-century Arabic philosopher Al Hazan to develop our idea of the eye as a passive receiver of light. Of course, the brain takes a much more active role in interpreting what we see but it can be easily fooled, as in the case of optical illusions (see **observation**).

F

FAIR TEST

A fair test is a type of scientific enquiry or investigation in which children systematically change one variable – the independent **variable** (factor) – whilst observing or measuring the effect of these changes on another factor (the dependent variable). To make the test 'fair' they need to keep all other factors that might have an effect on the outcome (the control variables) the same. This is appropriate when it is possible (and ethical) to control the different variables and when the purpose of the enquiry is to explore a causal relationship between one factor and another, for example exploring the effect of temperature on seed **germination** by putting pots of water and mung bean seeds in cool, warm and hot places and counting the number that sprout.

FERNS

A group of **plants** that don't have flowers. They reproduce instead by making spores, rather than **seeds**, which can often be found under their leaves. They do have **roots**, **leaves** and **stems**, and come in many shapes and sizes from tiny floating ones to tree ferns. Common ferns include bracken, shuttlecock ferns and hart's tongue ferns. They grow wild in the UK and are easy to grow – ideal for a damp and shady part of the school garden or conservation area. They need very little care and don't get attacked by many pests or diseases.

FISH

Members of the animal **kingdom**. They are cold-blooded **vertebrate** animals, covered with scales, and equipped with two sets of paired fins and several unpaired fins. They use gills to get oxygen from the water, and a few can also breathe air. Most reproduce (see **reproduction**) by laying eggs which are usually released into the water and sometimes cared for by a parent. The eggs hatch into larvae which grow into adult fish. Fish eat a wide range of things: algae, water plants, **invertebrates**, other fish. A shoal of fish is a loosely organised group – where they are 'hanging out' together. Schools of fish are tightly packed and synchronised groups which provide protection from predators. There is excellent video of fish behaviour on the BBC Nature website (www.bbc.co.uk/nature). Children gain knowledge of fish as pets or through fishing. Angling is the largest participant sport in the UK and anglers often have an excellent knowledge of fish ecology and behaviour, so you may well have a fish expert in your class or school community.

FLEXIBILITY – see **elasticity**

FLOATING AND SINKING

Exploring the science of floating and sinking is one of the most common activities in early years settings, where children can gain direct experience of the buoyancy of a range of familiar objects and materials in the water tray. Many practitioners like to develop young children's **prediction** skills during this activity, by asking them to say whether they think each object will float or sink before they put it in the water. Children may think that all heavy things will sink whilst all light things will float, which can be challenged by, for example cutting a small piece off a potato, which will still sink (see **concept map** and **restructuring**). Alternatively they may argue that it depends what the object is made of; for example, wood will float whilst metal sinks. But actually not all wood floats (ebony, pitch pine and licorice root are all examples of sinking wood) whilst most ships are made of metal! Whether an object floats or sinks depends on how much water it displaces (causing the water level to rise). Displaced water seeks to return to its original level, resulting in an upward **force** on the object immersed in it – this is called 'upthrust' and is equal to the **weight** of the water displaced. We can feel upthrust by trying to push an inflated balloon underwater. If the upthrust is enough to balance the weight of the object (i.e. the two forces are balanced) then it floats. So objects with a large volume for their weight – such as hollow balls and boats – will float, whilst dense objects which don't displace much water (i.e. they are denser than water) will sink. This is what Archimedes found when he famously jumped out of his bath and ran naked down a street in Athens – a nice link if you're studying Ancient Greece. It wasn't just that his bathwater rose in level, it was that the weight of the water he displaced balanced his own weight!

FLOOR BOOKS

A floor book is a way of recording children's work in science. They are often used as a means of capturing children's spoken thoughts as part of eliciting their existing ideas at the start of a new topic (see **elicitation**), but can also be used to document the progress of an **enquiry**. Floor books got their name because they are books made out of large sheets of paper that an adult or children can write on while sitting on the floor in a group. There are many possible variations on this format, but the important idea is that an adult (or child) records exactly what various children say, probably noting their name (see Figure F.1). Children generally like having their ideas valued in this way and it provides a record to return to later when reviewing learning. Children's drawings and photographs may also be included in the book. The website www.azteachscience.org.uk contains a full explanation of how to create floor books, along with examples.

FLOWERING PLANTS

Like most groups of living things, flowering plants come in a wide and wonderful array of sizes, colours and forms, therefore studying them is a great way to introduce children to the concept of **biodiversity**. Flowering plants include trees (e.g. horse chestnut), herbs (e.g. lavender), vegetables (e.g. pea), ornamental plants (e.g. tulip), grasses (e.g wheat) and 'weeds' (e.g. daisy; see **weed**). Children should have the opportunity to observe a wide variety of flowering plants, develop an understanding of the function of each part of the plant, discuss and explore their many uses as foods, construction materials, medicines, etc., and begin to understand the importance of this group of organisms. Digital microscopes or cameras can be put to very good use to capture and magnify (see **observation**) the amazing detail of petals,

What do you think will happen to the apple if we leave it alone?

Figure F.1 An example of a floor book.

anthers, stamens, seeds and fruit (see Figures F.2 and F.3). Flowers feature widely in many cultures as objects of beauty and symbolism. They appear in art and craft as paintings, jewellery, architecture and textile motifs. This cultural significance offers the teacher a range of opportunities for **cross-curricular** teaching.

Few flowers look like a scientific diagram and it is not required for children to draw and label such a diagram until Year 6. Flowers are reproductive structures (see **reproduction**) which use two basic strategies, wind or animal pollination, to unite the male and female sex cells. Many trees (e.g. oak) are wind pollinated,

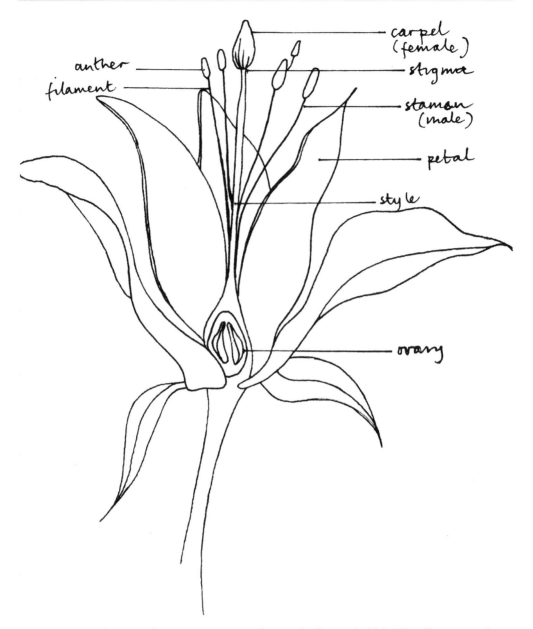

Figure F.2 The reproductive structures of a simple flower (a lily). The filament and anther are known collectively as the stamen (male part). The female part is known as the carpel and consists of the stigma, styie and ovary.

taking advantage of their height to distribute their pollen far and wide in the wind. The flowers of grasses are also wind pollinated and as such are usually held high on a stalk above the leaves so they can sway in any breeze. Insects, such as bees and butterflies are the main animal pollinators and are attracted to the flower by high visibility petals and/or delicious sweet scent and nectar. These events can be observed out in the garden, or there is some excellent footage on YouTube.

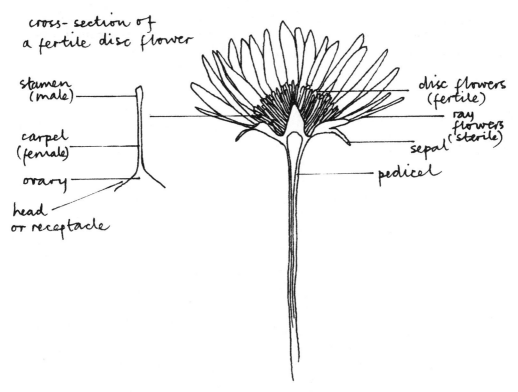

cross-section of
a fertile disc flower

stamen
(male)

carpel
(female)

ovary

head
or receptacle

disc flowers
(fertile)

ray
flowers
('sterile)

sepal

pedicel

Figure F.3 The reproductive parts of a composite flower (a daisy) showing sterile 'ray flowers' which make up the daisy's white petals and the mat of fertile yellow disc flowers.

These adaptations are all intended to facilitate the movement of pollen, containing the male reproductive cells, from the anther of one plant to the stigma of another. This is the process of pollination. The pollen grain then grows a tube down to the ovary to allow its valuable cargo to meet the female reproductive cell, the ovule. This is the process of fertilisation. The fertilised ovule grows into a **seed** which, given the right conditions for the species, will germinate (see **germination**) and grow into a mature plant to complete the life cycle.

FOOD CHAINS

Food chains or food webs indicate feeding relationships, as **energy** transfer, between organisms from producers (green plants) to consumers (animals). Arrows indicate the passing of food (chemical energy) from one living thing to another and therefore the direction is important. The chain generally begins with a green **plant** (e.g. stinging nettle → tortoiseshell butterfly caterpillar → sparrow → sparrowhawk) or with dead organic matter (detritus) (e.g. leaf litter → earthworm → blackbird → fox). Older children will be able to understand the more complex representation of a food web which shows that organisms can be food for a number of different consumers. Food chains need not always include a whole **animal** (e.g. grass → cow (milk) → human). A common mistake in making food chains is to use the arrow to mean 'eats' (e.g. cow → grass), which is wrong because the energy transfer is from grass to cow.

It is fun to model a food web. You need to do prior research into 'what eats what' and provide a dozen small balls of string or wool. Each child takes the role of an organism apart from one, who is the sun. Start with a range of producers who stand around the sun, 'collecting' the sun's energy (run string or wool from the sun to the producers). Continue the web by 'feeding' the strings from producers to consumers … this can get into quite a tangle. You could also model what might happen if a part of the web is destroyed (see **interdependence**): which consumers are affected if some plants die (e.g. through drought)?

FOOD TECHNOLOGY (D&T)

Food technology is an important and compulsory part of the D&T curriculum. It considers food ingredients as materials to work with and combine, and involves skills of food preparation, cooking, hygiene and safety (see **risk assessment**). Food technology is more than **cooking** as it requires children to follow a design process (see **designing**) where they may develop a recipe to meet a want or need. When doing this they will apply knowledge about food, health and **diet** and combine ingredients to produce something tasty and fit for a particular 'consumer' (including themselves). The national scheme of work for D&T includes a number of units that are food-based, including those on sandwiches, fruit salads, bread and biscuits. Other popular food projects include pizza, soups, yoghurts and cakes. There is excellent potential to make **cross-curricular** links with science:

- Exploring the senses of sight, taste and touch;
- Humans as organisms (see **diet**, **digestive system**, **food chains**, **teeth**);
- Similarities, differences and the **properties of materials**;
- Changing and separating materials (see **chemical changes to materials**);
- Nutrition and a healthy diet (see **fruit**, **vegetable**);
- **Micro-organisms**.

There are many online resources available on food technology, including those from:

- Active kids: www.activekidsgetcooking. org.uk/
- The Design and Technology Association: www.data.org.uk/
- The British Nutrition Foundation, who offer a framework of competence statements outlining how food, nutrition and cooking skills should develop for children aged 5 to 16: www.nutrition.org.uk.

For more information see also www. teachernet.gov.uk.

FORCE

In science, the concept of 'force' or 'impetus' is an abstract idea used to explain why objects might start or stop moving, speed up, slow down, change direction or change shape. Usually, some sort of **energy** transfer is involved, e.g. if a child rolls a ball along the floor, she has transferred some of the **kinetic energy** in her arm to the ball. However, in the case of **friction**, a force might not cause any movement at all, but might prevent something from moving (as in the case of bookends, which stop a row of books falling down because of the friction between the bookends and the shelf). For young children, it is usually sufficient to explain force as 'a push or a pull', since these are sensations they can easily experience directly (all forces are either pushes or pulls). Everyday use of the word 'force' to mean 'coercion' – as in 'he forced me to do it' – can be confusing for children, so it is important that they have a chance to experience and discuss pushing and pulling before attaching this 'special' scientific term to these phenomena. There are many kinds of forces; some work through direct contact between the objects concerned (such as friction) whereas others can act at a distance (e.g. **weight** due to **gravity**, magnetic attraction and repulsion – see **magnetic materials**). The topic of forces is widely regarded by primary and early years teachers as one of the most difficult to teach, partly because of its abstract nature and partly because some of the explanations in this area appear to be counterintuitive (they appear to defy 'common sense'). For example, many children (and adults) would say that a ball stops rolling because the force has 'run out', whereas scientists might argue that there is no 'forward' force acting on the ball after it has left the child's hand, only the 'backward' force of friction slowing it down.

FRICTION

Friction is a special kind of **force** acting between two surfaces, tending to reduce the speed at which they slide or slip past each other. Generally, the rougher the surfaces, the greater the force of friction between them, because the bumps and hollows of the surfaces can interlock. Children can experience this by rubbing two pieces of sandpaper together, then 'magnify' the surfaces by using two hairbrushes with bristles facing each other. There are two kinds of friction: static friction, in which the force between the surfaces is sufficient for them not to slide past each other, and sliding friction. Walking in shoes with good grip on a non-slippery surface is a good example of static friction, because the lack of sliding between our shoes and the floor gives us confidence to change speed or direction without slipping over. Children can test how well their shoes grip different surfaces by putting them on a ramp and gradually increasing its angle until the shoe begins to slide. Once surfaces are sliding past each other they still experience sliding friction – a force which tends to be less than static friction.

Often we want to reduce friction as much as possible – the **wheel** is a simple machine that enables us to do this as it replaces a large friction force between the load and the ground with a smaller force between the wheel and **axle**. This can be further reduced by lubrication, which can also cut down on the amount of **kinetic energy** that is transferred to heat energy, thus improving the efficiency of the machine. Children can demonstrate this by rubbing their hands together vigorously; fairly quickly their hands start to become warm. However, if they add some baby lotion or cooking oil their hands will slide more easily at a lower temperature. Even with lubrication a wheel still experiences a small amount of rolling friction between the small area which is in contact with the surface and the surface itself. One 6-year-old child described friction as 'the naughty force', because it stops things happening as we might want them to – balls and toys slow down, machines wear out, whereas according to Newton's first law of motion they should carry on for ever. However, friction is also essential to everyday life – just imagine walking around on ice all the time!

FRUIT

Biologists and cooks have different views about this. Biologists think fruits are ripened plant ovaries. For the purpose of primary science teaching it is useful to categorise anything that contains a **seed** or seeds as a fruit, so apples, apricots, pumpkins, peppers and pea pods are all fruits. Seedless fruits (e.g. bananas) are seedless because humans have selected and grown what would be naturally sterile varieties – they are grown from cuttings so could be thought of as designer clones!

Making a fruit salad is an appropriate **food technology** task – it could involve identifying, including and excluding certain fruits, looking at recipes and finding favourites. Food skills – peeling, cutting, slicing and basic hygiene – will need to be developed and applied. The salad may need some additives: lemon juice to preserve the fruit colour and texture or sugar to adjust sweetness.

FUNGI

A large group of living things – a **kingdom**. Mushrooms, moulds and yeasts are fungi. Many of them are tiny so fall into the category of **micro-organisms**. They perform a very important job in decomposing and recycling material (see **decay**). Fungi cannot photosynthesise (see **photosynthesis**) – they feed off dead or living things or organic matter

(e.g. sugar in wine-making). Children can experience fungi in everyday situations. Edible mushrooms are easy to find (in the supermarket) and can be examined closely, for example under the digital microscope (see **observation**). Bread-making involves the use of yeast – bread rises in a warm place as the yeast feeds on sugar and gives off carbon dioxide gas. Be careful if you grow mould or fungi in the classroom. Try this: take two slices of bread. Press an unwashed hand into one, then seal the slice in a clear bag. Now wash the hand very carefully and then press it into the other slice. Bag and seal that too. Leave both in a warm place. You should see mould develop on at least one of the slices. Can you see a hand shape? Don't open the bags – dispose of carefully (see **risk assessment**).

G

GALAXY

A galaxy is a vast cluster of billions of **stars**, often hundreds of thousands of light years across. We believe our sun is part of a galaxy we call the Milky Way, which can be seen as a faint pale smudge stretching across the sky on a clear night away from light pollution. We only became aware that there were other galaxies in the universe with the observations of Edwin Hubble (1889–1953) in the 1920s, who concluded that spiral 'nebulae' (gaseous clusters) such as Andromeda were outside the Milky Way. He speculated that our galaxy looks similar to Andromeda, which is the closest spiral galaxy to us and is actually visible as a faint 'blurry-looking' star on a moonless night – the furthest object we can see with the naked eye!

Whereas previously astronomers had assumed that our solar system lay at the centre of the Milky Way, it soon became clear that we are about two-thirds of the way out along one of its spiral arms, slowly revolving round the core about once every 220 million years, attracted by its huge gravitational field (see **gravity**) in the same way the planets **orbit** the sun. Hubble also discovered that galaxies themselves are in clusters – we are part of a 'local' cluster of around 30 galaxies including Andromeda. What is more, the other clusters of galaxies appear to be moving away from us at very high speeds, leading to the 'expanding universe' hypothesis which was then extrapolated back to a single 'Big Bang' event around 13.7 billion years ago. The eponymous Hubble Space Telescope has sent back many stunning images of galaxies, which can be viewed on the NASA website (www.nasa.gov). In one famous experiment, scientists pointed the telescope towards an apparently 'empty' part of the sky and left the camera shutter open for a long time. The resulting 'deep field' view showed millions of galaxies so far away as to be undetectable by any other telescope – the universe is a mind-bogglingly big place!

GERMINATION

This is the process by which a **seed** begins to grow after a period of dormancy. Germination requires an appropriate **temperature**, moisture level and oxygen, but not usually light. Conditions for each species are slightly different. When conditions are right the seed will begin to absorb water, swell and burst its coat or testa. There are a number of features that children can observe. From the testa, one or two seed leaves will emerge. The first seed leaves are a different shape to the leaves that will grow next – they are not true leaves but stores of **energy**, in the form of starch, to fuel the early growth. The **root** (radicle) heads for the soil and the shoot (plumule) grows in the opposite

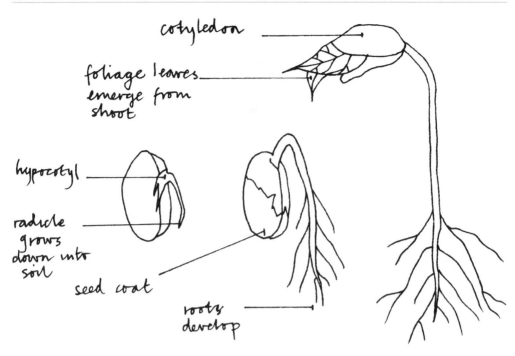

Figure G.1   A germinating bean. Eventually the hypocotyl develops into the plant's stem.

direction, even if the seed is planted upside down or rotated during germination (see Figure G.1). The plant will rely on the stored food until it can produce its first leaves and begin producing food through the process of **photosynthesis**. If it is kept in the dark it will grow tall, thin and yellowish, as it puts all its energy into looking for light. If a **light source** is sensed (e.g. a light to the side) the shoot will bend towards it. If all goes well, roots will draw up water, **leaves** will develop on the shoot and the plant can grow. There are some very good time-lapse films of germinating seeds available on YouTube (www.youtube.com).

GRAPH

Presenting data graphically helps with the processes of interpretation and communicating results (see **process skills**). The mathematical skills involved in drawing a graph are considerable and are likely to need explicit teaching. Younger children can do this physically, e.g. by putting a block in the stack next to a picture of their favourite food, or visually, e.g. by cutting a strip of paper to match the length of their foot and comparing it with those of others in the group. Older children can construct bar charts, line graphs, pie charts and scattergrams. Children can also be introduced to ICT tools such as databases or spreadsheets and use these to store and present data in graphical form. Using ICT in this way is a valuable skill and can speed up graph construction to allow more time for considering patterns in data. Deciding what kind of graph is most suitable for the data is a data-handling skill that children start to develop in the later primary years; before that, teachers can help children to make appropriate choices.

GRAVITY

Gravity is one of the four fundamental forces of the universe. It is a **force** that is always attractive (it always pulls, never pushes) and acts over vast distances; **galaxies** are held together by gravity. Although by comparison with the other three forces – electromagnetism and the two nuclear forces – gravity is very weak, nevertheless it is the force we experience most powerfully in our everyday lives. This is because the strength of a gravitational attraction between two objects is related to their **mass** and their distance apart. The main gravitational force we experience is that between ourselves and the Earth. Since the Earth is very massive and we are very close to it, this force is very large. Actually, gravity acts between all objects in the universe so we are very faintly attracted to all the things around us, but because they are all much less massive than the Earth we don't notice it. The two other gravitational forces that make a big difference to our lives are those between the Earth and the sun – which keeps us orbiting it at a safe distance – and between the **moon** and the oceans, which gives us tides. Children find the concept of gravity very hard to grasp; for them, the reason objects fall is because 'what goes up has to come down'. This notion of a 'universal down' makes it difficult to appreciate that for people in Australia, 'down' is actually in a different direction. Asking children to stick Lego figures into Plasticine models of the Earth can help them understand that what we call 'down' is actually caused by our gravitational attraction towards the centre of the Earth.

GROUP WORK

Children rarely do practical science on their own. Teachers tend to group children together to undertake scientific enquiry for a number of reasons (see **classroom organisation**). One of these is practicality; we tend not to have enough equipment and **resources** for each child to undertake an individual investigation. Another rationale is peer tutoring: if children can help each other solve the practical problems they encounter they are less likely to come to us for help and we can direct our scarce adult support to groups or individuals who find the activity difficult. Linked to this is the development of children's speaking and listening skills as they 'talk science' to each other in groups. Children's talk is fundamental to their scientific learning (see **learning**). Through talking to each other they can rehearse their own scientific explanations, debate different ideas about a phenomenon and construct shared understandings. Simply grouping children together does not guarantee that they will cooperate or discuss their scientific learning with each other. Part of the reason for this lies in group composition: teachers may need to try out several combinations of children with different temperaments, friendships, ideas and capabilities to find the optimum combination for groups to 'gel'. Group size is also crucial: many scientific activities work well in pairs, whilst more complex activities with clearly defined roles may need group sizes of up to five. However, teachers may also need to teach children how to co-operate, particularly if they have little previous experience of working in collaborative groups. Working in groups can develop in children a wide range of personal **attitudes** and dispositions which are essential for success in science as well as contributing to their broader well-being. Scientists in the twenty-first century tend to collaborate in multi-disciplinary, often international teams, with frequent informal communication in addition to the papers and conferences on which the scientific community depends.

GROWTH

For organisms to grow, their cells get bigger and also divide and multiply. A **plant** will usually grow for the whole of its life, although trees reach a maximum height determined by how well they can transport water to the tree top. In humans, rapid growth ceases in adulthood, although some cells (e.g. skin) continue to grow throughout life. Growth can also be a psychological concept – if the needs of humans are not met this may have emotional outcomes as well as physical. It could be an interesting classroom discussion to explore the emotional needs of other animals – what kind of care does a dog need compared with a fish?

H

HABITAT

In its narrowest definition this is simply the environment that a particular **population** of a species lives in, so that the habitat for a snail might be the damp parts of a wood or wall. But more broadly the term is used to describe the physical environment in which a collection of species live. For example, a grassland habitat may be characterised by the cover it provides or the **temperature** differences across its area. A habitat is distinct from an **ecosystem**, a study of which is specifically concerned with the interaction between the physical environment and the community of plants and animals within it. A popular way to study habitats in the primary school is through education for sustainable development (see **sustainability**), so that the focus is on the impact that change has on habitats in the local environment.

HANDS-ON SCIENCE CENTRES AND TECHNOLOGY CENTRES

Around the country there is a large number of centres dedicated to developing the public understanding of science and technology. These usually have the dual roles of being a visitor attraction and providing educational services such as school visits and courses for teachers. They provide opportunities for visitors to interact (see **practical (hands-on) activities**) with different exhibits to explore scientific and technological phenomena and often have special events such as talks and exhibitions. Some examples are: Explore@ Bristol, Inspire in Norwich, Stratosphere in Aberdeen, the Centre for Alternative Technology in mid-Wales and Investigate in the London Natural History Museum.

HARDNESS

One of the **mechanical properties of materials**. Put succinctly, hardness is the ease by which a material can be marked or indented. Children can be challenged to develop their own 'rub' test or scratch test to determine hardness. For one material to scratch another, it needs to be harder, a useful fact to know when ranking materials in order of hardness. When the hardness of two materials is nearly identical, children will need to make particularly careful **observations** to determine a rank order. Also be aware that soft materials will leave a mark or deposit (but not a scratch) on harder ones, like chalk on slate. Tests for hardness can be used to influence the choice of material for a particular job. For instance, which one of these would make the best surface for playing with a spinning top: wood, a sheet of metal or polystyrene? Tests that measure the hardness of a material and its reactivity to acid (e.g. reaction to vinegar to mimic acid rain) could be combined to determine which rocks or building materials will be most resistant to weathering.

HEALTH AND SAFETY – see **risk assessment**

HYDRAULICS (D&T)

A hydraulic system is one which controls movement by the means of compressed liquids (either water, oil or other fluids) moving between different cylinders by the motion of pistons. Since liquids are much less compressible than gases, hydraulic systems tend to be more precise and able to exert more force than pneumatic systems (see **pneumatics**), hence they have been widely adopted for heavy lifting machinery, fairground rides and a range of applications where large **forces** are required. Children can experience hydraulic forces by filling a plastic syringe with water and connecting it by flexible tubing to another empty syringe. Pushing the full syringe inwards results in an instant movement of the other, by comparison with the delay experienced when one is filled with air. However, the likelihood of getting wet has resulted in many fewer applications of hydraulics than pneumatics in primary design and technology.

HYPOTHESIS

A hypothesis in science is an explanation for an event based on some underlying theory. It is generally held that in science an acceptable hypothesis must be testable (see **evidence**). Of course, children have not yet formed the theories that scientists are working with, so their hypotheses will be based on their experiences and current ideas (see **constructivism**). Children in primary schools are not expected to develop formal testable hypotheses as such, but should be encouraged to provide explanations for their scientific ideas, and challenged when these are inconsistent with the evidence available to them. When making a **prediction** children may also be asked to offer an explanation. A child's explanation for their prediction could then become a testable hypothesis, for example 'Flowers grow better in pots because they are warmer.'

I

ILLUSTRATIVE ACTIVITIES

Sometimes teachers will set up a practical activity to illustrate a particular concept; for example, children might be asked to try heating a range of different materials (e.g. ice, butter, chocolate and sugar) to illustrate that different materials have different **melting** points. Another form of illustrative activity might be a teacher demonstration, which is particularly useful when it would be too dangerous for children to carry out an activity by themselves (such as burning materials) or to engage the children's interest (e.g. a bicarbonate of soda and vinegar 'volcano') (see **risk assessment**). If 'recipe' style instructions have been provided for the children then it is the teacher who has made the decisions about what will be done rather than the children, so this is an 'illustrative activity' rather than a full '**investigation**.'

INSULATOR (ELECTRICAL)

An electrical insulator is any material which does not allow an electrical **current** to pass through it. This is because the atoms within an insulator have **electrons** which are all tightly bound to their respective nuclei and are not free to flow even when given **energy** by a **battery** within an electrical **circuit**. This is not to say, however, that electrons *never* move within electrical insulators. They can be rubbed off the surface of an insulator (e.g. when rubbing a balloon on our jumper) leading to the accumulation of electrical charge – positive or negative depending on whether electrons have been removed or deposited. This is what we call static **electricity**, because it is 'stuck' on the surface of insulating materials and cannot flow away until put in contact with a **conductor** (e.g. the sweat on our fingers) leading to the small electrical shocks we sometimes experience when getting out of cars, etc. Even though the surface of a car is a conductor, it can build up a static charge because it is insulated from the ground by the non-conducting rubber tyres.

INTERDEPENDENCE

Each living thing depends on others to survive. Species are unable to survive without others (e.g. bean plants cannot grow without special bacteria). This interdependence includes food (one eats another – see **food chains**), provision of shelter (e.g. hermit crabs use the shells of other species), **seed dispersal** and the control of competitors. Competition can come from other individuals from the same species (the **population**) or from other species.

INTERPRETING AN ENQUIRY – see **process skills**

INVERTEBRATES

Invertebrates are 'spineless' – the term refers to a group of **animals** without a backbone (see **skeletal system**). They are a diverse group of small animals sometimes referred to in primary science as 'bugs', '**minibeasts**' or perhaps 'creepy crawlies.' They are easy to find in and around homes and schools and are therefore an ideal topic for study, as a way of exploring the diversity of life cycles, habits and **habitats** of the **animal** kingdom. In fact around 90 per cent of all animals are from this group. Common examples include spiders (arachnids), head lice (insects) and crabs (crustaceans) – all these animals also have jointed legs and hard exoskeletons. Molluscs such as slugs, snails and octopus have soft bodies, as do the worm family. Jellyfish, corals, sea anemones, sponges, starfish and sea urchins are also invertebrates. Invertebrates are a vital part of our ecosystem. Bees pollinate crops for us, worms improve the fertility of the soil and ladybirds feast on greenfly. A school conservation area can provide habitats and food plants for a wide range of invertebrates. The website www.buglife.org.uk is a useful starting point for further information about conservation and educational activities.

INTERVENTION – see **restructuring**

INVESTIGATION

In science education an 'investigation' is usually understood to be a specific form of a science **enquiry** that involves children in a complete process (see **process skills**). The term 'investigation' implies a more rigorous, systematic approach focused on a particular issue in comparison with a more open-ended **exploration**. First the children will be involved in raising a **question** and making a **prediction** based on some kind of **hypothesis** at a developmentally appropriate conceptual level. Then they will plan how to gather data, possibly planning a fair test or a survey. The next step would be to carry out the data collection (see **measurement**) and present it, maybe orally or pictorially, or as a table or **graph**. Having gathered the data, the children need to reflect on what it means. This may include **evaluation** of the process of data collection by asking if it was a **fair test**, or how accurate the measurement was, and considering whether they are able to answer their question. Reviewing how the investigation has developed the children's knowledge and conceptual understanding is the final stage and involves considering: 'What have we learned here?'

J

JELLY

How do you make a jelly? Take some cubes of jelly; break them in a bowl. Pour on hot water, stir and leave it to set. Clearly there are many **variables** to consider when making it: the **temperature** of the water, the amount of jelly, the size of the cubes, the number of stirs and the temperature of the location for setting the jelly. All ages can experiment at making jelly, although it may be older children that carry out a structured **investigation** into, for example, the factors that affect the time it takes for a jelly to set. Jelly has some fascinating properties. When making it, both **melting** and **dissolving** are happening. Once it has set the mixture formed is a **colloid** in which liquid is dispersed within a solid. Jelly is actually made up of gelatine, water, sugar, food colourings and flavourings, with the gelatine being the interesting bit, for it is this that is able to trap large amounts of water in pockets as it cools. It is this structure that gives jelly its most fascinating property – it wobbles!

JINKS JOINT (D&T)

The Jinks joint was named after David Jinks, former lecturer at Bishop Grosseteste College Lincoln and one of the pioneers of primary design and technology in the 1970s and 1980s. It is a means of reinforcing a glued join between two pieces of square-section wood – often the tropical softwood jelutong – to build a stronger framework for a model building, vehicle or other structure (see **materials, resistant**). Once children have glued two pieces of wood at right angles to each other, they can stick a cardboard triangle over the joint which, when dry, will brace the joint and make the resulting framework much stronger. Educational suppliers have also produced plastic jigs to hold the two pieces of wood at right angles whilst the glue is drying. Usually the best way of building a wooden framework quickly is to use a 'cool melt' glue gun to stick the pieces of wood together, since this type of glue dries very quickly. Adding card triangles with PVA glue – which is stronger but takes longer to dry – will then help to overcome the brittleness of the joints stuck with the glue gun.

JOINING FABRICS (D&T)

In design and technology fabric is one type of material (see **materials, sheet**) that children can learn to work with. The main techniques primary children use to join fabrics are stitching and gluing. A simple running stitch is made by pushing the needle in and out of the fabric. Another common method is oversewing, which is used to join the edges of two pieces of fabric and helps prevent them from fraying; the needle always goes in from the same side and the thread loops over the edge. Sewing machines can be used in primary schools but require careful supervision as fingers can get in the way of the rapidly moving needle. Fabrics may need some kind of preliminary holding in place, such as pinning, or tacking (a kind of rough stitching together which is taken out later), before joining in a more permanent form. Stitching – even a simple running stitch – takes space to create the seam and this may be important if you are designing a finger puppet or bag to fit a certain sized object. Glue can be used to join fabric (the most useful is Copydex), but the join is unlikely to be able to take much **force** and so gluing tends to be most suitable for adding on small pieces and decorations. Heat bonding, in the form of iron-on tape or decorations, can be useful, but again ironing would require very careful supervision (see **risk assessment**). Comparing the different methods of joining and deciding what is most suited for the purpose might be an important stage in the design process (see **designing**).

K

KINETIC ENERGY

Kinetic energy is a form of **energy** which is carried by moving objects. Like **momentum**, it is related to the **velocity** (or **speed** – see separate definitions for the differences between these) of the object and its **mass** (the amount of 'stuff' it contains), but it differs from momentum in being more affected by velocity; a car travelling twice as fast carries four times the kinetic energy. Like other forms of energy, kinetic energy can be transformed; for example, a dynamo changes some of the kinetic energy of a bicycle **wheel** into **electrical energy** (and some heat). A bouncing ball exhibits a series of changes between kinetic energy (when it is falling or rising) and gravitational potential energy (when it is at the top of the bounce). In collisions, kinetic energy may be transferred to other objects (such as when the white cue ball on a snooker table hits one of the others) or may be dissipated in heat (as in most traffic accidents). An understanding of kinetic energy can help us to understand why a car travelling at 40 mph is potentially 90 per cent more dangerous than one travelling at 30, since its kinetic energy which is transferred to the pedestrian on impact depends on the square of its velocity. Children can develop an understanding of kinetic energy by investigating impact craters made by dropping marbles into sand; the diameter of the crater is proportional to the kinetic energy of the marble at impact. See Figure K.1.

KINETIC THEORY – see **particle theory**

KINGDOM

A term describing a major group of living things. Scientists who classify organisms are called taxonomists. It is not possible to say how many kingdoms there are – as on many science topics, there is disagreement – but you could ask your class to decide based on their own knowledge. Children will learn about the **plant** and **animal** kingdoms in primary school; but where would they place pondweed, mushrooms or sea anemones?

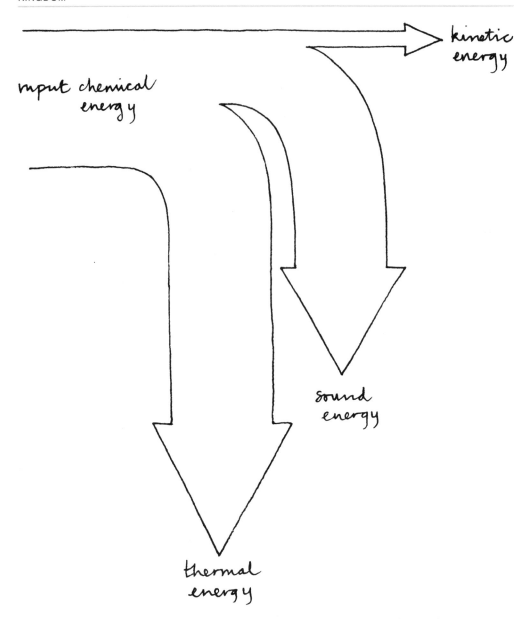

Figure K.1 Sankey diagram of a car in motion showing potential chemical energy (fuel) being transformed into kinetic energy as well as sound and thermal energy.

L

LEAF

New material for **plant** growth is made in leaves. By the process of **photosynthesis**, simple materials are made using the **energy** from the sun. Leaves come in all shapes and sizes and a great range of colours too, but whatever their appearance their main function is to catch light, and they are helped to achieve this by being held in position by the plant's **stem**. Children will be able to study leaves in three of the four main plant groups they might study: **ferns, conifers** and **flowering plants**. **Mosses**, however, do not have this particular plant part.

Box 3   Learning (theories of learning)

Primary science education has been influenced by a number of different theories of learning, including behaviourism, Piagetian constructivism, social constructivism and sociocultural theory. In this mini-essay we will examine each of these theories in turn and consider the extent to which they influence practice in primary science.

Behaviourist theories were the dominant psychological learning theories of the first half of the twentieth century. They emerged from a concern to study human learning scientifically, and have their roots in a Darwinian notion of the continuity between humans and animals. Human learning, argue behaviourists, is merely an extension of animal learning; in order to understand how humans learn we can conduct controlled experiments on animals. In the most famous of these early experiments, the Russian physiologist Ivan Pavlov (1849–1946) trained a dog to salivate at the sound of a bell. He called this 'conditioning'; by continually reinforcing the connection between the sound of the bell and the presence of food he was able to modify the dog's automatic reflex of salivating as a response to the stimulus of smell. For behaviourists, learning is a connection between stimulus – what enters the brain through the senses – and response: the behaviour triggered by that stimulus. The American behaviourist John Watson (1878–1958) rejected the idea of consciousness, since he regarded it as vague and subjective, whilst behaviour could be studied objectively. Behaviourists, he argued, should treat the mind and brain as a 'black box'; we know what goes in and what comes out but we cannot speculate on the nature of the processes going on inside. To an extent, this is what we do as teachers every time we set a learning objective with observable outcomes: for example, 'We are learning to predict which objects will float and which will sink.' In this case we can only tell if the objective has been met if the children speak, write or draw their predictions – all examples of behaviours. Watson also

---

introduced the ideas of 'frequency' and 'recency' into behaviourist learning theory; in other words, the strength of the new connections made between stimulus and response ('learning') is affected by how *frequently* the connection has been made, and how *recent* the last attempt was at making this connection. In primary science it might be associated with learning 'correct' scientific vocabulary or remembering the conventional symbols for electrical components.

Another significant contributor to behaviourist theory was Edward Thorndike (1874–1949) who introduced the notion of 'satisfiers' and 'annoyers' as reinforcing mechanisms for strengthening stimulus–response connections. If a rat in a maze receives a 'satisfier' (say, a piece of cheese) for going the right way and an 'annoyer' (say, an electric shock) for going the wrong way, it tends to 'learn' the maze more quickly! If we apply this principle to children learning science, giving them extrinsic rewards for 'right' answers (such as good work stickers or 'well done!' comments on their written work) might help to reinforce this appropriate behavioural response, whilst 'see me' or a red cross might deter them from an inappropriate response in future. Many computer quiz or revision games in science use cheers as satisfiers and boos as annoyers to reinforce the 'correct' answer. Preparing for tests tends to direct teachers down behaviourist approaches to teaching and learning. This idea of reinforcement was extended into verbal conditioning and training by B.F. Skinner (1904–90) who applied many behaviourist principles to the teacher's role in the classroom. Many teachers tend to engage in initiation–response–feedback (IRF) discourse with children, which is a form of verbal conditioning. For example, the sequence: initiation – 'What do plants need to grow?', response – 'water', feedback – 'water, good', is reinforcing the appropriate behavioural response through verbal praise. Knowledge for behaviourists is a behavioural potential; it is the capacity of the individual to give the correct response to a particular stimulus. We can never know whether the child 'knows' something until they actually produce the required behaviour in the form of an answer.

Over the past forty years, primary science education has been influenced by the learning theories of the Swiss psychologist Jean Piaget (1896–1980) and the Russian psychologist Lev Vygotsky (1896–1934). Broadly, Piaget saw children's learning as a product of their active interactions with the environment, through which they would assimilate new information within their existing *schemata* (conceptual frameworks about the world) or adapt these schemata to accommodate new evidence. This process has been adapted by Wynne Harlen (1996) into a model of learning in primary science. She gives the example of a child interpreting two wet wooden blocks stuck together as 'magnetic.' This idea would require testing by holding a magnet near them, which may then require accommodation of the child's concept of forces of attraction. Piagetian 'constructivism' – the process by which children construct knowledge in this way – was also influential, through the Plowden Report (CACE 1967), for popularising 'discovery learning' in primary science during the 1970s and 1980s. The assumption underlying discovery learning was that children would spontaneously 'discover' the laws of science by being presented with the right materials in the right environment by the teacher, acting in the role of 'facilitator.' Increasing dissatisfaction with this 'laissez-faire' approach to primary science education has led to a shift towards Vygotskian 'social constructivism', which places a greater importance on the role of talk in the development of children's scientific ideas. Vygotsky's 'zone of proximal development' (ZPD) is the gap between what a child knows or can do unaided and what they are capable of learning with the intervention of a 'more knowledgeable other' to help 'scaffold' their construction (Wood *et al.* 1976). Constructivist and social constructivist models of learning have been adapted by the Children's Learning in Science Project (Driver and Oldham 1986) into a 'generalised teaching sequence' for science education comprising five phases: orientation, elicitation, restructuring, application and review. During orientation, the teacher introduces children to the topic to be studied through exploration of objects, images or other materials that are designed to get them thinking about the concepts involved. Elicitation involves probing children's existing understandings – including their 'alternative frameworks' (Driver 1983) or misconceptions – about the topic area, whilst restructuring may involve gathering further evidence through scientific enquiry or scaffolding through discussion. Children can then apply their new understandings in different contexts, before reviewing their learning by reflecting upon how far their ideas have changed since elicitation. Depending on the outcomes from review, teachers may opt to revisit the elicitation–restructuring–application cycle several times.

Recent trends in learning theory have seen a shift away from a 'cognitive' view of teaching and learning in science to a more 'sociocultural' one. Whilst continuing to draw upon Vygotsky's ideas about learning, a sociocultural view of science education acknowledges a close relationship between cognition, identity and cultural values (Aikenhead 1996). Children in a classroom will each bring a set of cultural ways of knowing and relating to one another, which will affect their perceptions of what happens in that cultural space. From a sociocultural view, every classroom embodies a set of cultural norms that children need to adjust to and a set of cultural tools (such as specific vocabulary and ways of expressing themselves in speech and writing) that children need to appropriate in order to participate in joint meaning-making. These classroom cultures reflect the wider culture of society; for example, in a comparison between primary classroom culture in different countries, Alexander (2001) observed that there was more robust debate in Russian and French classrooms than in England, where concerns for children's self-esteem and wellbeing tended to avoid controversy or labelling ideas as 'wrong.' Science too has its own culture and its own specialist vocabulary, which children need to make their own in order to participate in the social learning of the classroom. In other words, learning science is learning to talk science (Lemke 1990). One of the central ideas in sociocultural theory is that of 'dialogue.' For Bakhtin (1986), all speech is dialogue, either with another or internally with ourselves. When children are talking together they are establishing a 'dialogic space' (Mercer and Littleton 2007) where ideas can be shared and meanings negotiated. This has led to the idea of 'dialogic teaching', which Alexander (2004) defines as communication between teacher and pupils in which ideas are developed cumulatively over sustained sequences of interactions. In the field of science education, Mortimer and Scott (2003) have distinguished teaching which is 'interactive' – in which a range of children contribute to discussion – from that which is 'dialogic' – in which children's ideas are given status.

References

Aikenhead, G. (1996) 'Science education: border crossing into the subculture of science', *Studies in Science Education*, 27 (1): 1–52.

Alexander, R. (2001) *Culture and Pedagogy: International Comparisons in Primary Education.* Oxford and Boston, MA: Blackwell.

Alexander, R. (2004) *Towards Dialogic Teaching: Rethinking Classroom Talk.* Cambridge: Dialogos.

Bakhtin, M. (1986) *Speech Genres and Other Late Essays.* Austin, TX: University of Texas Press.

Central Advisory Council for Education (CACE) (England) (ed.) (1967) *Children and their Primary Schools: The Plowden Report.* London: Her Majesty's Stationery Office.

Driver, R. (1983) *The Pupil as Scientist?* Milton Keynes: Open University Press.

Driver, R. and Oldham, V. (1986) 'A constructivist approach to curriculum development in science', *Studies in Science Education*, 5: 61–84.

Harlen, W. (1996) *The Teaching of Science*, second edition. London: David Fulton.

Lemke, J. (1990) *Talking Science: Language, Learning and Values.* Norwood: Ablex Publishing.

Mercer, N. and Littleton, K. (2007) *Dialogue and the Development of Children's Thinking.* London: Routledge.

Mortimer, E. and Scott, P. (2003) *Making Meaning in Secondary Science Lessons.* Maidenhead: Open University Press.

Wood, D., Bruner, J. and Ross, G. (1976) 'The role of tutoring in problem solving', *Journal of Child Psychology and Psychiatry*, 17: 89–100.

LEARNING OBJECTIVE

A learning objective for a science lesson may be focused either upon conceptual content (see **conceptual understanding**) – for example, 'I am looking for children who can tell me what a **seed** needs in order to germinate' – or upon the development of **process skills** – for example, 'I am looking for children who notice something about the **plant**.' Including a learning objective concerned with scientific **attitudes** such as: 'I am looking for children who show they are curious by asking questions about this collection' can help children to understand what kinds of thinking and behaviour help them to act as scientists.

LESSON STRUCTURE

There is no fixed length for a science or design and technology lesson and certainly no requirement to adopt the widely used 'three part' structure that begins and ends with the whole class. Children can work as individuals, pairs or groups (see **classroom organisation**) at different points of the lesson, depending on the activity and learning aims. Whole class time can play an important role in maintaining a shared sense of purpose and understanding if ideas are shared together frequently. Learning can take place at tables, on the carpet or floor, in a circle, or outdoors. The decision about how to group the children depends on the purposes of the lesson and what it is you want the children to learn; for example, is it essential that every children gets hands-on experience or is time for discussion of ideas more important? How can both be combined to best support learning? The availability of **resources** will also constrain the possibilities. The following are examples to illustrate the breadth of possibilities.

Example 1 Groups collaboratively explore and evaluate a collection of toys that move, ideas are discussed as a whole class and then individuals record an evaluation of one toy that particularly interested them.

Example 2 The teacher introduces a technique, such as using a thermometer, to the whole class. The children then work in pairs on a structured task to practise the technique. Next the whole class regroups in the middle of the lesson to discuss how to investigate a related question (how best to keep a drink cool) before working in small groups to devise an **enquiry** of their own.

Example 3 Pairs of children discuss a **question** (e.g. What do seeds need to germinate?) or a **concept cartoon** and then join with another pair to share their ideas. The class gather together to observe a phenomenon demonstrated by the teacher (e.g. cress grown on cotton wool or a bean seed sprouting under compost being dug up) and discuss their ideas further in response to this with talk partners and again as a class.

Example 4 There is a circus of 10 different activities (e.g. on making **sounds**) around the room. Pairs of children spend five minutes on each and move on.

Example 5 A ten-minute discussion in a circle about an interesting **rock** that a child has brought in leads to information-searching about rocks in small groups or individually.

Example 6 A small group works outside the classroom with a teaching assistant (e.g. to plant **seeds** in the school garden/bake bread).

LEVER (D&T)

A lever is a **mechanism** that consists of a beam or bar which turns about a point (the pivot). It enables a small force over a long distance to be changed to a large force over a short distance (consider here how a pair of nutcrackers work) or vice versa. Typically, for primary school projects the beam is thick card or possibly a lolly stick, and the pivot is made from a split pin or maybe a plastic

rivet. At its most simple this could be a strip of card fastened to a piece of card by a paper fastener (a fixed pivot). Moving one end of the strip to one side moves the other end of the strip in the opposite direction. Try experimenting by moving the pivot closer or further away from the handle end of the lever. More complicated levers have more than one bar joined together by fixed or loose pivots (loose pivots go through the levers only, but are not fastened to, for example, a piece of card) and guides to direct the movement of the bars. These can change up-and-down motion to side-to-side movements, or a pull to a push (see **force**). The teacher can construct a number of different lever mechanisms on a pin board, covering up all but the ends of the bars so that children attempt to work out how the movement is created before it is revealed to them. Figure L.1 shows a pair of possible arrangements that could be used for this purpose. Projects using levers in the primary school could include making greetings cards or moving storybooks.

LICHEN

Lichens are an amazing and curious group of plant-like things. They are actually two organisms – usually an **algae** and a **fungi** – living co-operatively and able to survive very harsh conditions. They can be found on **rocks**, walls, old gravestones, roofs, tree trunks, etc. They can look like blobs of white, yellow or grey paint. Reindeer eat lichen. Beatrix Potter studied lichens and was among the first people in England to understand that they were two organisms living together.

LIFE CYCLE – see **reproduction**

LIFE PROCESSES

We decide that living things are actually living when we establish they carry out seven different processes. For the purposes of primary science we can call these

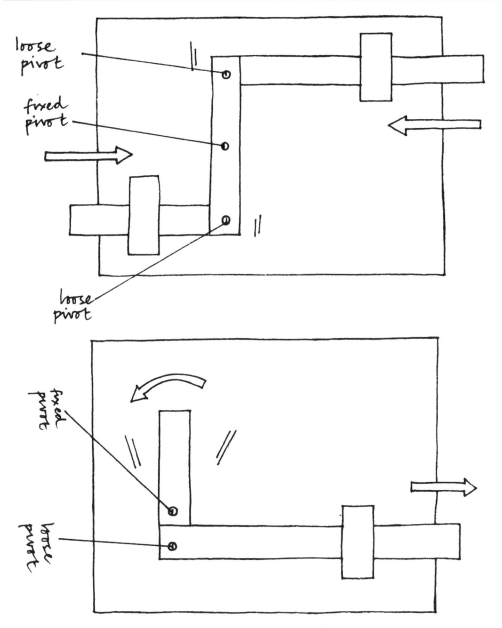

Figure L.1 Two possible lever arrangements (adapted from DATA 1999).

processes movement, **respiration**, sensitivity, **growth, reproduction, excretion,** and nutrition (the mnemonic is MRS GREN). In living things, each process is carried out by a system which consists of cells, tissues and organs with particular functions (see **digestive system, excretory** system, **nervous system, respiratory system** and **skeletal system**).

LIGHT

It is easier to say what light *does* than what it *is*. It is sufficient for primary-age children to know that light is a form of

energy which appears to travel in straight lines, can be reflected, refracted (bent) and split into different colours (see **rainbow**, **reflection** and **refraction**). It is these different properties of light which have led to two major theories about its nature – the wave and particle models. Isaac Newton (1642–1727) believed that light was a stream of tiny particles, a bit like coloured snooker balls, which travelled very fast in straight lines and bounced off objects in predictable ways. This view was challenged by the Dutch scientist Christian Huygens (1629–95), who proposed that light could be thought of as a wave, a bit like ripples on a pond. Its different wavelengths would correspond to different colours of the spectrum, and it could be refracted (bent round corners) or diffracted (spread out after travelling through a small hole) like other waves. Huygens' theory seemed to fit the experimental evidence better than Newton's, so for two centuries we thought of light as a *transverse* wave (one that ripples from side to side) and later as part of the electromagnetic spectrum alongside radio waves, X rays and microwaves. However, at the beginning of the twentieth century an experiment by Ernest Rutherford (1871–1937) on the photoelectric effect seemed to suggest that light did behave like a particle after all. This idea became incorporated into the new quantum physics: it seems that light has a dual nature in that sometimes it looks like a wave, sometimes like a particle!

LIGHT SOURCES

Light sources are objects or places that emit **light**, not to be confused with those that merely reflect it (see **reflection**). The most common sources of confusion for children are the **moon** and so-called 'shiny' objects such as foil and glossy coloured paper. The moon is not a source of light; we can only see it because it reflects light from the sun. Similarly, the **planets** we can see with the naked eye – Mercury, Venus, Mars and Jupiter – are not sources of light even though they look like **stars**, which do produce their own light. Most light is produced by heating or **burning**, for example the flame of a candle or glowing filament or gas of a light bulb. The sun and other stars emit light because of the nuclear reactions heating up their surfaces to many millions of degrees. Some chemical reactions (see **chemical changes to materials**) can produce light without heat, e.g. in a 'glow stick' or certain luminous creatures such as glow worms or deep sea **fish**.

LOUDNESS/VOLUME

The loudness or volume of a sound depends on the amplitude of **vibrations** that cause it: in other words, how much the object which is the source of the sound is 'shaking.' For example, if we strike a drum softly it will only vibrate gently (with a small amplitude) and the volume will be low, whilst if we beat it hard the vigorous vibration will cause a loud sound. Although some scientists have found a small effect of sound pressure (loudness) on frequency, it is probably simpler for primary children to learn to clearly distinguish between changing the **pitch** (frequency) of a sound – how 'high' it is – and its volume – how loud it is. This can be confusing for children if they equate the word 'high' with 'loud', an understandable misconception as many high frequency sounds are also quite piercing (actually, if anything, a very loud low note can apparently sound lower!).

M

MAGNETIC MATERIALS

A **property of materials**. Objects can be classified in one of three categories. First, there are permanently magnetic objects, such as bar and horseshoe magnets. Secondly there are those objects which become temporarily magnetic when placed in a magnetic field, such as objects made from iron, nickel and cobalt. And finally there are non-magnetic objects that show no response in a magnetic field and include many metallic as well as non-metallic objects. A **model** can help explain our **observations**. At a particle level materials can be thought of as being made of numerous 'mini-magnets', each mini-magnet having a north and a south pole. The mini-magnets of a permanently magnetic material are well ordered so that the material creates a magnetic field. The organised pattern is quite difficult to disturb, although hammering a permanent magnet or heating it up will disrupt its alignment. Temporary magnets have randomly orientated mini-magnets when outside the influence of a magnetic field, creating a neutral net overall effect. They are not attracted to each other nor do they attract other materials. However, within a magnetic field the mini-magnets become temporarily aligned so that they behave like a magnet (see Figures M.1 and M.2). The mini-magnets are aligned so that their poles are lined up towards the opposite pole of the permanent magnet, which

means that they are always attracted to it (repulsion only happens between two permanent magnets). Finally, the mini-magnets of non-magnetic materials are randomly orientated no matter where they are placed; they are not attracted to a magnet. Testing magnetic materials is very easy for children to do – simply use a permanent magnet and observe how the material responds. Explanation (see **exposition**) of observations can be made through drama. Children can line themselves up as mini-magnets and pull (or push) in one direction to model magnetic materials, or can be randomly arranged when modelling non-magnetic materials.

MAMMALS

Mammals are a class of **vertebrate** animals. Males and females have hair or fur and three middle-ear bones used in hearing. Females have mammary glands to feed their young. There are three main groups: monotremes (five species of egg-layers), marsupials (with pouches) and placentals (young develop in the womb). Most mammals have specialised **teeth** and a four-chambered heart (see **circulatory system**). There are over 5,400 species of mammals ranging in size from the 30–40 mm bumblebee bat to the 33 m blue whale. Children may confuse the term 'mammal' with '**animal**.' All mammals are animals but not all animals are mammals.

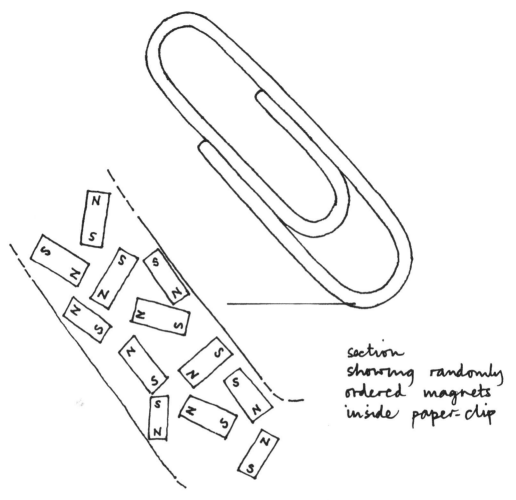

section showing randomly ordered magnets inside paper-clip

Figure M.1 The paper clip's mini-magnets are randomly orientated when it is outside the influence of a permanent magnet.

MANUFACTURED MATERIALS

Manufactured materials are made from **natural materials** which have been changed so that the structure and composition of the original materials have been modified. There are many manufacturing processes that could be studied in the classroom by using secondary sources of information. For example, metals are refined from ores found in **rocks** and alloys are produced by combining metals with other metals or non-metallic materials. For example, steel is a combination of carbon and iron; bronze is copper combined with tin. Synthetic materials such as plastics are made from products of the oil industry. As well as doing research from books and the internet, there is also scope for first-hand investigation of some processes. For example, the manufacture of ceramic products can be investigated if the school has access to a kiln. Also it is possible for children to make their own paper. Links could be made between this topic and history (see **cross-curricular**) by studying the development of materials

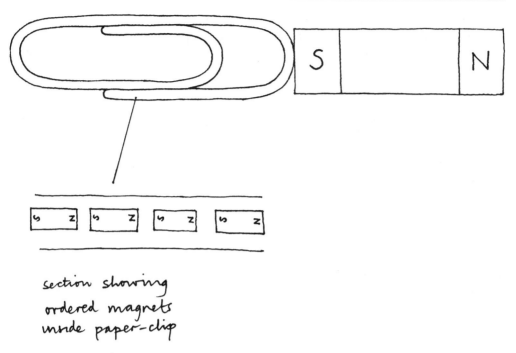

section showing
ordered magnets
inside paper-clip

Figure M.2 When placed near the permanent magnet, the paper clip's mini-magnets become aligned and it is attracted to the magnet.

from early history to the present day. Important stages in the development of humankind are described by the names of materials (Stone Age, Bronze Age and Iron Age). In more recent times, steel and plastics have been manufactured (although historians haven't yet coined the term 'the Plastic Age'!).

MASS

The mass of an object can be thought of as the amount of 'stuff' it contains (literally, a measure of the total number of particles in it – see **particle theory**), measured in grams (g) or kilograms (kg) (1 kg being 1,000 g). We often talk about **'weight'** when we mean mass since it is the **force** between that mass and the Earth which we experience in everyday life. Heavier things are more massive, which matters when we try to move or stop them, even in the zero-gravity environment of outer space where they are

effectively weightless. It is worth getting children to refer to mass rather than weight when they are considering, say, two vehicles rolling down a slope or dropping a pair of film canisters, one of which has a piece of Plasticine in it. In the latter case, children should notice the rather surprising outcome that the two canisters hit the floor at the same time, even though one has a greater mass than the other. This remarkable outcome, noticed by Galileo and explained by Newton, is because, even though the more 'massive' canister has a greater force pulling it towards the ground (its weight), it needs that greater force to accelerate it at the same rate as the other canister as objects with more mass are harder to pull!

MATERIAL (SCIENCE)

The term 'material' has a very specific scientific use. It refers to the form of matter from which substances are made. Usually this matter is in solid form but it can also be in the form of a liquid or gas. These are known as **states of matter**. However, everyday usage of the word 'materials' usually refers specifically to fabric, and this is probably the understanding of the term that young children will bring to school. There are two main areas of learning of materials: their properties (see **properties of materials**) and how they change (see **chemical changes to materials** and **physical changes to materials**); but underpinning each area is the big idea of the particulate nature of matter (see **particle theory**). Teachers can provide experiences that eventually lead to children developing an understanding of particle theory, although this may not occur until after the end of primary school with some children. Nevertheless, being aware of it helps teachers to question, respond and provide experiences that build towards this explanation in the future. Grounding these experiences in everyday contexts makes learning meaningful for children (see **contexts for science**). Topics that can be usefully addressed might include the **weather**, **cooking** and testing materials for design and technology projects.

MATERIALS, MOULDABLE (D&T)

A mouldable material is a solid which children can fashion into a desired shape without the need for cutting or shaping tools – though children may wish to use such tools to give more precision or detail to their models. At a molecular level, this is because the particles of the material (see **particle theory**) can slide over each other, whilst retaining sufficient cohesive **force** to retain the new shape. Another term for 'mouldable' might be 'plastic' (see **plasticity**), though this can easily be confused with the more everyday usage of this term to refer to synthetic materials manufactured from hydrocarbons. One of the benefits of mouldable materials for children's designs

is that they permit many reshapings as ideas emerge and evolve. Some, such as Plasticine or playdough, offer opportunities for endless reworking and recycling into new models, whilst others such as clay or plaster of Paris enable children to fix their ideas in a permanent form by drying or firing. Mouldable materials are particularly useful for designing objects with organic shapes such as model animals or bowls that would be impractical to make from resistant or sheet materials.

MATERIALS, RESISTANT (D&T)

A resistant material is a hard solid (see **hardness**) which requires the use of specialist cutting and shaping tools (saws, snips, files) to change its shape to that which children may require for their models. The main resistant materials children will encounter in primary design and technology are wood (in the form of balsa, lolly sticks, dowel or thin square-section jelutong), metal (in the form of stiff wire or aluminium cans) and plastic (in the form of stiff, corrugated board). Such materials can be used by children to design a range of structures and **mechanisms** such as vehicles, buildings, windmills and fairground rides. An obvious advantage of using resistant materials over the easier cardboard boxes joined with sticky tape is that the resulting **artefacts** are more robust and are likely to have a higher quality of finish. However, they will also take longer to make and children will probably encounter more difficulties in joining resistant materials in permanent ways (see **Jinks joint**), for example using a hot glue gun, staples or screws. Many secondary D&T teachers may prefer to see children develop the necessary craft skills to develop well-finished outcomes using resistant materials, whilst primary teachers may be anxious about the health and safety issues associated with using saws and drills in the classroom (see **risk assessment**), together with the relative expense of such materials. In practice, given the right training, even very young children are able to cope with using basic woodwork tools safely in the classroom and gain a great deal of satisfaction through working with resistant materials.

MATERIALS, SHEET (D&T)

A sheet material is a solid which may be rigid or flexible, but which is supplied in a thin sheet. Examples include card, fabric, corrugated plastic, aluminium foil, polythene and cellophane. Children tend to use sheet materials to clad the outer surface of their designs, providing a lightweight skin over a rigid frame which gives an aesthetic finish to the model. For example, when **designing** a toy which moves using a **cam** mechanism, children may choose to cover the framework containing the cam in sheets of card to hide the mechanism, whilst the actual moving part of the toy (a lifting hat or rocking boat) may also be made from sheet materials since they are light and easy to cut. Sheet materials also tend to be relatively easy to join together, either temporarily using sticky tape, pins or Blu-Tack, or more permanently using PVA glue, staples or sewing. Whilst not always classified as sheet materials, fabrics such as felt can be cut, folded and shaped in a variety of ways by children to design wallets, bags, hats or shoes.

MEASUREMENT

Measurement enables scientists to explore relationships between **variables** in more depth: for example, measuring the **temperature** of a hot potato as it cools results in a temperature–time **graph** which is not a simple straight line but a curve. Plotting a scattergram to look at the relationship between the thickness of a material and the volume of **sound** that travels through it would help test the idea that thick materials block more sound than thin ones, and any materials that don't fit the general pattern might trigger further enquiries. The need for measurement may not be evident to primary-age children; it is possible to see which car went furthest down the ramp without getting a tape measure out. Here technological contexts can be useful to make measurement more meaningful: for example, designing a game for a summer fair might involve measuring how far a ball could roll, repeating measurements to see what the likely range of outcomes would be. Measuring skills (see **process skills**) may need to be taught explicitly (Goldsworthy and Holmes 1999). Time spent, for example, in learning to use a stop clock, thermometer or Newton meter reduces frustrations and will increase the accuracy of children's results.

MECHANICAL PROPERTIES OF MATERIALS

The mechanical properties of materials all have one thing in common: they describe the way a material responds to a **force**. It is possible to divide mechanical properties into those of the material itself and those of the object (see **properties of objects**). Although such a fine line is not usually drawn in primary teaching, it is as well that we are aware of the difference. The mechanical properties that are commonly investigated in the primary classroom are:

- **elasticity/plasticity** – elastic materials return to their original shape when the force squashing them is removed; plastic materials retain their shape;
- flexibility/rigidity – objects which cannot be deformed are rigid; those that can be deformed are flexible;
- brittleness/toughness – brittle materials break suddenly; tough materials break slowly;
- strength – how much force a material can withstand before it breaks;
- **hardness** – how easy it is to indent or scratch a material.

Ductility and malleability are mechanical properties which are specifically used to describe metallic materials. It is often but not always when primary school children are investigating solid materials that they might use these terms. An example of a mechanical property that can be used to describe liquids and gases is **compressibility** (indeed, this property could be used to distinguish these two **states of matter**).

MECHANISM (D&T)

A mechanism consists of components acting together to make an action take place. It is the part of the machine that enables it to perform its function more easily. It uses **energy** and needs controlling (see **control system**). In primary school, the types of mechanisms children commonly use in their design-and-make projects include **cams** and **cranks**, **levers** and **sliders**, **axles** and **wheels**, **pulleys** and gears, and **pneumatic** and **hydraulic** systems. Younger children will learn how mechanisms can make things move. Older children will explore a range of mechanisms enabling them to discover how **forces** can be changed in size or direction, and how one type of movement can be converted to another.

MELTING

When a solid is heated, the thermal **energy** that is transferred to it causes its particles to vibrate more rapidly (see **particle theory**). As they do so, they move apart, causing the solid to expand. If enough energy is transferred, the particles vibrate rapidly enough to break free from their fixed positions and they are able to move around relative to each other. At this point the solid has melted and become a liquid. Children should be encouraged to notice that for some materials the change is gradual (e.g. chocolate melts over a range of

temperatures) but for other materials it is almost instant (e.g. ice). Chocolate behaves as it does because it consists of a number of fats that melt at different temperatures. Presented with an ice balloon (a balloon filled with water then frozen), children will soon be observing and testing it in lots of different ways. What happens if salt, sugar or powder paint is sprinkled on its surface? How can the balloon be made to melt faster? Close observation of ice cubes, chocolate or cheese in plastic bags immersed in hot water encourages the development of **vocabulary** to describe what is happening. Teacher **questions** can help to focus on change of shape or colour and on what happens when the substance cools again. Keeping the sample in a bag throughout can show that no material is added or taken away (see **conservation of matter**). Another 'unbagged' sample can be melted to allow children to feel and smell as well as see the changes. It is particularly important to use a bagged sample of jelly if the purpose is to only study melting, as jelly will dissolve (see **dissolving**) as well as melt when it comes into contact with hot water. During freezing weather the outdoors may be used to extend children's understanding of melting (see **contexts for science**). If it is snowy, children can test which snowman melts first (size of snowman, its location, the compactness of the snow and clothing might be important factors that can be investigated). When it is icy children could consider how they can make the path safe to walk on.

MICRO-ORGANISMS

Tiny living things, such as bacteria and some **fungi** which cannot be seen individually with the naked eye, are present almost everywhere in their millions and billions. We may be able to see groups or 'colonies' of them. Many micro-organisms are completely harmless and some are beneficial, such as those that help to recycle garden waste. Some are not helpful, such as the mould that appears in a damp bathroom. Some are harmful, such as those that cause disease and food poisoning. Children need to learn that good personal hygiene such as handwashing is important in reducing the transmission of micro-organisms (often called 'germs' in this context) between people. We need to store food in such a way that harmful micro-organisms do not grow, so we refrigerate or freeze foods at temperatures below which they can reproduce. We preserve foods in sugar or salt or vinegar – all chemical environments in which the cells of micro-organisms cannot survive. Processes such as bottling and canning (tinning) keep out the oxygen that micro-organisms need to live. However, some micro-organisms have a positive role in health. 'Bio-yoghurts' are marketed as having benefits because the digestive system contains some micro-organisms that are helpful to the processes of digestion and the **yoghurts** might increase these.

MINIBEASTS

An **animal** 'group' that includes slugs, snails, worms, centipedes, insects and spiders, all of which are examples of **invertebrates**.

MIXTURES

When two or more substances are combined without a chemical reaction taking place a mixture is formed. For example, instant coffee is a mixture of the chemicals in coffee granules and hot water. Mixtures can be made of elements – air is a mixture of gases – or of compounds: sea water is a mixture of water and dissolved salts. Mixtures do not form new substances. The substances that are part of a mixture remain chemically distinct; this means they can be separated from each other by physical changes so that, for example, sieving can separate a mixture of solids such

as sand and rice (see **physical changes to materials**). A suspension is formed by solids which are insoluble in liquid (e.g. flour in water). One way of separating this mixture is by filtering, another way is by sedimentation (allowing the solid to settle out) and a third way is by flotation (only if the solid floats in the liquid). Soluble solids form a solution when dissolved in a liquid (e.g. sugar in water). The solute can be recovered by **evaporation**. For instance, in the case of instant coffee, the water can be evaporated so that the coffee grains are retrieved. When a solvent is evaporated, the solute (solid) remains behind. The solvent can be collected by allowing it to condense on a cold surface such as glass, a process known as distillation. Some mixtures of solutes can be separated into their components by paper **chromatography**. To separate inks into constituent colours, the solvent soaks through filter or blotting paper and the coloured inks separate out as they travel at different rates across the paper.

MODEL

A model is a way of explaining a scientific theory to a particular audience at a particular time, e.g. a Year 3 class in Birmingham next Tuesday. Its effectiveness depends upon the sociocultural backgrounds (see **sociocultural perspective**) of the audience concerned – i.e. what experiences and understandings they share in common – and upon the prevailing scientific culture within the classroom. If children are used to talking about abstract ideas and illustrating them in different ways then using models can be very effective pedagogy in supporting their learning. A model can be physical, for example a 'body apron' to which children can attach different organs in order to learn their relative positions in the human torso; mathematical, for example Ohm's law – the bigger the **resistance** the lower the **current** in a circuit); or conceptual, for example our 'mental picture' of the particles in a cube of ice or drop of water (see **particle theory**). Conceptual models are probably the most common in the primary classroom, as the SPACE research has suggested that children all carry with them mental pictures of practically every scientific phenomenon they are likely to encounter, which teachers ignore at their peril! For example, Osborne's research into children's conceptual models of electric circuits (Osborne *et al.* 1991) found that they tended to fall into three types: the 'source-sink' model in which children consider the battery as a source of **electricity**, which flows down a single wire to 'drain away' in the bulb; the 'clashing currents' model in which they imagine two streams of electricity emerging from the battery along separate wires, 'clashing' together when they meet at the bulb to produce light; and the 'consumption' model, which involves the current flowing in a loop but some of it being 'used up' in the bulb. The 'scientific' model – of small particles called **electrons** present throughout the circuit, which the battery starts moving simultaneously to transfer **energy** to the bulb without it being used up – can make little sense to children with another conceptual model firmly embedded. This is where carefully chosen **illustrative activities** and meaningful **analogies** can help.

MOMENTUM (INERTIA)

A moving object carries momentum by virtue of its **velocity** (or **speed** – see separate definitions for the differences between these) and its **mass** (the amount of 'stuff' it contains). If two objects are travelling with the same speed towards you (say, a shopping trolley and a railway locomotive) the more massive of the two will carry more momentum and therefore will be more difficult to stop! This is why

momentum is sometimes called 'inertia' because it is a measure of how difficult it is to change the velocity of a moving object. Young children need plenty of experience of pushing and pulling wheeled toys with different weights placed in them, because this will lay the foundations for grasping the concept of momentum, and ultimately to the understanding of Newton's second law of motion. To paraphrase, this law states that heavy things are harder to get moving, and also harder to stop. Newton expressed it rather more elegantly as force = mass × acceleration ($F = ma$), which provides a powerful way of understanding how objects move. For example, it provides an explanation for Galileo's observation that objects of different **weights** fall at the same rate (in the absence of **air resistance**), since a heavier object will be attracted to the Earth by a larger force (its weight) but it requires this larger force to get it moving – so the two cancel each other out and it falls at the same rate as the lighter object.

MOON

A moon is a heavenly body which **orbits** a **planet**: in other words, a natural satellite. In our solar system, the inner two planets, Mercury and Venus, do not have moons, but all the other planets have varying numbers from one (Earth) to 62 (Jupiter). We do not yet know whether planets in other solar systems have moons, but it is probably safe to assume that some of them do. Most moons are much smaller than their planet (our moon is one-sixth as massive as the Earth) but Charon, the moon of the recently demoted 'dwarf planet' Pluto, is nearly the same size, so they effectively orbit around each other. There are two principal theories to explain the formation of moons: one that they coalesced out of the swirling disc of dust around the same time as the planets during the formation of the solar system, and the second that they were formed by massive impacts knocking large chunks off their parent planet. After the excitement of the Apollo lunar landings (1969–72) our moon was reckoned to be a fairly dull, lifeless place which had changed little for millions of years. However, it continues to be a source of wonder, fascination and romance for those of us trapped on the Earth! There are many extraordinary things about our moon; for example, it appears to be exactly the same size in the sky as the sun, despite being very much smaller and very much closer. This can give us spectacular total solar **eclipses**, such as that observed from Cornwall on 11 August 1999. It also orbits the Earth with the same face pointing towards us all the time – its period of rotation is the same as its period of orbit. We had never seen the other side until Apollo 8 flew round it in 1968, producing the iconic 'Earthrise' photograph as

it emerged from the other side. Its gravitational force pulls the water in all the oceans and seas on Earth, giving us tides (see **gravity**). Finally, our moon appears to constantly change shape in the sky on a regular monthly cycle – the lunar phases (see **phases, lunar**). Children may believe that the moon really changes shape, or that the Earth casts different amounts of shadow on its surface. However, the explanation for this curious phenomenon is that half of the moon is always lit by the sun, but that we see different proportions of this lit half as the moon orbits us.

MOSS

Mosses are **plants** that have no flowers, **stems** or real **leaves**. They keep low to the ground as they are non-vascular, which means they cannot transport water and food around their 'bodies.' They **reproduce** by making spores, rather than **seeds**.

N

NATURAL MATERIALS

All materials ultimately originate from the Earth (apart from small quantities of extraterrestrial materials captured from the **moon** and asteroids). In some cases, these materials require little or no modification to be of use to us and are called natural materials. They may be from the biological world (wood, vegetable or animal fibres) or from the physical world (stone, soil) but all have one thing in common: they require little or no processing to be of use apart from possibly shaping, sorting or cleaning. A common activity in the primary classroom is for children to sort a range of materials (see **sorting activities**) into those that are natural and those that are man-made (see **manufactured materials**). This seemingly straightforward task is actually quite difficult without reference books being available to support children's observations (think how similar natural and man-made yarns can appear). It may also help children's learning if the natural material is available to refer to just as it would be found in nature (maybe a tuft of sheep's wool or a log).

NERVOUS SYSTEM

This consists of the brain and spinal cord, nerves, sense organs (e.g. ears, **eyes**, tongue). Information from the sense organs travels along nerves to the spinal cord and then, usually, to the brain. Other information is sent to muscles and other organs. The brain is a complex network of nerve cells whose function results in thinking, feeling, controlling movement and some hormones. The details of brain function are not well understood and it is a huge field of current research. Children can explore how we use our senses and react to different stimuli by asking and answering, through **investigation**, such **questions** as: Can everybody distinguish the taste of green sweets from yellow ones? What is easier to see – white words on a blackboard or black words on a whiteboard? Are fingers, thumbs or palms more sensitive to touch? Can we smell two smells at once? How quick are our reactions? The last question can be answered by a 'catch the ruler' test. Child A sits with her hand outstretched as if holding a cup. Child B holds a ruler so it dangles vertically just above the open fingers. Without warning child B drops the ruler and child A catches it. A reading can be taken – how many centimetres passed through the fingers?

O

OBSERVATION

Although observation may seem to be about looking, science takes a broader view; all five human senses can be involved in observation in primary classrooms, with children feeling, listening, smelling and – when safe – tasting as well as using their sense of sight. Technology can help us to sense what is beyond the limits of the human body; microscopes, telescopes, light meters and stop clocks are all tools that enable us to observe and sometimes measure aspects of natural phenomena we may not be able to perceive otherwise. Observation is not a neutral, disinterested activity as we always make some kind of selection of what to focus on, which means that our ideas and preconceptions will always influence what is observed. Making sense of data, such as an **x-ray** image of the human body, requires interpretation skills (see **process skills**). Looking at a visual illusion tells us that even with something as apparently objective as whether a pair of lines are parallel or not, or the same length (see Figure O.1), our brain is working hard to make sense of what we are observing and is using a model of how the world is in order to interpret it.

As part of a teaching activity children may be asked to make an observation of, say, a **plant** as it grows, and may notice all kinds of features that the teacher was not expecting whilst not apparently paying attention to the parts that are the focus

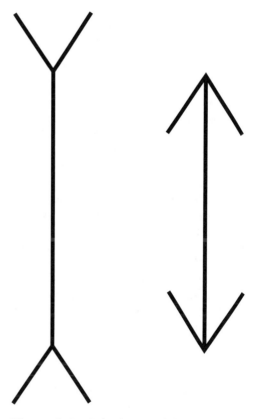

Figure O.1   Which one of these two lines appears to be the longer?

of our learning objectives! Here sensitive responses are required to both help children focus on the salient features and value the new perspectives that the children bring.

ORIENTATION

Orientation is the initial phase in the Constructivist Teaching Sequence (see **learning**) formalised in the 1980s as part of the Children's Learning in Science Project (CLIS) at the University of Leeds (Scott 1987). At the start of a new sequence of work, orientation sets the scene for the work to come and hopefully raises the interest of the learner in what is to follow. Typically it might include reading a book or exploring a collection of artefacts. Orientation might involve a provocation for learning that the teacher introduces, such as reading a story, exploring a collection or discussing a local event. Alternatively, it might be a response to something that the children have initiated. It could take the form of a discussion, involving children in sharing their perspectives on a topic or relating it to their interests. The class as a whole can benefit from the breadth of ideas and questions that different children might bring. Planning a thoughtful orientation with time for the children to respond by talking together can help to establish a shared commitment to the topic for the class. Although the orientation phase may be a distinct experience for the learner, often it merges with **elicitation**, as ideas held are explicitly considered by the learner and reviewed by the teacher.

OPAQUE

An opaque object is one which will not allow any **light** to pass through it, and therefore forms a dark **shadow** on the opposite side from the light source. In practice, some objects which appear opaque at first glance (e.g. flat plastic shapes) will actually allow some light to pass through if it is bright enough. We say that opaque objects absorb 100 per cent of the light and transmit none of it, in contrast to those which are **translucent** or **transparent**.

OPTICAL PROPERTIES OF MATERIALS

Materials respond to light in a variety of ways (see **properties of materials**). **Transparent** materials such as air and glass transmit **light** so that it is not distorted to any great extent. To the observer, the image seen is crisply defined. A **translucent** material allows light to pass through it but scatters it as it does so that the image seen is indistinct. **Opaque** materials, which allow little or no light through, instead might absorb light or reflect it. The observer might see the clear image of objects when light reflects (see **reflection**) from a material with a very smooth surface (such as a mirror or a calm lake). If the surface is rough a matt appearance is produced. Additionally, the material may absorb only some of the visible spectrum of light, with the part of the spectrum that is reflected being the material's colour. If only red light is reflected, the object will appear red. If the entire spectrum is absorbed, the material appears black. Materials can be tested by children using a torch to see how they respond to light. It's worth noting that the division of materials into transparent, translucent and opaque is somewhat arbitrary. However, children could be encouraged to come up with their own way of 'drawing the line' between each category.

ORBIT

The word 'orbit' has two specific meanings in science. The first is to name a part of the **eye**, but the more common usage describes the path of a heavenly body such as a **moon** or **planet** around a much more massive object. For example, our moon orbits the Earth, whilst the Earth in turn orbits the sun. We can take this further, since the sun itself orbits the centre of the Milky Way **galaxy**. The first-century Greek–Egyptian astronomer Ptolemy developed a model of the universe in which all the heavenly bodies orbit the Earth, which was not challenged until Nicolaus Copernicus (1473–1543) suggested the idea that they actually orbit the sun. Isaac Newton (1643–1727) suggested that the **force** which made the planets orbit the sun was the same force which causes objects to fall from the sky – **gravity**. His universal law of gravitation predicted that orbits would be slightly elliptical rather than perfectly circular; hence the Earth is slightly closer to the sun at certain times of the year (though this is not the explanation for seasonal variations in temperature – see **seasons**). The orbits of the Earth and moon are closely linked to our concepts of time, specifically the length of the year (the time it takes for the Earth to orbit the sun – 365.25 times the Earth's period of rotation) and lunar month (the time it takes for the moon to orbit the Earth, which is 28 times as long as it takes us to spin round once – see **phases, lunar**). Children may confuse the idea of orbit and rotation: it is the 'spin' of the Earth on its axis which gives us day and night, not its orbit around the sun.

P

PARALLEL CIRCUITS – see **series and parallel circuits**

PARTICLE THEORY (KINETIC THEORY)

Understanding the particulate nature of materials helps explain the **properties of materials** and the processes that change them; it is one of science's 'big ideas.' The theory goes that all materials are made from tiny particles that bond to each other in various ways which determine the properties of materials. It also helps us understand phenomena such as **condensation**, **evaporation**, **melting**, **dissolving** and the processes of chemical change such as **burning**.

The individual particles are not visible, so by introducing this theory to primary children we are asking them to think in an abstract way. As such there is controversy about the teaching of the kinetic theory of matter in the primary classroom. However, many primary teachers believe that the concepts of solid, liquid and gas (see **states of matter**), change of state and reversible and irreversible reactions can be more easily explained with reference to a theoretical model, albeit a much simplified one. A way forward that may help children appreciate the microscopic size of the particles is for them to imagine or try to find out what would happen if we cut something in half, in half again, and again … What would we end up with? To appreciate the structure of solids, liquids and gases and the energy transfer needed to change from one state to another, drama might be used, with the children 'being' particles tightly packed but 'vibrating' in a group with elbows linked, to represent a solid. When the teacher applies (imaginary) heat **energy**, the 'particles' become a little excited and move slightly apart; their bonds constantly break and re-form so the particles of a once-ordered solid, for example boy–girl–boy–girl, mix and flow into the spaces of a container (for example a shape marked out on the floor) rather like a liquid. As more heat is applied, some particles have sufficient energy to break loose and run off (evaporate) as 'gas particles' to distant parts of the room.

Starting from the **model** for a gas (see Figure P.1), it is possible to model the changes in reverse. As heat is lost, gas particles form bonds becoming a liquid (the process of condensation – see Figure P.2). As further heat is lost, the liquid particles once again become tightly packed and unable to move relative to each other (see Figure P.3). A solid has formed by the process of solidification. Other ideas include making a 'mobile' for the classroom using polystyrene balls, glued together for the solid, connected with short lengths of dowel for the liquid and hung freely to represent the gas.

An understanding of this model can be developed further by asking children

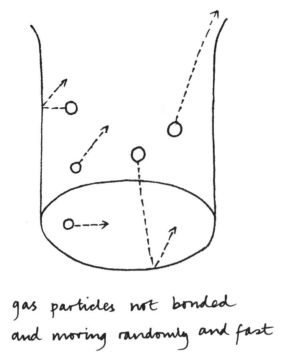

gas particles not bonded
and moving randomly and fast

Figure P.1 Diagram of a gas, showing the particles are not bonded to each other.

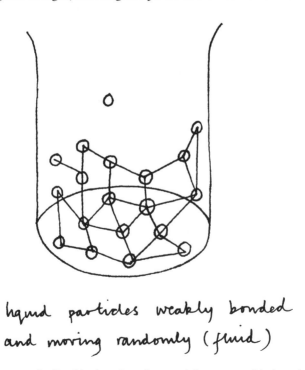

liquid particles weakly bonded
and moving randomly (fluid)

Figure P.2 Diagram of a liquid, showing the particles are weakly bonded and able to move relative to each other.

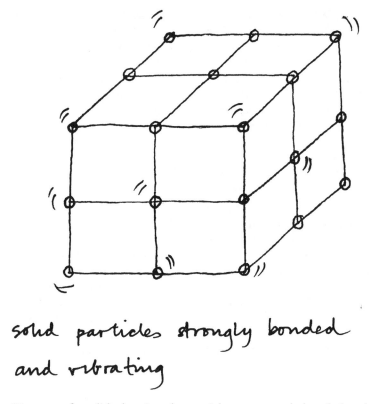

solid particles strongly bonded
and vibrating

Figure P.3 Diagram of a solid, showing the particles are strongly bonded and vibrating.

to devise their own dramatic representations of changes that happen in materials which they observe. For example, they could show what they believe is happening when condensation forms on the classroom's windows on a cold day, or why the top layer of **soil** is dry even though deeper down the soil is damp.

PATTERN-SEEKING ENQUIRY

One form of scientific **enquiry** is to conduct a survey, or keep a record of lots of examples and look for patterns in the data collected. This is particularly appropriate when **variables** cannot be controlled, such as when investigating living things in their environment. Monitoring **climate change** is a topical example of this form of scientific enquiry, as is phenology –

noting occurrences of regular events such as the flowering of a kind of **plant**, or the migration of a species of **bird**. Children can take part in nationwide surveys (e.g. BBC's *Springwatch* – see www.bbc.co.uk) and make real contributions to scientific knowledge. The outcomes are often descriptive, and may describe correlations, but provide weaker evidence for establishing a cause-and-effect relationship than a **fair test**.

PHASES, LUNAR (OF THE MOON)

The apparent shape of the **moon** in the sky changes over a predictable 28-day cycle. We have one night of 'new moon' when it is completely invisible, followed by seven days when it 'waxes' from a thin sliver to a semicircle – somewhat confusingly called the 'first quarter', referring to the period in the month rather than the shape. Over the next seven days it continues to wax through the 'gibbous' phases to 'full moon', in which it appears as a bright disc on clear nights. During the third period of seven days it 'wanes' to a semicircle again ('third quarter') then continues to wane back to 'new.' This regular pattern has been linked to – among other things – women's menstrual periods and mental health; the word 'lunatic' was coined to refer to someone behaving strangely on the night of a full moon. The explanation for lunar phases is beyond the scope of the primary curriculum, but is worth knowing as it often crops up in class discussion during topics on 'the Earth and beyond.' As we know, the moon does not produce its own **light** but reflects the light of the sun (see **reflection**). As it is spherical, exactly half of the moon is lit by the sun at any one time. However, as the moon **orbits** the Earth in its 28-day cycle, we see different proportions of this lit side. At 'new moon' the moon is on the same side of the Earth as the sun – not directly between them, however, as this would produce a solar **eclipse**. As the lit side of the moon is facing the sun we can't see it so the moon appears completely dark to us and blends into the sky. At this time of the month the 'dark side of the moon' is the side we can actually see! As the moon moves through the first 14 days of its orbit it gradually reveals more of its illuminated half until we see all of it at 'full moon' – at this point it is at the opposite side of the Earth from the sun so the half we can't see is the 'dark side.' The process is effectively reversed as the moon completes its orbit. To simulate this process in the classroom (see **model**), use a white polystyrene ball on a stick held in the light from an overhead projector (see Figure P.4). If we rotate in a swivel chair whilst holding the ball at arm's

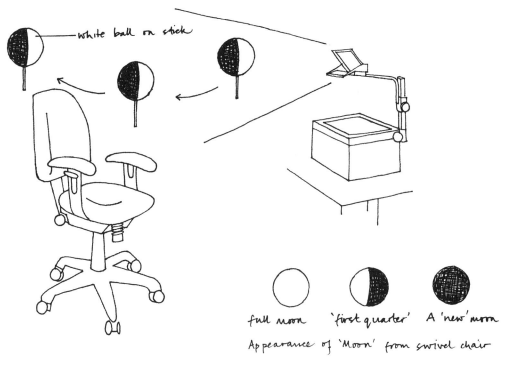

Figure P.4 Modelling the phases of the moon.

length above eye level, the phases of the moon appear before our eyes!

PHOTOSYNTHESIS

Plants make their own food by this process. 'Photosynthesis' literally means 'assembly by light.' In simple terms, carbon and oxygen from carbon dioxide gas and hydrogen from water are combined to make a sugar molecule of carbon, hydrogen and oxygen (i.e a carbo-hydr-ate, where '-ate' refers to oxygen). The useful by-product of photosynthesis is oxygen gas released into the atmosphere. **Leaves** could be described as factories in which simple raw materials are changed, using the **energy** from the sun, into new plant material. This material is then transported around the plant so new **roots**, **stems** and flowers can be made. Gardeners have 'green fingers' because they are stained by a pigment called chlorophyll, vital to photosynthesis, which comes from crushed plant cells. The idea that plants make solid material like wood from water and gas is counterintuitive, so many people, including teachers, have difficulty in understanding the concept. The other confusion is the idea of 'plant food' or fertiliser – if plants make their own food, why do we feed them? Plants need to get certain chemicals from **soil** and water in order to thrive (like iron or potassium), rather like the vitamins and minerals we need in our diet. By adding soluble chemicals to the soil we can supplement naturally occurring minerals.

PHYSICAL CHANGES TO MATERIALS

From an early age, children experience materials changing from solid to liquid, liquid to gas and vice versa. Melting of chocolate and ice cream, watching ice form, puddles evaporating, steam coming from kettles and condensation forming on car windows all provide everyday experiences of materials changing state through physical processes. Physical changes are defined as those that involve a change of state (solid to liquid, etc.) and do not produce new materials (unlike chemical changes in which new substances are formed). **Dissolving** is also a physical change because the materials mixed together remain chemically distinct. With all physical changes, the appearance of the material might have changed but the particles that make up the material remain chemically identical (see **chemical changes to materials** by contrast). This is because the particles are simply rearranged without being fundamentally changed. During physical change, the mass of the material remains the same before and after the change (although when liquid water becomes solid ice, its volume will change). The reversible nature of the processes (**evaporation** and **condensation**, **melting** and solidification, or freezing) can be quite easily investigated in the classroom. Melted chocolate can be cooled until it sets as a solid once more. Water vapour can be condensed to a liquid again, for example when it comes into contact with a cold pane of glass. Clay that has been shaped into a pot and left to harden can be reconstituted by adding the water that has evaporated from it. An understanding of these changes can be developed in the classroom through **observation**, questioning, demonstration (see **illustrative activities**) and **investigation** so that children begin to understand the role of heating and cooling in bringing about these changes (see **temperature**). One investigation is to study what happens to ice cubes when placed in different locations. This lends itself to a discussion of a **fair test** (for example, were the ice cubes all the same size?). Measurements can be taken using data loggers so that a continuous trace of the rise and fall in temperature is recorded.

105

PITCH

The pitch of a **sound** (how 'high' or 'low' it is) depends on the frequency with which the source of the sound vibrates (see **vibration**). The higher the frequency of vibration (measured in hertz or Hz for short) the higher the pitch. For example, a whistle will have a high frequency of vibration, hence will make a high-pitched note. Conversely, a didgeridoo will vibrate much more slowly and hence produce a low-pitched sound. Most musical instruments can change the pitch of the note they produce by altering the length of the string or air column which vibrates, using either a fretboard or strategically placed holes. There are several ways of demonstrating that the longer the vibrating object the lower the pitch; for example, cutting a drinking straw into a point at one end and blowing through it whilst compressing the lips can make a sort of 'clarinet.' By cutting the length of the straw as we blow, the pitch of the note increases by steps producing a dramatic and amusing effect!

PLANET

A planet is a spherical body – usually solid or gaseous – orbiting a **star**. Planets do not produce their own **light** (except in the case of volcanoes); rather, they reflect the light from the star they **orbit**. We live on a planet and are aware of seven (formerly eight) more in our solar system orbiting our sun. Five of these – Mercury, Venus, Mars, Jupiter and Saturn – are visible to the naked eye and share their names with Roman gods, since their 'wandering' movements across the night sky made it appear that they had a life of their own. Until the sixteenth century it was assumed that the planets – together with the sun and **stars** – moved around the Earth, but Nicolaus Copernicus (1473–1543) suggested the idea that they actually orbited the sun. Later, the outer planets of Uranus, Neptune and Pluto were discovered, but in 2005 Pluto was demoted to the status of 'minor planet' following the discovery of several larger bodies even further out in the solar system. This controversial decision rested on a number of features which make Pluto rather different from the other eight 'major' planets and similar to the newly discovered planets which would otherwise have to be admitted to the 'club.' Children in the later years of primary school can have their own debate about Pluto's status, which illustrates some important features of 'how science works' (see **scientific literacy**). In order to get a sense of the scale of the solar system, they can also **model** it using beads, marbles and balls with appropriate relative dimensions, placed at their scaled distances from a large exercise ball to represent the sun. They will find that they need to group the first four fairly close together, with vastly increasing distances from Jupiter onwards. Over the last ten years, scientists have begun to infer the existence of 'extra-solar' planets: that is, planets which orbit other stars in our **galaxy**. So far, only large 'gas giant' planets like Jupiter and Saturn have been found, but there remains the possibility that somewhere there is a planet like Earth, at the 'right' distance away from its star for life to exist.

PLANNING – see **scheme of work**

PLANNING AN ENQUIRY – see **process skills**

PLANT

'Green plants' as they are referred to in the National Curriculum (although few plants are uniformly green) are one of the two main **kingdoms** of living things studied in primary school (**animals** being the other). Scientists disagree about many things and the definition of a plant is no exception (see **tentative nature of science**). One way to identify a member of this kingdom is to check it out at cell level. A plant cell will have a cell wall made of cellulose, a sap-filled space within the cell and some tiny grains called chloroplasts which contain the green pigment chlorophyll, vital for **photosynthesis**. If all these features are present then you probably have a plant. This knowledge about cells is, however, reserved for the Key Stage 3 curriculum. It is usually obvious to children that something green with **leaves**, a **stem**, **roots** and flowers is a plant, although children are likely to hold alternative ideas about what is and what is not a living plant. To complicate matters, not all plants have features that children usually associate with plants (see **algae**, **moss**, **ferns**). Although young children have trouble seeing plants as 'alive' in the same way as animals, they are classified as living things because they carry out all of the **life processes**. Plants can reproduce sexually or asexually (without sex; see **flowering plants** and **reproduction**). Leaves, designed to catch as much light as possible, can be little or large, smooth or rough, veined, ribbed, hairy, spotty, striped, fleshy, prickly, needle-like, jagged, split or holed. They can be green, red, yellow, purple, even black. Leaves are held on stems that are equally diverse – round or square, hollow or solid, horizontal, twisting or vertical, edible or poisonous. Roots can be delicate, thick and swollen or like branches of a tree. They do not get up and walk, but plants will move their leaves, stems or flowers (e.g. sunflowers) to find the light or a support (e.g. beans). Plants can sense **light**, **gravity** and water. Some can sense if they have been damaged. Plants use food they make themselves to get **energy** to do all of the above.

PLASTICITY

A **mechanical property of materials**; when the **force** that was deforming a material is removed, if the material remains deformed it is said to be plastic (the opposite is elastic; see **elasticity**). Plastic (the material) was named after plasticity (the property) because of the plasticity this material shows during its manufacture which enables it to be formed into a variety of shapes (see **manufactured materials**). However, plasticity is a property of many materials other than just plastic. Furthermore, some plastics in their finished form are elastic!

PNEUMATICS (D&T)

A pneumatic **control system** is one that uses compressed air to control movement (see **mechanism**). Simple examples include party blowers and bicycle pumps. Children can experience pneumatic control using a flexible plastic bottle connected to a length of tubing, which can then be used to inflate a balloon, or two plastic syringes (obviously not ones that have been previously used for medical purposes) again connected by a length of flexible tubing. If one is connected compressed whilst the other is extended, pushing the one full of air will result in the plunger in the other syringe moving outwards, and vice versa. Children enjoy this experience of influencing movement at a distance and can readily adapt it to numerous models, such as a clown whose hat elevates or a monster whose mouth is opened by the expanding syringe.

POPULATION

In **ecology**, the population is the number of individuals of a **species** in a particular **habitat**. For example we might talk about the population of frogs in a pond or seagulls in a town. Children could survey populations of different living things in the school grounds by sampling and estimating using a variety of techniques, such as regular **observation** of a wall for snails, counting **invertebrates** under logs, listening for birdsong, counting daisies within a square metre (see **pattern-seeking enquiry**).

POWER

Power defines how rapidly **energy** is being converted. The watt is the unit of power, and 1 watt is equal to 1 joule of energy conversion every second. Raising a 1 kg object (that's 10 newtons of **weight**) by 1 metre transfers 10 joules of energy to potential energy. If it takes one second to perform this lift, your arm will be producing 10 watts of power. More power is needed to lift the same object through the same distance but in less time. If the object weighs less, then less power is needed to lift it by the same distance in one second. For more information on light bulbs and their power rating, see **power (electrical)**.

POWER (ELECTRICAL)

The power of an electrical **circuit** is defined as the rate at which **energy** is transformed within it. Electrical current carries energy from the **battery** to components such as lamps, motors and buzzers where this energy is transferred into **light**, movement, **sound** and heat. The faster this occurs, the more powerful the component. Power is measured in watts, named after the Scottish inventor and mechanical engineer James Watt (1736–1819); 1 watt is defined as 1 joule of energy per second. We are familiar with domestic light bulbs being rated in watts – a 100 watt bulb transfers 100 joules of electrical energy to light and (mostly) heat energy per second. The development of new low-energy bulbs makes this process much more efficient since a far greater proportion of the electrical energy is transferred to light and much less to heat.

PRACTICAL (HANDS-ON) ACTIVITIES

Asked what they enjoy about science, many primary-age children will cite the hands-on element of their classroom experience. They see practical activities – whether referred to as 'experiments', 'investigations' or 'enquiry' – as interesting, fun and sometimes surprising. As teachers we ignore this at our peril; the more formal written elements we bring into classroom science – perhaps in a bid to provide better **assessment** evidence or to revise for a test – the less children are likely to enjoy it and hence the less they will probably learn. Practical activities engage children's kinaesthetic learning styles and are also usually collaborative, so they lead to plenty of social learning as children discuss how best to go about an investigation (see **learning**). We need to make primary science as practical as possible, but also to remember that there are many different kinds of practical work within the heading of 'scientific enquiry.' One under-used type of hands-on experience is **exploration**: literally 'play' with intrinsically fascinating objects such as magnets. Whilst we may be willing to allow younger children to play in science, it is tempting to assume that older children need to get straight into more systematic forms of investigation, including the control of **variables** needed in a **fair test**. However, without the initial opportunity to play, children may not acquire a 'feel' for the phenomena in question or develop some of the more creative ideas for their own investigations. Practical work in science should be 'minds-on' as well as 'hands-on'; simply following a set of instructions to undertake an experiment to 'prove' a scientific **theory** is likely to be a less rich learning experience than a relatively open-ended task in which children have a degree of choice over what they investigate and how. As teachers, we need not be afraid that our experiments 'won't work' as many of the most important discoveries in science (e.g. penicillin) have come from 'failed' experiments. Clearly, we need to provide children with guidance and scaffolding in planning and carrying out their own enquiries, but unexpected results should be shared and discussed in a spirit of respect for **evidence**, rather than dismissed in favour of 'what ought to have happened.'

PREDICTION

A prediction in science is a statement of what outcomes are expected from a scientific **enquiry**. This should not be a guess, but based on a logical following-through of a premise, or **hypothesis**. For primary-age children, however, the thinking behind a prediction may not be made explicit, and may be more linked with children's prior experiences. Children's predictions can actually provide teachers with useful insights into their thinking. Asking children to develop a prediction with the causal connective 'because' can help to make the reasoning behind it more explicit (see **thinking skills**). Another way of developing predictions is to make sure that both the independent and dependent **variables** are included: for example, 'I predict that the greater the height I drop the parachute from, the longer it will take to fall', so that the predicted relationship between cause and effect is made clear. Older children can be challenged to make more complex predictions, such as producing a graph to show what general trend of pattern in their results they expect.

PROCESS SKILLS

Science is a complex activity that is carried out through a combination of thinking and doing. Some process skills are *thinking skills* (see **thinking skills**) – for example, hypothesising, interpreting and evaluating – while others are physical or motor skills, such as using **measurement** or using magnifying equipment. Some of these involve manual dexterity – holding, pouring, cutting – and also have a conceptual component. For example, to use a hand lens, a thermometer or a Newton meter requires a combination of physical manipulative skills and an understanding of what the tool does.

Scientific processes can be presented as distinct elements – **exploration**, **questions**, **prediction**, establishing a **hypothesis**, planning, testing, **observation**, measuring, recording, interpretation, **evaluation**, drawing **conclusions** and communicating – that make up a whole **enquiry**. However, in practice these processes are not as separate as the labels suggest and often flow from one to the next or become intertwined; planning the range and intervals of the independent **variable** depends on a prediction of what may be significant, and evaluation may change the plan as you go along. In short, there is no neat sequence that is the 'scientific method.'

PROGRESSION

Progression in science falls into one of three areas: progress in the development of **attitudes**, procedures (see **process skills**) or concepts (see **conceptual understanding**). A list of the kinds of attitudes that teachers may look for in their pupils might include curiosity, willingness to consider evidence, sensitivity to living things in the environment, critical reflection, perseverance, **creativity** and inventiveness, and co-operation with others. Harlen and Qualter (2009) identified important indicators of development in key scientific attitudes. For example, when considering a child's willingness to consider evidence, she may develop from 'recognising when evidence does not fit a conclusion' to 'relinquishing or changing ideas after considering evidence.' The progress a child is making in procedural understanding can be judged against the individual process skills such as **observation**, planning and considering evidence. AKSIS research materials (Goldsworthy *et al.* 2000) have been produced for progression across a range of skills such as raising questions and the use of **fair tests**. For example, in fair testing children progress from recognising when a test is clearly unfair to recognising which variables

109

need to be controlled. Probably the area where most information on progress has been published is in children's development of conceptual understanding. The SPACE reports (see www.nuffieldcurriculumcentre. org) provide a great deal of information on ideas held by children as they move towards a more scientific view of science topics. In general children's scientific ideas move from description to explanation, from small ideas to big ideas, and from personal to shared ideas.

PROPERTIES OF MATERIALS

Each material has its own characteristics that are used to distinguish it from other materials. These characteristics influence our choice of material for a particular job. The property of a material, put simply, is how it reacts to a variety of external influences. These include: the **mechanical properties of materials** (response to a force) such as **hardness**, **elasticity**, toughness; **thermal properties of materials** such as conductivity (how well a material will conduct heat); electrical properties such as **electrical conductivity**; **chemical properties of materials** such as reactivity; **optical properties of materials** such as transparency, **reflectivity**, refractivity; magnetic properties; acoustical properties (the material's response to **sound**) such as sound absorption; and environmental properties such as **biodegradability**.

Young children are inclined to describe a material by how it feels. Some children go further by describing **observations** made using a range of their senses. For example, some describe what noises the materials make or what the materials look like in terms of colour. It can be the case that children describe the material in terms of how it is used rather than by its properties. Older primary school children are more able to identify the material from

which objects are made and the uses to which objects could be put. Sorting games based on collections of objects can be used in a variety of ways to develop both the skills and an understanding of the properties of materials, helping children to become aware of the variety of materials that form the world around them (see **sorting activities**). A useful and cheap starting point is to put together a collection of (clean) household packaging, with a variety of cartons, yoghurt pots, plastic bottles, bottle tops, corks, rubber bands, polystyrene, bubble wrap and anything else to hand. A collection designed to sort metal and plastic objects into two groups could include a metal ruler, spoon, scissors with plastic handle, plastic coat hanger with a metal hook, etc. Plastic PE hoops can be used to show each group – metal and plastic. There are a number of other sorting games:

- *Guess the criterion*: One child sorts the collection without disclosing to the others the criterion she has used. Children study the groupings and guess the criterion used.
- *Domino game*: Each child has an object; one of these is placed on the floor and others try to add to the chain by putting down their object if it has the same property (for example, both objects are **transparent** or both objects are very hard).
- *Making a key*: Children work in groups, each with a small collection of 5–10 objects and a large sheet of paper. They are asked to develop an identification key using yes/no questions (e.g. Does the object conduct electricity? Is the object elastic?). Groups move round and try each other's identification keys.

There are many other games that can be played, including ones using sorting diagrams (Venn, Carroll and branching databases) which have **cross-curricular** links with mathematics.

PROPERTIES OF OBJECTS

Strictly speaking the property of a material is different from the property of an object as the former is intrinsic to the material and is independent of its size and shape. For example, the **hardness** of a material is not dependent on the shape of the object. However, the ease with which an object can be bent (its flexibility) is determined not only by what the material is made from but also by its thickness. Children can investigate this property by testing a variety of objects made from the same material but with different thicknesses.

PULLEY (D&T)

A pulley is a grooved **wheel** over which a cord or belt can run. Commonly primary school children encounter pulleys when constructing winding **mechanisms**. At its simplest, the winder is a cord attached to an **axle** which is turned by a handle to raise and lower an object such as a bucket in a well (consider here possible links with the nursery rhyme 'Jack and Jill'). A more advanced winder can be fitted to a crane so that the cord is directed over a pulley at the end of the crane's arm. Yet more advanced are pulley systems fitted with continuous belts that run between the driver (the wheel that is turned) and the follower (the wheel to which the movement is transmitted). Children can investigate changing the direction of rotation by crossing over the drive belt between the driver and follower. Changing the size of pulleys affects the speed that they rotate, so that a small pulley rotates more quickly than a large pulley but with less turning **force**, or torque. The Design and Technology Association have produced a helpsheet to aid the teaching of pulleys that suggests giving children the opportunity to produce a model fairground ride (Design and Technology Association 1999).

Q

QUESTIONS

Children naturally ask questions about their surroundings and science education seeks to encourage and develop this desire to understand the world around them. Question-raising enables children to capture their curiosity in a way that can lead to scientific and technological learning. The formulation of questions generated from **observation** and **exploration** is an important part of developing a scientific or technological enquiry and is a requirement of the English Primary National Curriculum (DfEE 1999). Teachers can seek to both capture children's questions as they emerge naturally and stimulate them through introducing new objects or experiences or challenging children to explore familiar objects from a different perspective. Different kinds of questions lead to different kinds of answers and stimulate different approaches to seeking answers. By the end of the primary phase children should be able to make decisions about how to go about answering their questions. For activities to support this see Goldsworthy *et al.* (2000). Children can be helped to rephrase questions in a way that emphasises the relationship between the variables concerned; for example, 'What makes the best raincoat?' can be rephrased as 'Which material lets the least water through?'

(Goldsworthy *et al.* 2000). Some questions, particularly those with a philosophical or moral dimension, such as 'Can we keep butterflies in our classroom?' may not be answered by direct enquiry, but may be good starting points for debates about the wider applications of science and technology in people's lives.

Teacher questions have a key role to play in children's learning, but can have a range of purposes. The form and content of the question need to match the purpose. For example, open-ended questions explore children's ideas initially, but a more direct, focused question might be needed to challenge those ideas (see **elicitation**). An opening question might be 'What do you think plants need to stay alive?' whilst initial ideas about plants 'eating soil' might be challenged by asking: 'Can you think of any examples of when plants live without soil?' In both of these examples the focus is on discussing the children's ideas, not testing them to see if they match a predetermined 'correct' answer. Teacher questions also help children to develop their thinking about scientific **enquiry**, e.g. 'What could you do to find out if plants need soil to grow well?' or 'Have you found any connection between how well the plants grow and how much soil they had?'

R

RAINBOW

A rainbow is one of the most beautiful sights we can see in the sky and always produces excitement and wonder amongst children. Typically, it occurs when the sun comes out just after – or even during – a rain shower, and can also be produced artificially using a fine spray from a hose on a sunny day. It almost seems a shame to demystify this awe-inspiring phenomenon by attempting to explain it scientifically, which is actually quite difficult. In a nutshell, each droplet of water both reflects the sunlight internally, refracts (bends) it and disperses its colours into a spectrum (see **reflectivity** and **refraction**). The combined effect of millions of droplets each reflecting, refracting and dispersing sunlight in a predictable, coherent way produces the full rainbow (see Figure R.1). Rainbows are semicircular because water droplets are spherical – the 'missing half'

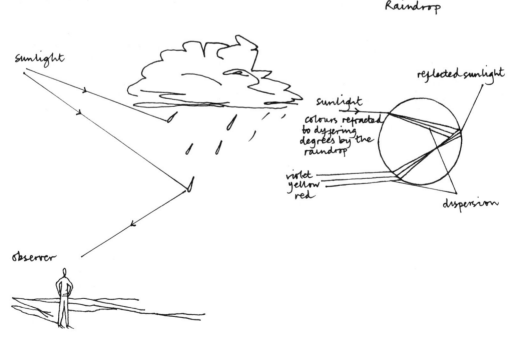

Figure R.1 How light is refracted and reflected by a raindrop producing a rainbow.

of the full, circular rainbow is theoretically under the ground!

RECORDING AN ENQUIRY – see **process skills**

REFLECTION

Reflection is one of the properties of light, the process by which **light** appears to 'bounce off' surfaces. It is usually used to refer to the predictable way in which light bounces off very smooth, highly polished surfaces like mirrors or pools of still water. In this case, the angle of reflection of each light ray is the same as its angle of incidence (the angle it made with the mirror as it arrived), a bit like a snooker ball bouncing in a predictable way off a cushion at the side of the table. This kind of predictable reflection forms images because all the reflected light rays maintain their juxtaposition from when they left the object – hence we can see our reflection in a mirror. Children can investigate this using a torch, mirror, protractor and a pair of cardboard tubes; shining the torch down one of the tubes at a particular angle to the mirror will require them to place the other tube at a corresponding angle to see the light. However, reflection is also sometimes used to refer to the random scattering of light from 'rough', non-shiny objects (i.e. all the objects you can't see your face in). It is this scattering of light which enables us to see the object, because some of the light which hits it from a source such as the sun or a light bulb is scattered ('reflected') towards our eyes. Because most objects scatter some frequencies (colours) of light and absorb others, we see them as having a particular colour.

REFLECTIVITY

A **property of materials** that is dependent on the shape of the object. When light hits an object, the proportion of it that is not absorbed by the material or transmitted through it will be reflected. An uneven surface will scatter the light, giving a matt appearance. Polished surfaces will reflect light in a uniform way so that an image of the **light source** or objects will be visible. We call objects with highly polished surfaces 'reflectors.'

REFRACTION

Refraction is the bending of **light**. This might at first appear strange as we are taught that light travels in straight lines, but its direction can be changed by passing through different **transparent** materials such as glass and water. We can easily observe this by looking at a spoon in a glass of water; it appears to be 'bent' because the water changes the direction of light from the part of the spoon below the water surface. These changes of direction actually occur at the boundaries between different **materials**, e.g. the surface of the water or the edge of the glass. Prisms refract light by having outer surfaces at different angles to each other, thus magnifying the bending effect at each surface. This also has the effect of *dispersing* the colours within the white light entering the prism, producing a spectrum. Lenses are effectively a series of prisms stuck together, so are able to focus parallel beams of light passing through them by making these converge or diverge, creating an image which can be very useful for those of us whose **eyes** no longer do the same job so effectively!

REPRODUCTION

The process by which living things make new individuals like themselves. It can be sexual, involving a combination of male and female cells, or asexual – for example when a strawberry **plant** sends out a 'runner' at the end of which is a new plant which can eventually survive independently of its parent. Asexually produced individuals are clones and genetically identical to the parent. For some **micro-organisms**, reproduction is achieved by dividing one cell into two (cell division).

Sexual reproduction involves the mixing of genes from a mother and a father through the combining of sex cells or gametes (a Key Stage 3 concept). At Key Stage 2 children will learn about pollen (male) and the ovum (plural ova; female). The flower's anther makes pollen and the ova are contained within the ovary, usually found at the base of a **flowering plant**. Plants have devised a wonderful variety of ways to get these two cells together through a process called pollination. Pollen does the travelling, therefore it is usually as light and small as dust – and can make some of us sneeze. Pollen is carried by the wind (as in the case of grasses), by bees and other insects. The pollen is caught by the feathery or sticky stigma found at the centre of most flowers. Once on a stigma, the pollen grain grows a tube that finds its way through the stigma and style to the female ovum. The male sex cell, containing half the information to make a new, unique individual, will unite with the female half of the genetic information to produce a **seed**. This is called fertilisation. The ovary then swells and changes to become the fruit. A pea pod is the fruit and the 'pea' is the seed. The peas may look identical, but they will each grow into a unique individual with characteristics combined from their parents. The mother will be the same but the fathers could be different. Gregor Mendel discovered all about heredity and sex in peas, his ground-breaking work conducted, somewhat ironically, in a monastery garden.

Children will begin to learn before primary school that **animals** have babies which grow into adults. Through school they will become familiar with the life cycle of plants and animals through experience and some charming books. They will learn that butterflies have life cycles in which the animal takes distinctly different forms, i.e. a caterpillar (larva), then a pupa, then a butterfly (imago). **Birds** and **reptiles** lay eggs from which smaller, immature versions of the adult hatch. **Amphibians**, such as frogs, lay eggs which turn into tadpoles which then develop in tiny adult forms.

Human reproduction needs to be taught with great sensitivity according to the school's sex and relationships policy. Parents have a right to withdraw children from sex and relationships education except the parts that are statutory in the current **curriculum**. The government publishes clear guidance for teachers and governors on this topic (see http://publications.dcsf.gov.uk).

An essential feature of human reproduction is that it is sexual – that cells from the male with half of his genes fertilise cells from the female with half of her genes, so the resulting offspring has inherited genetic material from both parents. The cells with half the genetic information are called gametes. In the testes of the man cells divide in a special way to split the genetic information on chromosomes and produce sperm cells (see **DNA**). A similar process happens in the ovaries of the woman producing the egg cells or ova. Bringing the two together is achieved by sexual intercourse, when sperm from the man's penis travels up into the uterus. At the midpoint of the woman's menstrual cycle an egg cell will be released from one of the ovaries and travel down a fallopian tube (oviduct) to the uterus, where one sperm cell may fuse with it, fertilising the egg cell. For a wonderful account of how this is achieved see Babette Cole's book *Mummy Laid an Egg!* (Cole 1995). The fertilised egg now has the full set of genetic information that is a unique combination of each parent. This cell divides repeatedly, forming more and more cells, all with the same genetic information and, in a process that is only partially understood, different cells become different parts of the developing foetus. This all takes place in the uterus (womb) of the mother until the birth of the baby. Most **mammals** give birth to live young.

REPTILE

A member of the **animal kingdom**, e.g. lizard, snake, turtle. A cold-blooded **vertebrate** with a dry smooth skin made from scales. Eggs are usually laid on land and hatch into live young. Adults can range in size from the tiny gecko (16 mm) to the crocodile (6 m). Dinosaurs (literally 'terrible lizards') such as the meat-eating tyrannosaurus and the herbivorous diplodocus were reptiles. Children may well be very familiar with them through stories, films and TV. There are a number of dinosaur museums around the UK, for example in Hull, Dorchester and London.

All reptiles should be treated with care, and it is illegal to disturb, kill, injure or catch many UK species (see **risk assessment**). You must not sell them or damage, destroy or obstruct their **habitat** – so if you find a reptile species in your school take advice, e.g. from your local wildlife trust.

REPULSION

Unsurprisingly, in the world of **forces** as elsewhere, repulsion is the opposite of **attraction**. A repulsive force between two objects is one tending to drive them apart. This is most clearly seen when playing with magnets or magnetic toys (see **magnetic materials**). If two 'like poles' (a north and north, or south and south) are brought close together they push each other apart. So, two 'Brio' train carriages with magnetic couplings can push each other along

the track without touching, whilst if one of them is turned round they immediately stick together. Another 'magic' demonstration of magnetic repulsion is 'floating' ring magnets on a pole, which appear to hover unsupported. In this case the repulsive force of the two like poles of the ring magnet are sufficient to balance the attractive gravitational force between the upper magnet and the Earth (its **weight**). This is the principle behind the Maglev trains running in Shanghai, which hover just above the track thus minimising **friction** and enabling high speeds.

RESISTANCE (ELECTRICAL)

Resistance is a measure of how difficult it is for an electrical **current** to flow around a **circuit**. It is measured in ohms (Ω), named after the German scientist Georg Ohm (1787–1854). Most electrical **conductors**, such as copper or steel, have very low resistances, so the main source of resistance in an electrical circuit will be the components rather than the wires. For example, lamps (bulbs) have a filament of very thin wire, often made from a poor conductor such as tungsten. The thinness of the filament will introduce resistance (think of a busy motorway filtering from three lanes to one lane of traffic) and so will the large tungsten atoms which the **electrons** will tend to collide with. As a result of this resistance, the filament will heat up rapidly until it is white-hot, thus producing the desired glow. However, the resistance will also slow the current down all the way around the circuit (not just in the filament), in a similar way to that in which a single set of roadworks can produce 'gridlock' in a busy city, or on a circular motorway such as the M25 (though this **analogy** breaks down when we consider the difference in the flow of traffic before and after the roadworks). Thus, the greater the resistance, the smaller the flow of current in a simple circuit (see **series and parallel circuits**). Two lamps will have twice the resistance of one, thus halving the current if they are placed in series. The only ways of increasing the current again are either to place the lamps in parallel so that they each have their own connection to the **battery**, or to double the number of batteries, thus doubling the **voltage** ('push') that the electrons receive. This relationship was expressed by Georg Ohm in the law named after him: voltage = current x resistance.

RESOURCES

Several different kinds of classroom resources are needed to teach and learn science effectively. First, we need sources of information, such as reference books, the internet and CD-ROMs in order to pursue scientific **questions** which may not be answerable through **practical (hands-on) activities**. Second, there are a series of general resources available in most classrooms which children can use to carry out and record practical activities. Examples of these include paper, card, scissors, balloons, paper clips, elastic bands, Blu-Tack, Post-It notes and sticky tape. Third, there is the more 'specialist' scientific equipment – including ICT resources – needed for particular topics. This might include magnifying glasses, a digital microscope, data loggers, digital stills and video cameras, Newton meters, thermometers, scales, stopwatches, pond-dipping nets and pooters to collect small insects. Some resources, such as **batteries** and bulbs, come under the heading of 'consumables' and will need regular checking and replenishment by the science subject leader. How these resources are organised varies from school to school and is dependent on the science programme followed and the funding available. Until recently, many schools chose to organise specialist equipment and topic-specific books into 'topic boxes', each

related to a specific science unit of work (see **scheme of work**). These could be stored centrally and checked out by individual teachers for the duration of the unit before being returned and replenished. However, increasingly primary schools are adopting a 'creative curriculum' with more whole-school **cross-curricular** themes, which may require all classes to use the same set of resources in a particular term, necessitating multiple sets. Other approaches include providing a generic set of science resources to each classroom, to enable children to carry out investigations as and when required. Whichever approach is taken, there will always be a significant job of monitoring and replenishing science resources, which can be minimised by giving children greater ownership and responsibility for the storage and organisation of the science equipment in their own classroom (see **classroom organisation**).

RESPIRATION

One of the **life processes** that define 'living.' The word has two meanings, the first describing the transport of oxygen from the air to living cells, with carbon dioxide removed as a waste product (see **excretory system**). The second describes the reaction that takes place in the cells that enables **energy** from food to be released and used by the body.

RESPIRATORY SYSTEM

In humans the respiratory system includes the lungs, nose and mouth. We breathe in air through our mouths and noses, and this goes down our airway (trachea) into the lungs. There are tiny blood vessels running close to the surface of the lungs and oxygen from the air goes into the blood, latching on to the red blood cells; carbon dioxide dissolved in the blood plasma goes into the air in the lungs and is breathed out. Blood (see **circulatory**

119

system) then takes the oxygen to where it is needed in the cells all around the body. Children will be familiar with a number of phenomena associated with breathing. They may know that 'breath' can be seen on a cold day – this is due to water in the warm exhaled air condensing in the cold atmosphere. They will know a breath can extinguish a **burning** candle (as it takes away the heat of the flame) and that it can be used to play an instrument or blow something down. They may know that holding a breath is uncomfortable, or that sneezing and coughing makes air come out very quickly. They may know someone who has asthma (a condition where the tubes in the lung become swollen and therefore narrow, restricting the flow of air and making breathing difficult). Respiration can be investigated by counting breaths per minute or by measuring chest expansion and contraction with a tape measure (see **pattern-seeking enquiry**). Special bags are available that can measure lung capacity in litres – children will have a capacity of 3–4 litres and will breathe 8–20 times per minute.

RESTRUCTURING

Having elicited children's ideas (see **elicitation**), the teacher can then decide how to help move children's understandings forward. Restructuring is the label given to this phase of the Constructivist Teaching Sequence (see **learning**), formalised in the 1980s as part of the Children's Learning in Science Project (CLIS). Different children have different starting points, and meeting the needs of the whole class can be quite challenging. Some may need to extend and develop existing ideas, while others may have alternative ideas that need to be challenged and significantly restructured. Sometimes children's alternative ideas can be very resistant to change (see

alternative **frameworks**). Restructuring is an active process for the teacher, requiring careful analysis of the children's ideas and selection of appropriate kinds of intervention activities.

In an approach based on **social constructivism**, the most important intervention is to encourage children to test their ideas through the processes of scientific **enquiry** to extend, develop or replace them. This is not suggesting that children can 'discover' theories which have taken thousands of years of experimentation and thinking to develop. The role of the teacher is crucial in helping to identify productive lines of enquiry. Practical work to support the restructuring of ideas may not always be in the form of a full investigation. For example, first-hand observation of children's own **teeth** might be combined with the teacher initiating a discussion about why food needs to be broken into smaller bits. Children might then be invited to generate further **questions** and research different kinds of teeth. (Do **birds** have teeth? Are snake fangs teeth? Has everyone still got their baby teeth?)

Not all forms of intervention to support restructuring directly involve scientific enquiries. Challenges to existing ideas might come from various sources: other children, books, videos, visits, visitors or the teacher, who might use phrases such as: 'The way I see it is that … Does that make any sense to you?' The use of **models** and **analogies** can be very helpful in discussing ideas that are not immediately accessible to children. Taking a sociocultural view (see **sociocultural perspective**), the process of restructuring could be seen as a collaborative gathering of relevant experience and sources of evidence, together with a communal evaluation of the possibilities. It mirrors a view of scientists, not as brilliant loners, but as a community with a collective responsibility to criticise each other's interpretations of data, to look for exceptions to rules and to find the best possible explanations.

REVIEW

Reviewing is sometimes seen as what is done at the end of an activity, but can be a much more continuous process. The Constructivist Teaching Sequence developed by the Children's Learning in Science Project (CLIS) identifies reviewing as a distinct stage, linked with **elicitation** (see **learning**). A better way of seeing review might be as part of the ongoing dialogue with and between children about their changing ideas. This thinking about thinking, or metacognition, is an important theme of other approaches to learning in science, such as CASE (**Cognitive Acceleration through Science Education**). Children can be challenged to reflect on both how their ideas might be different now from ones they held previously, and how the change in their ideas came about. This is an important time for teachers to help children make the link between ideas and **evidence** and how scientific knowledge is continually changing (see **tentative nature of science**). Part of **progression** in learning science is moving from personal knowledge to a shared knowledge (Harlen 2006). The process of reviewing ideas collectively enables the class to decide which ideas are thought to be particularly significant and give them the special status of shared knowledge. However, time for individuals to reflect on their personal learning is also important.

RISK ASSESSMENT

All lesson-planning should involve a risk assessment. This simply means that thought needs to be given to any possible sources of risk and that action needs to be taken to minimise any danger. It may involve discussing safety issues with children, or it may mean checking that certain materials are suitable for use in a primary classroom. Detailed guidance is provided in the publication *Be Safe! Health and Safety in Primary School Science and Technology* (ASE 2001). Schools and local authoritites have their own risk assesment procedures and documentation to complete for taking children on off-site visits.

ROCKS

Rocks fall into one of three groups (igneous, metamorphic or sedimentary) depending on the processes that formed them. Igneous rocks (e.g. granite) are formed by the melting and subsequent cooling of geological materials, and are often characterised by randomly orientated, angular, interlocking grains (see **crystal**). Metamorphic rocks (e.g. schist) are formed by heat and pressure acting on an existing rock so that over a long period of time the rock recrystallises with grains often in a banded or layered orientation. Sedimentary rocks result from material at the Earth's surface being broken down by weathering, transported (e.g. by water), deposited and then compacted and cemented into rock, so that grains are often rounded and non-interlocking.

Primary school children can gain a procedural understanding of how to classify rocks (see **classifying and identifying**) by being encouraged to make detailed **observations** of grain relationships. They might notice that in a granite the grains are angular and interlocking whereas in a sandstone the grains are rounded with a 'glue' holding them together (see Figure R.2). Following careful observation, children could develop **models** of the rocks in 2D (using angular and rounded shapes) and 3D (construction kits such as Lego, and marbles). There are usually plenty of opportunities to study rocks

121

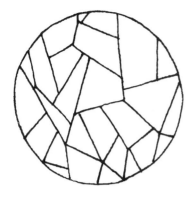
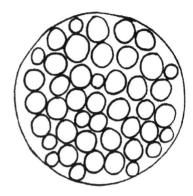

Interlocking grains

Rounded grains held together by 'rock glue'

Figure R.2 Rock grain relationships, showing an igneous rock formed by interlocking grains (left) and a sedimentary rock formed by rounded grains held together by 'rock glue' (right).

in the outdoor environment. Maybe on visiting a shopping area children will discover that a variety of building stones have been used to construct the shop fronts. Alternatively a visit to a cemetery might reveal that the gravestones have been constructed out of a number of different rock types.

ROOT

Plant roots have two main functions – to anchor the plant and to take up water and dissolved minerals to be transported through the **stem** to other parts of the plant.

ROTATION OF THE EARTH – see **day and night**

S

SCHEME OF WORK

A scheme of work (SoW) for science is a long-term and medium-term teaching plan. The key purpose of a SoW is to ensure that, as pupils move through a school, their science experiences are balanced, coherent and comprehensive. It should also show how science relates to the **curriculum** as a whole.

A SoW is usually prepared by the school's science co-ordinator or subject leader in consultation with other staff. The co-ordinator will take into consideration the statutory requirements of the National Curriculum, the particular needs of the children in the school, the curriculum time, the **resources** and expertise available for science teaching. The resultant SoW will typically identify when each science topic is to be taught and for how long. The scheme of work will consist of a number of 'blocks' or *units of work* which are 'medium-term' plans. Each unit will indicate the subject knowledge (see **conceptual understanding**) and enquiry skills (see **process skills**) to be developed, possible activities, resource requirements, **differentiation** and **assessment** opportunities. Teachers will then use the scheme to develop medium-term plans and lesson plans for their class.

The Department for Education and Employment (DfEE) and Qualification and Curriculum Authority (QCA) co-published the first national scheme of work for primary science in 1998, with an update in 2000 (DfEE/QCA 1998). It is a non-statutory document – schools can implement as little or as much as they like. The document is a good place to start when thinking about planning for science, although experienced teachers can find it rather restrictive and repetitive. The DfES/QCA encourages schools to adapt the national SoW to match the needs of their children. It also suggests combining units from other subjects, so encouraging **cross-curricular** planning. The national SoW is available at www.standards.dfes.gov.uk.

Box 4   Science and design and technology: their relationship

The relationship between science and technology in the primary curriculum has shifted backwards and forwards a number of times over the past twenty years. An original intention to create a single subject in the National Curriculum (DES 1987) was resisted by those who wished to champion design and technology (D&T) as a separate discipline and not merely an application of scientific knowledge (Davies

123

1997). This led to the development of separate subject areas. However, more recent reviews of the primary curriculum in England recommend a joint learning area of 'scientific and technological understanding' (Alexander 2009; Rose 2009). In some ways, the debate concerning the relationship between science and D&T in the primary curriculum reflects a wider debate about the relationship between science and technology in society, characterised by Gardner (1994) as follows:

(i)   Science precedes technology, i.e. technological capability grows out of scientific knowledge; this position, often called the technology as applied science (TAS) view, is widely held and influential.
(ii) Science and technology are independent, with differing goals, methods and outcomes (the demarcationist view).
(iii) Technology precedes science; this materialist view asserts that technology is historically and ontologically prior to science, that experience with tools, instruments and other artefacts is necessary for conceptual development.
(iv) Technology and science engage in two-way interaction; this interactionist view considers scientists and technologists as groups of people who learn from each other in mutually beneficial ways. (Gardner 1994: 5)

The recent proposals for the establishment of a single learning area for science and technology, whilst they may appear to adopt a view of the two subjects as indistinguishable from each other and therefore equal in status, would probably result in a TAS model (see Gardner above) in which science education takes precedence over technological applications of children's scientific knowledge. Drawbacks of such an approach include the undervaluing of design skills (Gardner 1994) which risks sending messages to children that scientific knowledge is more important than D&T capability in gaining access to technological careers. Science is not the only source of knowledge upon which D&T needs to draw, and the necessity of children understanding the scientific principles within a D&T project is unproven. Furthermore, the assumption that children are able to transfer knowledge in a 'raw state' from science lessons to D&T activities has been called into question. The alternative, 'demarcationist' model has arguably been applied to the primary curriculum over the past twenty years, by establishing two distinct subjects, with only very limited links between them. However, by treating the subjects entirely separately, teachers may be missing out on opportunities for contextualising and applying scientific learning through D&T activities, or vice versa.

The development of specific knowledge in context is central to a 'materialist' model of the interaction between science and D&T in the primary curriculum. Siraj-Blatchford (1996) argues that the historical basis for such a view should be taught explicitly, since scientific development often occurs directly as a result of the introduction of new technology. One consequence of adopting a 'materialist' model is to elevate D&T to a leading role in the relationship, and teach science concepts through the contexts provided by evaluating products and solving design problems during making. So, for example, teachers might adopt a challenge-based approach to teaching electricity by asking children to design a greetings card that lights up or a fully functioning door buzzer. Another version of a D&T-dominated relationship is to regard science as a 'service' subject (Layton 1993), contributing ideas and techniques within the framework of a design-and-make assignment. For example, when designing a torch, children may need to undertake a short investigation into the effect of adding batteries to a circuit, in order to help them in selecting an appropriate power source and case size. Adopting Gardner's fourth category above – an 'interactionist' view of the relationship – emphasises the equal and complementary nature of science and D&T, seen as mutually dependent in some respects yet distinct in others. An interactionist perspective highlights the role of D&T in reworking scientific knowledge to make it more 'useful' (McCormick *et al.* 1995). In a 'constructivist' model of conceptual change (see **Box 3 Learning**), D&T activities can have a role in restructuring children's alternative frameworks (Driver 1983) concerning scientific concepts. For example, a project to design a torch may result in clarification of the distinction between transparency and reflectivity in the optical properties of materials. Any interactionist model must also consider the role that science may have in broadening children's 'device knowledge' (McCormick 1999) by, for example, developing general principles of electrical circuits from children's understanding of the workings of a torch. Whilst appreciating the differences between processes used in science and D&T, it is important in an interactionist model to seek ways in which they can 'feed into' one another. Scientific procedural knowledge, particularly that of designing 'fair tests' as part of investigations, can support the development of design processes. Conversely, the imaging and modelling skills children develop during D&T activities (Baynes 1992) can support them in developing mental models and analogies for scientific purposes (for example, a bicycle chain to simulate the flow of electricity in a circuit).

References

Alexander, R. (ed.) (2009) *Children, Their World, Their Education: Final Report and Recommendations of the Cambridge Primary Review.* London: Routledge.

Baynes, K. (1992) *Children Designing – Learning Design: Occasional Paper No. 1.* Loughborough: Loughborough University of Technology.

Davies, D. (1997) 'The relationship between science and technology in the primary curriculum – alternative perspectives', *Journal of Design and Technology Education*, 2 (2): 101–11.

Department of Education and Science (1987) *The National Curriculum 5–16: A Consultation Document.* London: Her Majesty's Stationery Office.

Driver, R. (1983) *The Pupil as Scientist?* Milton Keynes: Open University Press.

Gardner, P. (1994) 'Representations of the relationship between science and technology in the curriculum', *Studies in Science Education*, 24 (1): 1–13.

Layton, D. (1993) *Technology's Challenge to Science Education.* Milton Keynes: Open University Press.

McCormick, R. (1999) 'Practical knowledge; a view from the snooker table', in R. McCormick and C. Paechter (eds) *Learning and Knowledge.* London: Paul Chapman.

McCormick, R., Davidson, M. and Levinson, R. (1995) 'Making connections: students' scientific understanding of electric currents in design and technology', in J.S. Smith (ed.) *IDATER 95.* Loughborough: Loughborough University of Technology.

Rose, J. (ed.) (2009) *Independent Review of the Primary Curriculum: Final Report.* Nottingham: DCSF Publications.

Siraj-Blatchford, J. (1996) *Learning Technology, Science and Social Justice.* Nottingham: Education Now Publishing.

SCIENCE LEARNING CENTRES

There are nine Science Learning Centres located in regions around England whose central purpose is to support the professional development of teachers of science, both in primary and secondary schools. A national Science Learning Centre based in York leads the network of regional centres. They are run by different institutions, such as universities and **hands-on science and technology centres**, often working in collaboration and frequently supported by industrial partners. The centres offer a variety of courses and one-off events as well as drop-in support and useful webpages with online resources and reports of innovative projects. Information about the regional centres can be found through the main website www.sciencelearningcentres.org.uk.

SCIENTIFIC LITERACY

An important aim of science education as a whole is establishing 'scientific literacy' across the population. In a scientifically literate society people would engage with science issues that affect society as a whole and take an active role through democratic processes and personal decisions. They would understand enough about scientific processes to evaluate (see **evaluation**) the work of scientists and have sufficient understanding of scientific concepts (see **conceptual understanding**) to be able to engage with issues and make sense of information in the media. Science is not something scientists do in isolation from the rest of society, and it is not just scientists that need to make decisions about science and the directions in which science goes. A lack of scientific literacy can lead to either an acceptance or a mistrust of all science rather than an approach which is critical but is also open to new possibilities. Primary-age children are already developing viewpoints on issues that have an ethical as well as a scientific basis, and may have very strong views on issues such as how farm animals should be treated and how **habitats** should be protected.

SEASONS

The seasons – particularly the transitional seasons of autumn and spring – are a popular topic of study in primary schools since the aesthetic experience of holding a shiny conker or rustling fallen leaves is not to be missed (see **contexts for science**). The explanation for seasonal changes in **temperature** and daylight hours – the 'reasons for the seasons' – is, however, quite difficult and beyond the scope of the current primary science curriculum. This is not to say that questions will not arise in the classroom requiring some sort of explanation! So it is probably worth knowing that seasonal variations occur because of the tilt of the Earth's axis and not – as widely believed – changes in distance between the Earth and the sun. Since this tilt of approximately 23 degrees from the perpendicular remains the same throughout the Earth's **orbit** it results in the North Pole being tilted towards the sun on one side of the orbit (Northern Hemisphere summer) whilst six months later it is tilted away from the sun giving us winter (see Figure S.1). The tilt affects both the number of hours of daylight at different times of year – the area around the North Pole called the Arctic Circle receives 24 hours of daylight in midsummer – and also the angle at which the sun's rays strike the ground. In our summer, because our hemisphere is tilted towards the sun, it appears to be relatively 'high' in the sky and its rays strike us from a higher angle, making them more intense. Conversely, in our winter, the sun appears relatively 'low' in the sky and its rays strike us from a lower angle, giving

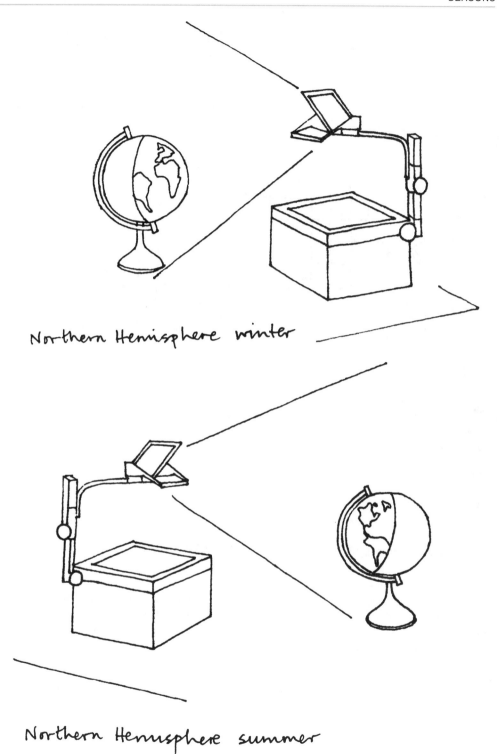

Northern Hemisphere winter

Northern Hemisphere summer

Figure S.1 Modelling a Northern Hemisphere summer and winter.

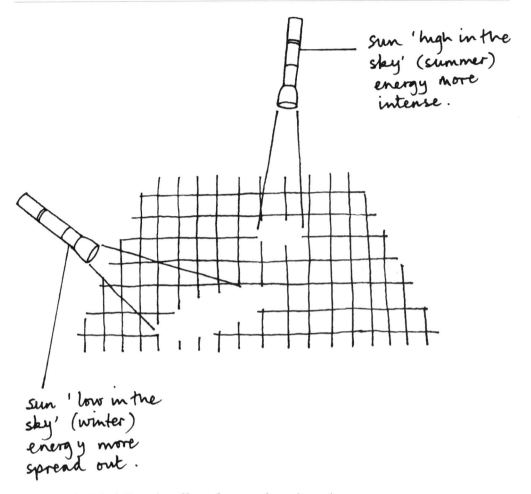

sun 'high in the sky' (summer) energy more intense.

sun 'low in the sky' (winter) energy more spread out.

Figure S.2 Modelling the effect of sun angle on intensity.

that beautiful winter light but with much less intensity (see Figure S.2). The seasons are of course reversed in the Southern Hemisphere since, when the North Pole is tilted towards the sun, the South Pole tilts away and vice versa. Tropical areas near the equator experience fewer seasonal variations since the sun is relatively high in the sky all year round.

SEED

A small embryonic **plant** wrapped up with some stored food in a seed coat (see **reproduction** and **seed dispersal**).

SEED DISPERSAL

Once **seed** is produced, plants encourage their progeny to leave home – the adult **plant** doesn't want to be overcrowded. Seed dispersal is a fun aspect of plant biology to study in the primary school as plants have evolved a variety of methods.

Wind dispersal: The sycamore, ash and maple drop their winged 'keys' from a height, while the dandelion's seeds are launched in feathery parachutes on a gust of wind. Poppies have long wobbly stems topped with 'pepper pots' that shake seeds out as they wave in the wind.

Water dispersal: Many water plants and shore dwellers (e.g. the coconut palm) have floating fruits that are carried by water currents to new desirable destinations.

Hitchhikers: The 'sticky' cleavers and hooked burdock achieve dispersal of their seeds by hooking to the coat (or clothing) of a passing animal.

Edible fruits: Juicy **fruits** entice animals to eat them. The seeds pass through the digestive tract unharmed and are deposited in a new location (see **digestive system**). Nuts lend themselves to being stored, buried and forgotten.

Exploding fruits: Some fruits, as they dry, suddenly explode open when ripe, expelling their seeds. The gorse, broom, wisteria and busy lizzie (impatiens, also a herbal cure for impatience!) are examples. Once the seeds find themselves in a suitable spot they may lie dormant for some time before **germination** takes place.

SEEING – see **eye**

SERIES AND PARALLEL CIRCUITS

A series circuit is one in which all the components (**battery**, lamp(s), motor(s), buzzer(s), etc.) are connected in sequence one after the other – there is only one loop in the **circuit** (see Figure S.3 top). Because each of the components resists the flow of current around the circuit, the more components we connect in series the greater the overall **resistance** of the circuit and so the lower the **current** that flows (Ohm's law). For example, if we connect two lamps with equal resistance in series each will be only half as bright as it is when connected on its own in the circuit. If, however, we connect the lamps in parallel so that each has its own pathway to the battery (they are on separate loops of the circuit) they will each be equally as bright as when on

their own (see Figure S.3 bottom). This is because a parallel circuit is in effect two circuits – the negligible resistance of the wires means that we can think of each lamp's mini-circuit as having the resistance of only one lamp. Of course, having to provide **energy** for two lamps of equal brightness means that the battery life will be shorter in a parallel circuit than it would be if the lamps were connected in circuit – we can't get something for nothing!

SHADOW

A shadow is an area of partial or total darkness caused by an **opaque** or **translucent** object blocking the **light** from a source. Children tend to confuse shadows with **reflections**, but by describing the two they will begin to notice the differences between them. Shadows have no features and occur on the opposite side of the object from the light source, whilst reflections typically include the surface details of the object (e.g. our face) in the image and occur on the same side of the object as the source. Opaque objects tend to cast dark shadows if there is only one source of light (e.g. a sunny day in the playground), whilst translucent objects can cast pale grey or coloured shadows. Shadow puppets are great fun to make and can help children understand this confusing phenomenon.

SKELETAL SYSTEM

The skeletal system physically protects and supports an animal's body. **Vertebrates** have a backbone made from a series of individual vertebrae which contains and protects the spinal column – an important bundle of nerves which form part of the **nervous system**. From the vertebrae 'hang' a framework of bones. The adult human skeleton consists of 206 bones from the largest (femur) to the smallest (stapes, in the middle ear). Babies have 300 bones, some of which join or fuse

129

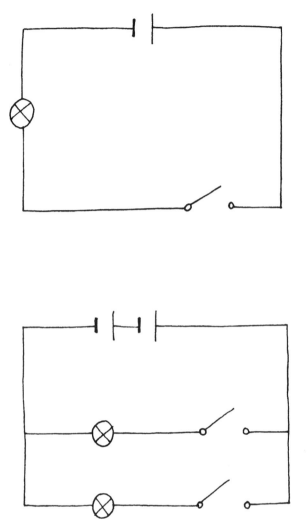

Figure S.3 Diagrams of a series circuit with one battery and one lamp, and a parallel circuit with two batteries and two lamps. If the voltage in the parallel circuit is twice that in the series circuit, which lamp(s) do you think will be the brightest?

together during development. Some **invertebrates** (crabs, insects) have a skeleton outside their body – an exoskeleton. In humans the skull and ribs protect the vital organs, while all bones form a framework to support the body and provide something for muscles to pull on to produce movement. Tendons connect muscle to bone. Ligaments join bones together, such as the cruciate ligaments in the knee. When a muscle gets a signal to act, it contracts and gets shorter, pulling on the bone it is attached to. Muscle cannot lengthen unless pulled by another muscle, so muscles are organised in pairs. Bones meet in joints (see Figure S.4). There are lots of different joints in the human body, including those which are rather like a hinge (elbow, knee), a 'ball and socket' (which may need further explaining to

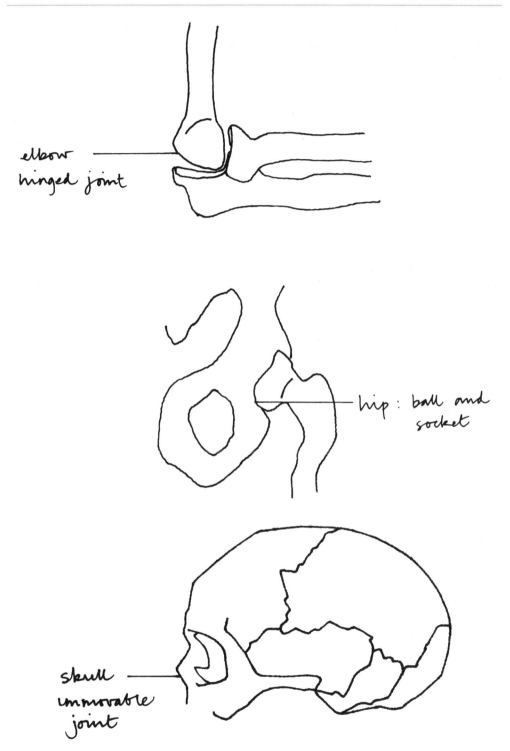

Figure S.4 Different types of joints.

children) such as found in the hip, and immovable joints (skull). Children could explore the range of movement in different joints by comparing the elbow, the wrist and the middle joint of the middle finger. During PE lessons children can explore how muscles work together to produce a huge range of movements from a tiny twitch to a great leap, or how limbs can be used to balance, twist and turn. They can feel their muscles move and change shape.

SLIDER (D&T)

Simple sliding **mechanisms** allow side-to-side or up-and-down movement but differ from **levers** as they do not have a pivot. Guides or slits ensure the movement is linear. They are a relatively simple mechanism for children to construct and enable them to create movement in their designs. Typically they might be used to make greetings cards or storybooks more interesting, or might turn a classroom display into something with which children can interact.

SOCIAL CONSTRUCTIVISM

Social constructivist views of learning (see **learning**) in science emphasise the central role of first-hand experience and the role of practical investigations (see **practical (hands-on) activities**) in constructing children's ideas but in addition they stress the importance of learning with and from others, both peers and adults. Children develop their existing ideas when they encounter new evidence, which could be in the form of new physical experiences or new ideas from other people.

SOCIOCULTURAL PERSPECTIVE

As well as recognising that ideas are developed within individual minds, a sociocultural approach to understanding learning sets out to understand how ideas are developed

between minds. Vygotsky (1978) proposed the existence of an individual and a 'social plane' across which ideas are shared, to which he gave the terms 'intramental' and 'intermental' planes. His theory was that learning occurs when concepts developed on the 'intermental' plane between people are then internalised by individuals to their 'intramental space.' Other authors (Rogoff 1990) use the term 'appropriated' instead of internalised to make the point that this is an active process for the learner which transforms the ideas of the social plane, not a copying process, which would take us back to a transmission view of learning. Sociocultural views of learning in science stress the importance of the cultural context for learning (see **contexts for science**). One implication of this is that teachers need to beware of making assumptions about children's understanding of the language they use. The teacher needs to make an effort to understand children's ideas in their own terms and in relation to their own cultural identities, not just expect them to see things from the teacher's perspective.

SOIL

Soil consists of the weathered remains of **rock** and the decaying remains of dead organisms (humus). It contains the minerals needed for plant **growth**. Soil also contains water from rainfall and air from the atmosphere. These different fractions can be separated by flotation and sedimentation (see **floating and sinking**) by placing some soil in a container and adding water. Organic matter will probably float to the surface, whereas the rock particles will settle out into a graded bed, coarser grains at the base and finer particles above. Air bubbles may be noticed escaping from the soil.

Links can be made between the home and school in the teaching of soils by encouraging children to bring in soil samples from home so that the constituents of a range of samples can be compared. Those who don't have access to a garden could take samples from the school grounds. This work could be taken further by considering the types of soil found (clay-rich, sandy, etc.) and how a gardener might go about improving its quality.

SORTING ACTIVITIES

Children can be asked to sort a collection of objects in order to elicit their ideas about a topic (see **elicitation**). For example, if a child sorted a collection of objects into 'living and non-living' groups (see **life processes**), they might classify a car as 'living because it moves and "eats" petrol', but a seed as 'not living because it "doesn't do" anything.' Rather than the teacher providing the criteria for children, children can decide on their own criteria, providing further insights into their thinking. Asking children to sort a collection can broaden their experience by introducing new objects or materials, or by considering familiar **materials** in a new way; for example considering whether to classify sand as a solid or liquid (see **states of matter**). Sorting can also provide an opportunity to apply new understanding, such as **classifying and identifying** a collection of photographs of **minibeasts** as insects or spiders. The outcomes of sorting can be recorded in different ways, such as listing or drawing, or by photographing the outcomes. However, more sophisticated mathematical representations such as Venn or Carroll diagrams can develop the process of sorting by showing more details about the relationships between different categories.

SOUND

Sound is a form of **energy**, transmitted through materials by longitudinal waves (sometimes called compression waves) causing the particles in the material to vibrate (move rapidly backwards and forwards a small distance). Sound is produced when an object vibrates, and travels outwards away from the source in all directions, getting fainter as it gets further away. We can detect sounds when the vibrations of the air (or water if we're swimming) reach our eardrums, thin layers of skin stretched across a hole in our outer ears. This **vibration** is amplified by three small bones in the middle ear and detected by a series of fine hairs in a spiral structure in our inner ears called the *cochlea*. The vibrations of these hairs send electrical signals to the brain (see **nervous system**) which interprets the type of sound, its **loudness** (how much the air is vibrating), which direction it is coming from and its **pitch** (how fast the air is vibrating). Because sound, like light, travels as a wave it can refract (bend round corners; see **refraction**) and reflect (**echo** back from a hard surface). However, sound travels about 100,000 times more slowly than **light**, which is why we almost always hear a clap of thunder several seconds after we see it in the form of lightning.

SPECIES

It is generally agreed that a species is a group of organisms that are so alike that they can interbreed and produce fertile offspring similar to themselves. Biologists do disagree about this, but children need to develop a basic understanding of this concept if they are to understand ecological concepts such as **biodiversity** and **population**.

SPEED

Speed is defined as the distance travelled in a given period of time. In scientific contexts, speed is usually measured in metres per second, though children will probably be more familiar in their lives outside school with the imperial measurement of miles per hour. Speed is very closely related to the more 'scientific-sounding' concept of **velocity**, which is defined as speed in a particular direction. In other words, velocity is a 'vector' quantity (you can have a negative velocity if you are travelling backwards) which contains more information than speed. To work out the average speed of a moving object we need to divide the distance it has travelled by the time it takes to travel this distance, but it is important to remember that the speed could have changed during its travel so this is only an average. If something is changing its speed it is said to be accelerating – either speeding up or slowing down. Actually, **acceleration** is strictly speaking a change in velocity; by changing direction a car can be accelerating even if its speed stays the same. In the primary classroom, children will rarely be asked to calculate average speeds and investigative work is usually limited to making direct observational comparisons between objects travelling at different speeds – 'the red car is moving faster down the ramp than the blue one.'

STAR

A star is a very large, immensely hot ball of gas which radiates **light** and heat over millions of miles. Our local star, the sun, is at the centre of our solar system and provides almost all the energy needed to sustain life on our planet – the only extra-solar sources of energy are nuclear power and geothermal heat from the Earth's core which sustains life around volcanic vents in the deep ocean. We might get this message across to children as we teach **food chains**. At the start of each chain are producers (**plants**) that make their own food by **photosynthesis** using the **energy** from the sun. Our sun is a medium-sized, middle-aged yellow star which is sustained by a process of nuclear fusion, releasing massive amounts of radiation and creating new

elements as it does so. Other older stars which have nearly exhausted their supply of hydrogen swell up into 'red giants', shrink into 'white dwarfs' or explode as supernovae before collapsing in on themselves as 'neutron stars' or 'black holes.' Astronomers believe that all the 100 or so naturally occurring elements are manufactured by nuclear fusion inside stars, then sprayed out into space by supernova explosions. The resulting dust and debris coalesce into other stars and **planets** – in the case of the Earth eventually producing the complex organic chemistry which has led to life. So, in one sense, we are all made of stardust!

STATES OF MATTER

In theory all substances can exist as solids, liquids or gases (see **particle theory**). For most substances it is not easy to demonstrate this, but water provides an example that can be studied in the classroom. An ice cube, as it is warmed up, changes from a solid to a liquid (water). If it is heated further, the liquid will turn into a gas (steam or water vapour). The **temperature** at which a solid melts to form a liquid is called its melting point. For pure water this is 0 degrees Celsius. This is the same as the freezing point: the temperature at which pure water changes to ice when it is cooled. Change of state can be explained by the particles from which they are made and the arrangement of these particles. This is summarised in Table S.1.

Asking children to sort a collection of solids, liquids and gases will stimulate thinking and challenge their understanding of states of matter (see **sorting activities**). Asking careful **questions** will help children identify criteria that can be used to distinguish between solids, liquids and gases. Collections could include objects made from metal, plastic, wax, chalk, paper and wood, for example. More problematic solids that may raise

Table S.1 The arrangement of particles and the properties of a solid, liquid and gas

Solid	Liquid	Gas
The particles are: • closely packed • arranged in a regular pattern • able to vibrate about a fixed point but not move from place to place • strongly bonded by forces of attraction to neighbouring particles.	The particles are: • fairly closely spaced • in a random arrangement • bonded to neighbouring particles by weaker forces, so able to move from place to place.	The particles are: • widely spread out • in a random arrangement • moving about at high speeds • not bonded to neighbouring particles by forces of attraction.
Its properties are: • not easily compressed • fixed shape • fixed volume.	Its properties are: • not easily compressed • no fixed shape • fixed volume.	Its properties are: • can be compressed • no fixed shape • variable volume.

questions include powders such as flour and dry sand, fabrics, wool and cotton wool, steel wool, Plasticine or Blu-Tack. Liquids could include water, washing-up liquid, honey, milk and cooking oil. Discussion about the viscosity (ease of flow) of a liquid can be encouraged and apparent anomalies explored (see **properties of materials**). Dry sand might be seen to 'flow' like a liquid and children need help to recognise that the individual grains have the properties of a solid. Providing examples of gases in the primary classroom is difficult but not impossible. Blowing up balloons, helium-filled balloons, cans of fizzy drink and air fresheners can be used to introduce the concept of gas and its associated vocabulary: air, carbon dioxide, oxygen.

STEM

A part of a **flowering plant** which supports and allows fluids to be transported.

SUBJECT LEADER, SCIENCE

Many schools have a teacher designated as science subject leader (more often known as a co-ordinator). Science subject leaders are responsible for the strategic direction of the subject, such as developing approaches to teaching and learning science in the school, and managing change in this area. They may lead staff meetings on science or support colleagues in planning (see **scheme of work**) and teaching. They are likely to be responsible for the management of science **resources**.

SUSTAINABILITY

Sustainability is a much used term these days but has a special meaning in relation to the future of planet Earth. One way to describe it is to think of a planetary bank balance that lists the amount of resources we still have, including **soil**, water, air, fossil fuel and all our different **species**. These resources are finite. If we are to behave in a

135

sustainable way then the bank balance should be just as healthy when we leave this planet to our children as it was when we inherited it from our ancestors. Unfortunately, current generations are likely to leave less for future generations – our level of consumption is not sustainable and it cannot go on like this forever. Governments around the world agree that we need to concentrate our efforts on saving the planet from destruction. Recently the international community came together in an effort to address **climate change**, culminating in the United Nations Climate Change Conference in Copenhagen.

SWITCH

A switch is a controllable gap in an electric **circuit**. When the switch is open it breaks the circuit so that no **current** can flow. When it is closed the circuit is reconnected and – assuming there is a source of **electrical energy** such as a **battery** present – the current can flow again. The idea of a switch is generally straightforward for children to grasp, but the fact that the inner workings of most switches (e.g. those in torches) are not visible makes it difficult for them to see how it works. It is therefore a good idea for children to have a go at bridging gaps in circuits by trying out different **conductors**, and to make different sorts of switches using paper clips, aluminium foil, etc. They can then be introduced to a range of specialist switches, such as two- and three-way switches to control more than one circuit, reed switches which operate in the presence of a magnet and pressure pads for designing security devices. We can also present children with circuit design problems such as the requirement to switch on and off two lamps independently within the same circuit.

SYSTEM

A system is a whole made up of parts that interact or are interdependent in some way. In science one example would be the solar system – the movement of the **planets** and **moons** are all interrelated as the pull of **gravity** on one affects the movement of another. Humans are made up of integrated systems, such as the **skeletal system** in which bones, muscle, tendons and nerves act together to produce movement. A system is an important concept in technology and engineering. For example, suppose you were designing a lorry to transport food aid across the globe; as well as the design of the lorry itself you would need to consider whether the fuel would be available at all destinations, what specialist loading equipment might be needed, how repairs could be carried out and how the drivers might be trained (see **designing**). If different component parts are to be made by different people, is everyone using the same unit of measurement? Developing systems such as a stage production or a tea party for guests provides children with opportunities to develop skills such as collaboration and clear communication.

T

TEETH

Teeth are at the sharp end of the **digestive system** of **vertebrates**. They are an excellent topic for study in primary school as children will be learning how to care for their permanent teeth as their first set begins to wobble and fall out. Teeth are to be found in the jaws (or mouths) of many vertebrates and come in different shapes and sizes according to their function – they can tear, scrape and chew food or stab, grip and cut in attack or defence. They break food into small bits which can be mixed with saliva, with the help of the tongue, and swallowed comfortably. The shapes of the animal's teeth are related to its diet. Herbivores (plant eaters) have lots of grinding molars for chewing plants, which are hard to digest (see Figure T.1). Carnivores have sharp canines to kill prey and slicing incisors to rip meat from bone (see Figure T.2).

Teeth are not made of bone, but rather of tissues of varying density and hardness including enamel, dentine and pulp. Because teeth are very hard and durable archaeologists and fossil experts can use teeth to identify **species** and find out about an animal's habits, diet and lifestyle. Children could be given the skulls and teeth of animals (or **models**, or pictures) and asked to deduce what the animal ate or how it lived.

Humans have two sets of teeth. The first set (the 'milk', 'baby' or 'deciduous' set) normally starts to appear at about six months. When teeth 'erupt' it is known as teething, which can be very painful. These baby teeth begin to fall out when the adult teeth begin to develop and push through. The roots of the milk teeth are usually reabsorbed in the gum so the only the crown falls out.

Some vertebrates develop only one set of teeth while others develop lots of sets. Rodent incisors grow and wear away continually through gnawing. If pet rats are not able to gnaw, the teeth will become uncomfortably long. Walrus tusks are long canines. Sharks grow a new set of teeth every few weeks to replace worn teeth. Tortoises have no teeth.

Tooth care: The outer coating of teeth is called enamel. Enamel can be damaged by acid which is created in the mouth by bacteria that feed on remnants of sugary and starchy foods stuck on and around the teeth. This mixture of food, bacteria and the acid they produce is called plaque. The acid will eventually eat through a tooth to cause a hole or cavity. **Diet** can therefore have an effect on oral health. Dentists also say it is best to avoid eating too many foods that have high sugar content and it is important to remove plaque regularly by brushing the teeth. Saliva helps prevent tooth decay by neutralising the acid. Keeping the teeth clean and free from plaque also protects our gums. If left, plaque can harden into 'tartar.'

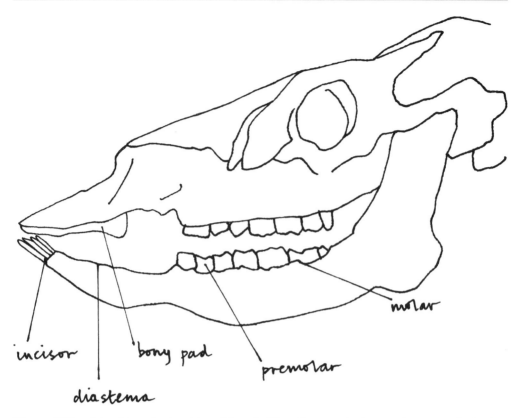

Figure T.1 A herbivore's dentition (sheep). The diastema is the gap between the incisors and premolars marking an absence of canine teeth.

This coating will make cleaning the teeth difficult as it can harbour more plaque, which attacks the gums and cause them to bleed (gingivitis). This is the beginning of gum disease, which can lead to tooth loss.

TEMPERATURE

All matter is composed of particles that are constantly in motion (see **particle theory**). When an object is heated its particles move more quickly, with the reverse happening when it is cooled. Temperature is a measure of the motion of these particles. The more rapidly particles move, the higher the temperature; the less rapidly they are moving, the lower the temperature. Heat and temperature are closely linked. Imagine a pan

of water being brought to the boil. Heating the water (that is transferring **energy** to it to cause its particles to vibrate faster) will result in an increase in its temperature. However, once the water reaches boiling point, transferring more heat energy to the water will not raise its temperature any further. At this point, the additional heat will convert the water into steam.

TENSILE STRENGTH

A **property of materials**. Tensile strength is a measurement of the pulling **force** a material can stand before it breaks. Children may consider which cord or thread is best for tying a parcel or for pulling a go-cart. They might conduct a 'pull' test

138

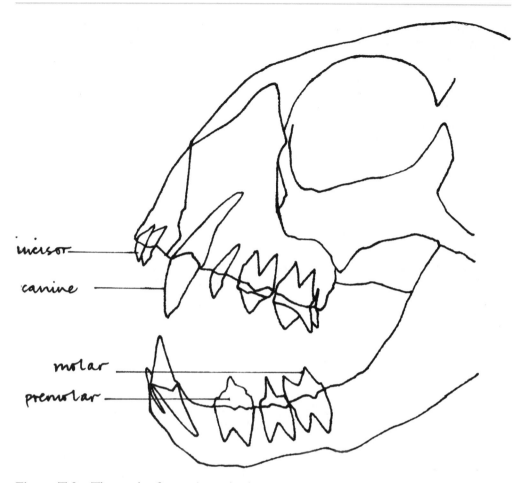

Figure T.2 The teeth of a carnivore (cat).

by using a Newton meter or a range of weights. However, do consider carefully how weights can be added safely to the point when the string snaps (possibly by tying each cord to a strong rod suspended between two tables, and adding weights to them in a boxed and cushioned area so the weights don't fall on children's toes or damage the floor – see **risk assessment**).

TENTATIVE NATURE OF SCIENCE

Scientific knowledge can be described as tentative because it is not certain; it is always just the best idea we have about something at the time based on the available evidence and explanations that scientists have come up with so far. This means that rather than presenting science as a set of fixed facts, to help children understand how science works (see **scientific literacy**) teachers need to help them see that scientific ideas are explanations that are made by people on the basis of the **evidence**, and that these are always open to be challenged.

TERMINAL VELOCITY – see **velocity**

TESTING AN EXPLANATION

According to the AKSIS Project (Goldsworthy *et al.* 2000), testing an explanation is one type of scientific **enquiry**. Children can test out a particular explanation, which might be their own or someone else's, and see if it works and makes sense. An example of this might be testing the view that a bulb in an electric **circuit** 'uses up' **electricity** by putting a second bulb in the circuit and seeing if it is dimmer than the first (it isn't). It is a good means of introducing a scientific view that the children are unlikely to suggest for themselves, such as **'light** travels in straight lines' and helping them to take ownership of it by developing a way of testing out the idea (see **exposition**). This testing may involve constructing a **fair test**, but it has a different starting point. This kind of enquiry is useful for supporting children's development of scientific concepts, challenging their ideas by presenting them with alternatives (see **alternative frameworks**). Testing an explanatory model could involve making a physical **model** of a situation, for example a version of the **water cycle** in a sealed container, and this has strong links with design and technology.

TEXTILE TECHNOLOGY (D&T)

Textiles (fabrics) are part of the range of materials that children should encounter and use in design and technology (see **materials, sheet**). Textiles can be created by fusing or weaving threads together and children can explore designing textiles themselves as well as using ready-made fabrics to make different **artefacts**. Children can evaluate existing products such as purses or PE bags, though teachers should beware of children making negative judgements about each other's belongings. Common textile-based design briefs for primary children are puppets, hats or slippers, and children could identify their own design opportunities. Also, textiles may be mixed with other types of material for a range of products.

Children can look at different fabrics under a magnifier to see how they have been constructed, relating this to their properties and uses to link science with technology (see **science and design and technology**).

THEORY, SCIENTIFIC

The activity of science produces tested knowledge, which is one of the attributes distinguishing it from the problem-solving outcomes of technology (see **science and design and technology: their relationship**). The status of scientific knowledge is not 'fact' or 'truth' (see **tentative nature of science**) – we never know when one very useful set of ideas (e.g. Newton's laws of motion) might be augmented, displaced or superseded by another (in this case, Einstein's special relativity). Instead, scientific knowledge takes the form of 'theories' – organised bodies of thought which seek to explain an aspect of the physical universe and make predictions which can be tested by experiment. Certainly, many scientific theories are enduring and widely accepted by the scientific community, but in the philosopher Karl Popper's view it can take only one piece of experimental evidence which contradicts a theory to bring it crashing down – indeed, scientists should be actively trying to *disprove* their theories. However, as Thomas Kuhn (1970) has argued, scientists operate within a sociocultural context which tends to be quite conservative (see **sociocultural perspective**), so it often takes a long period of what he described as 'normal science' before a radical new theory comes to be accepted, producing a 'paradigm shift' in the whole community. Theories lie at the root of the primary science **curriculum** (though they are often presented as 'facts' to be learned) and one of the ways in which children need to achieve **scientific literacy** is to understand 'how science works' – how the processes of scientific enquiry (see **process skills**) can support or undermine theoretical knowledge, and how this is undertaken by real people with real prejudices, sometimes funded by vested interests! Establishing a culture within the classroom where experimental **evidence** is taken seriously – even if it seems to give the 'wrong' result – can help children to discuss and modify their own theories about the world, whilst promoting the important scientific attitudes of scepticism and respect for evidence.

THERMAL PROPERTIES OF MATERIALS

The thermal properties of a **material** are concerned with how it responds to heat. The principal properties that might be investigated in the primary classroom are thermal conductivity, **boiling** and **melting** point, and flammability. Thermal conductivity is a measure of the ease with which a material will transmit heat. One activity that investigates this property is for children to design and make a mug-holder that will keep a teacher's mid-morning coffee warm while on playground duty. The best material for the job will be a good thermal insulator. This is also the case if the task is to design a holder that keeps a cold drink cool in warm weather. Boiling and melting points for water can most obviously be studied. Flammability (the ease with which a material catches fire) is difficult to study in the primary classroom because of the danger of scalds and fumes (see **risk assessment**). However, by choosing a suitable source of heat and a material which isn't going to give off harmful fumes and by using an appropriate technique for heating the material, it should be possible to conduct a test. See the Association for Science Education publication *Be Safe!* (ASE 2001) for further details about how to do this safely.

Box 5   Thinking skills

In recent years there has been a change in the priorities for science education reflected in a need for classroom debate and controversy (Trend 2009). A development that might be viewed as a response to this is the introduction of systematic teaching of thinking skills in science lessons. The current National Curriculum for England (DfEE/QCA 1999) promotes the development of thinking skills for primary children so that pupils, in the words of the curriculum, are 'learning how to learn.'

Higher order thinking skills such as hypothesising, evaluating and analysing are a fundamental part of scientific activity, and science can provide a rich context for their development. Oxford Brookes University have devised a number of activities to encourage higher order thinking (see http://www.azteachscience.co.uk):

- *Positive, minus and interesting*:   Children consider the positive, negative and interesting aspects of a specific scenario, e.g. a world without coal.
- *Asking the big question*:   There are many examples of 'big questions' that promote thinking and further questioning, e.g. why is it cold at the top of a mountain?
- *Odd one out*:   Children are presented with three different objects, materials or images and asked to say which they think is the odd one out and why, e.g. dolphin, shark, snake.

Prominent researchers in thinking skill development, Shayer and Adey, wondered whether primary school teachers should be concerned about teaching thinking skills, or whether cognitive development is an inevitability so that the teacher is left just 'waiting until the child is ready' (Adey and Shayer 1994). If a nativist approach to learning was adopted (a view that certain skills are hard-wired into the brain) then it could be argued that teachers should just wait for maturation of the central nervous system to occur. However, once an empirical view of learning is accepted and cognitive development is seen as the result of the learner's interactions with her environment, then the way is open for learning to be maximised through the manipulation of the environment by intervention. McGregor (2007) is also clear that teachers should support development of thinking through teaching that involves nurturing its development with motivating learning opportunities and reflection. What this might mean in relation to teaching of primary science is explored a little further here.

There are a number of intervention programmes designed to support the development of thinking skills in the primary classroom. Some are not subject-specific, yet parts of them have clear links to science teaching (for example, the Cognitive Research Trust – CoRT – programme devised by Edward de Bono, see www.debonofoundation. co.uk). Others, most notably the Cognitive Acceleration through Science Education (CASE) programme, are linked directly to science lessons. CASE in primary schools promotes cognitive development through two published programmes: *Let's Think!* (2001) in Key Stage 1 (Adey *et al.* 2001); and *Let's Think Through Science!* (Adey *et al.* 2003) in Key Stage 2. Another programme, *Thinking Together* is aimed at Key Stage 2 and focuses specifically on the use of talk to promote thinking (Dawes *et al.* 2000).

Underpinning CASE is the work of Piaget and Vygotsky. It has at its heart three main pillars of cognitive acceleration that are central to the stimulation of thinking abilities. First, 'Cognitive conflict' is the stage when the child is introduced to a challenge of their current understanding. This part of the programme draws on the work of Piaget in particular. Pitching the challenge at the correct level for the learner is of great importance. During the next stage, 'Social constructivism', the learner is actively encouraged to work together with others to solve the problem, seen as a Vygotskian approach by the authors of CASE. Later the child is asked to reflect on the approach they took to solve a particular problem, a stage which is known as 'metacognition' (Adey *et al.* 2003).

The types of thinking ability that are developed by CASE activities are grouped together by their underlying reasoning patterns (schemata). They provide a clear set of types of thinking that can applied in many different scientific contexts (Adey and Shayer 2002; Adey *et al.* 2003) and include:

- *Classification*: Putting things into groups based on common characteristics, for example, by grouping a selection of materials using a particular property.
- *Causality*: Developing an understanding of what is the cause and what is the effect. So, for example, does the vibration of the drum cause the sound or is it the sound that makes the drum vibrate?
- *Combinatorial thinking*: Identifying combinations in a systematic way.
- *Seriation*: Putting things in order, such as rocks in order of hardness.
- *Concrete modelling*: Building simple models based on real parameters to explain observations, e.g. developing an interlocking/non-interlocking grain model for rocks based on observations made when specimens are immersed in water.
- *Relationship between variables*: Exploring the relationship between variables, such as leg length and the distance people can jump.

- *Conservation*: Understanding that the amount of a material stays the same even if its shape or location changes (e.g. studying the same volume of water put in different containers of different shapes).

As well as the specific support intervention programmes may provide in developing scientific reasoning, they may also contribute to the development of aspects of creative thinking by making connections between one area of learning and another (McGregor 2007). One aspect of the CASE programme is bridging ideas developed through one activity to other situations.

At the stage when learners apply a general way of thinking developed in one context to another, different context, they need to evaluate the reasonableness of the bridge they are forming (McGregor 2007). This is a core aspect of critical thinking skills development, along with other skills such as explaining (or reasoning), generalising, inferring, analysing, synthesising, summarising and evaluating, or judging. All of these could be taught through primary science. So, for example, throughout primary school, learners are encouraged to move from description of events to explaining them ('the sweet is sticky' develops into 'it is melting'). They are asked to make generalisations as they interpret their findings (such as 'the more concentrated the bubble mixture, the bigger the bubbles that can be blown').

Finally the importance of metacognition in thinking skill development is underlined by a review of the methods employed during the teaching of thinking skills. It revealed that the methods used all relied on metacognition to a lesser or greater extent (McGuinness 1993). It was the primary tool for cognitive instruction. The CASE programme describes this stage as the point when the child consciously thinks about his or her own thinking. It is thinking about the process followed in order to find a solution. In science this may involve returning to predictions and thoughts held at the start, then reflecting on changes in thinking as a result of a particular activity. It may involve considering which information was used or what it was in particular that led to any change of mind that happened. What seems clear is that research over a number of years has found a positive correlation between metacognition and cognition (Larkin 2002). The conclusion is therefore drawn that children need to be provided with an opportunity to reflect on their thinking as they learn in science.

References

Adey, P. and Shayer, M. (1994) *Really Raising Standards*. London: Routledge.

Adey, P. and Shayer, M. (2002) 'Cognitive acceleration comes of age', in M. Shayer and P. Adey (eds) *Learning Intelligence: Cognitive Acceleration Across the Curriculum from 5 to 15 Years*. Buckingham: Open University Press.

Adey, P., Robertson, A. and Venville, G. (2001) *Let's Think! A Programme for Developing Thinking in Five and Six Year Olds*. London: nferNelson.

Adey, P., Nagy, F., Robertson, A., Serret, N. and Wadsworth, P. (2003) *Let's Think Through Science!* London: nferNelson.

Dawes, L., Mercer, N. and Wegerif, R. (2000) *Thinking Together: A Programme of Activities for Developing Speaking, Listening and Thinking Skills for children aged 8–11*. Birmingham: Imaginative Minds.

Department for Education and Employment (DfEE)/Qualifications and Curriculum Authority (QCA) (1999) *The National Curriculum Handbook for Primary Teachers in England: Key Stages 1 and 2*. London: DfEE/QCA.

Larkin, S. (2002) 'Creating metacognitive experiences for 5- and 6-year-old children', in M. Shayer and P. Adey (eds) *Learning Intelligence: Cognitive Acceleration Across the Curriculum from 5 to 15 Years*. Buckingham: Open University Press.

McGregor, D. (2007) *Developing Thinking; Developing Learning: A Guide to Thinking Skills in Education*. Maidenhead: Open University Press.

McGuinness, C. (1993) 'Teaching thinking: new signs for theories of cognition', *Educational Psychology*, 13 (3 and 4): 305–16.

Shayer, M. (2002) 'Not just Piaget, not just Vygotsky, and certainly not Vygotsky as an alternative to Piaget', in M. Shayer and P. Adey (eds) *Learning Intelligence: Cognitive Acceleration Across the Curriculum from 5 to 15 Years*. Buckingham: Open University Press.

Trend, R. (2009) 'Commentary: fostering students' argumentation skills in geoscience', *Journal of Geoscience Education*, 57 (4): 224–32.

Websites

AstraZeneca Science Teaching Trust: www.azteachscience.co.uk (last accessed 7 July 2010).

Edward de Bono Foundation: www.debonofoundation.co.uk (last accessed 7 July 2010).

TRANSLUCENT

A translucent object is one which allows *some* **light** to pass through it, and therefore casts a grey or coloured **shadow**. A coloured translucent object such as a sweet wrapper or piece of tissue paper transmits only certain colours of light and absorbs others, leading us to see the world through 'rose-coloured spectacles', for example. Tracing paper has the effect of scattering light so that the images of objects viewed through it have an indistinct outline. Translucent materials can be very effective when incorporated in shadow puppets since they produce beautifully coloured shadows.

TRANSPARENT

A transparent object is one which, in theory, will allow *all* **light** to pass through it, and therefore casts no **shadow**. We say that transparent objects transmit 100 per cent of the light and absorb none of it, in contrast to those which are **translucent** or **opaque**. In practice, however, there is no such thing as a completely transparent material. Even clear glass absorbs a small percentage of light. However, for the purpose of primary science activities we can think of it as transparent, though children may wonder why they can see a faint shadow from a clear plastic shape. Because light travels through transparent objects with little interference, objects beyond the material are seen as sharp images by the observer.

U

UPTHRUST

Upthrust is an upward **force** experienced by an object which is immersed in a liquid. It is caused by the displacement of some of the liquid by the object. The easiest way for children to 'feel' upthrust is to try and push a ball or balloon down under the surface of the water in a tank, water tray or swimming pool. The water really appears to 'push back' with quite a strong force, and if we let go of the balloon or ball it immediately pops to the surface. The Ancient Greek philosopher Archimedes (c. 287–212 BC) is widely credited with linking the force of upthrust to the **weight** of displaced water. In his famous 'bath' experiment he is alleged to have noticed that the amount by which the water level rose when he got into the bath (i.e. the displacement of water) was related to his own weight and volume. So Archimedes' principle states that if an object is floating in water, the upthrust force is equal to its weight – the two forces balance (see Figure U.1). If, however, the object sinks then the upthrust from the weight of water displaced is unable to balance its weight (because it is denser than water and therefore weighs more than the equivalent volume of water). We can make materials that normally sink (such as Plasticine)

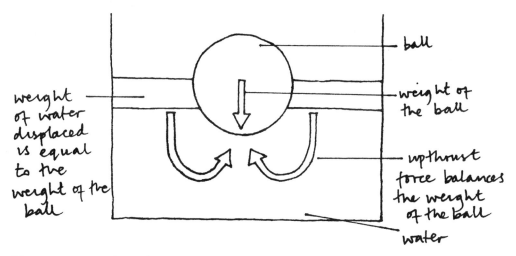

Figure U.1 Upthrust force balancing the weight of a floating ball.

float by changing their shape to increase the amount of water they displace – making them into a 'boat.' This is why we can build ships from dense materials like steel, because they are able to displace enough water for the upthrust from that water to balance their own weight. When shaped, the average density of a boat (the combination of steel and air) is small compared to the density of water.

V

VARIABLE

By identifying any factors that might be affecting a particular phenomenon, scientists can begin to control them and isolate one variable at time to order to find out more about its effects. This is known in primary science education as a **fair test**. The variable the child is deliberately changing is known as the independent variable and the ones she is keeping the same are the control variables. The outcome that she is observing or measuring is called the dependent variable. For example, in a fair test to find out which denier stocking is the stretchiest by putting masses (**weights**) in the feet, the independent variable is the denier (e.g. 10, 20, 30, 40), the dependent variable is the length of the stocking and control variables could be where the mass was attached on each occasion, the stocking size, brand or even (as children might suggest) the colour.

VEGETABLE

Vegetable is not a scientifically definable word – it can refer to **leaves** (cabbage, onion), **stems** (celery, potato), **roots** (carrot, parsnip), flowers (broccoli) or **fruit** (marrow, pumpkin). Vegetables are, however, an important part of our **diet** because they are excellent sources of fibre, vitamins A and C, potassium, calcium and iron. Legumes (e.g. dried beans, peas and lentils) are a good source of complex carbohydrates and have a high protein content. Vegetables come in all shapes, sizes and colours and many are easily grown from seeds. Growing food and gardening is an excellent way to engage children in learning about **plants**, **life processes**, life cycles, **ecology** and diet. Lots of help is available for schools wishing to set up school gardens and allotments. The Royal Horticulture Society (RHS) Campaign for School Gardening provides lesson plans and ideas for funding applications (see www.rhs.org.uk).

VELOCITY (TERMINAL VELOCITY)

It is sometimes difficult to understand the difference between velocity and **speed**. Velocity is the speed something is travelling in a certain direction. For example, two ice skaters could both be moving at 10 metres per second (m/s), but one might be travelling forwards in a straight line whilst the other might be moving in circles or even skating backwards! So even though they have the same speed, their velocities will be different. In the case of the skater moving backwards, we could say that her velocity was −10 m/s. This distinction is important when we think of objects falling through air. The **weight** of the object (the **force** between it and the Earth due to **gravity**) will cause it to start accelerating towards the ground (see **acceleration**). As its downward velocity increases, so will the air resistance it experiences, until it reaches a point where the downward force of its weight is balanced by the upward force of the air. At this point it stops accelerating, so its downward velocity stays the same until it hits the ground. This is known as its *terminal* velocity, which has nothing to do with what will happen to a living thing when it hits the ground, but refers to the highest velocity reached whilst falling. Terminal velocity depends on the shape of the object, since this determines the surface area which the **air resistance** can 'push against.' In the case of a sky-diver, her terminal velocity will be higher when free-falling than when she activates her parachute, which increases her surface area. At the moment the parachute opens, she will experience a negative acceleration until she reaches the new, lower, terminal velocity, which ideally will be low enough so that her subsequent contact with the ground will not be 'terminal'!

VERTEBRATE

Animals with backbones (see **skeletal system**) or spinal columns are known as vertebrates. Vertebrates have a backbone made from a series of individual vertebrae which contains and protects the spinal column – an important bundle of nerves which forms part of the **nervous system**. From the vertebrae 'hang' a framework of bones. Five per cent of animals are vertebrates, including **fish**, **amphibians**, **reptiles**, **birds** and **mammals**.

VIBRATION

All **sounds** are caused by vibrations, which we can think of as a very fast shaking movement. A good way to 'see' vibrations is to put some rice on a drum, where it will jump up and down when we beat the skin. To show that this vibration is picked up by the air particles around the drum and travels outwards in the form of sound waves,

we can beat another drum near the one covered with rice. The rice should jump around less vigorously, showing that some of the **energy** of the beat has been dissipated in the air. Different objects vibrate at different *frequencies* – the rate at which the particles of the object move backwards and forwards (see **pitch**). Generally, smaller objects vibrate more rapidly than large ones, so the vibrations may be more difficult to see. One way to make these invisible movements apparent is to suspend a ping-pong ball on a thread and hold it next to a tuning fork which has been struck. The ball bounces violently, much to the amusement of watching children, who also enjoy the spectacle of a vibrating tuning fork being dipped in water to produce spray.

VISITS

A visit off-site can provide children with an experience of the world it is not possible to recreate in the classroom. Different **habitats** can be studied at first hand, such as woodland, wildflower meadows or even the pond in the local park. At educational centres such as the Big Pit in South Wales children can experience new and challenging environments by going down into an old coal mine to gain an understanding of materials and what the earth is made of (see also **hands-on science centres and technology centres**). Looking at familiar areas in new ways helps to make some more abstract concepts relevant to everyday life, such as exploring **mechanisms** and **forces** in the playground, or examining the uses of different **materials** in the garden centre. Before undertaking any school trip you are legally required to carry out a written **risk assessment**. Schools have a duty of care towards pupils, and in an activity where there is an element of risk you will need to show that you have considered the possibilities, and as a result taken 'all reasonable precautions.' Different local authorities and schools will have specific procedures to follow and risk assessment documentation to complete prior to a school visit. Part of a risk assessment is likely to involve a preliminary visit to the location, during which you look for the hazards and the implications for organisation and think about the place in relation to any particular needs of the children. A preliminary visit can help to identify opportunities for learning and how these can be supported and developed before and after the visit. There is no definitive staff to pupil ratio for school trips as this will depend on a number of factors such as: the age of the pupils; any special educational or medical needs; the type of visit and the nature of the activities involved; and the experience and quality of the staff available (see www.rospa.com and www.teachernet.gov.uk).

VOCABULARY, SCIENTIFIC

Science has lots of 'special words', many of which appear long and complex, such as **'photosynthesis'** or **'evaporation.'** Children may find these words difficult to understand, say or spell! Additionally, there are some words with both 'everyday' and specific 'scientific' meanings. One of these is **'material'** which in an everyday context is often used to refer to fabrics or textiles, whilst the scientific meaning is much broader to embrace all forms of matter including solids, liquids and gases. Another example is the word **'force'** which many children associate with coercion, as in the sentence 'He forced me to do it', whilst the scientific usage refers to a push or pull. It is perhaps hardly surprising that children often use words that *sound* scientific but that may disguise major misunderstandings. The question, 'What do you mean by …?' is useful to ask when a child has given an explanation using scientific-sounding language which may or may not make sense. Exploring what children mean by the words

they are using can be useful in clarifying joint understandings of significant vocabulary. When introducing a specialist scientific word it is usually a good idea to get children to express the idea in their own language first, to ensure they have developed the concept before attaching a label to it. For example, a child might notice the drops of water collecting on a mirror held over a steaming kettle and identify them as having come from the 'wet air' coming out of the kettle. We might then introduce the word **'condensation'** and link it to the more common usage of the word to describe water droplets collecting on window panes on cold days.

VOLTAGE

Voltage can be thought of as the 'push' which a **battery** is able to give to the 'tiny bits of electricity' (**electrons**) in a circuit, causing them to start flowing in a **current**. It is more scientifically defined as the energy per unit charge – in other words, the **energy** which the battery is able to give to each charged particle. Voltage, unsurprisingly, is measured in volts (V) and is named after the Italian scientist Alessandro Volta (1745–1827). Voltage is sometimes called 'potential difference', which is analogous to gravitational potential energy: by picking up a ball from the floor we give it potential energy in a similar way that a battery can give an electron potential energy by raising it from 0 to 1.5 V. The potential difference across a standard electrical cell (what we tend to call a 'battery') is 1.5 V and it is this that causes an electron to 'fall' around the circuit (conventionally from positive to negative, though we now know that it moves towards the positive terminal). By increasing the number of cells (making a real 'battery' of more than one) we can increase this potential difference or voltage, giving the electrons more potential energy and increasing their rate of flow (current) through the circuit.

W

WATER CYCLE

The water cycle is the circulation of water in the atmosphere, the Earth's surface and **rocks** beneath it. Studying it in the primary classroom provides an opportunity to contextualise teaching of **evaporation** and **condensation**, and it can be linked to geographical course work on rivers and seas. What follows is a simplified description of how water circulates (see also Figure W.1).

Water evaporates from variety of sources (seas, oceans, lakes, as well as the Earth's land surface and from **plants**) into the atmosphere. As warm, humid air cools, water held as a gas (water vapour) will form tiny water droplets, leading to cloud formation. This cooling of the humid air mass may be because it is forced to rise up higher in the atmosphere or because it comes into contact with cooler air. If many tiny droplets (or tiny ice crystals) merge together, large drops may form and these fall to the ground as rain. Some of the rainwater may flow quickly across the surface or near surface of the ground to a water course, and then return to the sea. Another fraction of rainfall may contribute to ground water resources at depths below the surface. Ground water takes longer to reach rivers and streams, possibly emerging as springs. Some rainfall may be evaporated directly from the land surface back to the atmosphere, and yet more of the rainfall may be absorbed by plant **roots** and evaporated from their

leaves, or made into solid plant material (see **photosynthesis**). In the primary classroom it is possible to illustrate this through a simplified physical **model**. This may consist of a sealed tank in which there is a model of the land with a river network that drains to the sea. There is a visual representation of a cloud in the roof of the tank under which ice is placed. First of all water is placed in the space simulating the sea. Then the tank is placed in direct sunlight or under a strong desk lamp. After a while the water will evaporate from the sea, condense as it comes in contact with the cold cloud, drip back to the land and flow to the rivers and back to the sea.

WATERPROOFNESS

Waterproofness is the extent to which a material prevents water from passing through it. Children can be encouraged to design their own investigations to test this **property of materials** which may involve covering a beaker with the material being tested, then pouring water on it and measuring how much passes through in a given period of time. **Observations** will reveal that water soaks into some materials, sits on the surface of others or passes right through some. Links can be made to design and make projects such as choosing the best material to make a raincoat or umbrella for a teddy bear. At the design stage it is worth

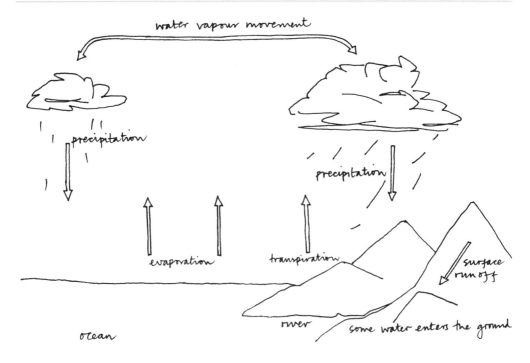

Figure W.1 A simplified representation of the water cycle.

explaining that waterproofness is only one consideration that needs to be taken into account when selecting a suitable material for the job. Other factors to consider include flexibility and toughness. Children may also consider how they can improve the waterproofness of materials. Candle wax or crayons on paper can be used to create water-resistant drawings. Links can be made with the natural world because some plants have **leaves** that are covered with a waxy coating so that water runs off them or forms round globules.

WAVE, LONGITUDINAL – see **sound** and **analogy**

WAVE/PARTICLE THEORY OF LIGHT – see **light**

WEATHER

When studying the weather, flexibility in planning enables spontaneous opportunities

for learning to be taken advantage of. It also helps if **resources** are prepared in advance and are ready to use. One way to organise resources is into boxes, one for each weather type, with each box containing the resources needed to carry out a number of **investigations**. Table W.1 provides a far from exhaustive list of the resources and possible activities that could be used to support the study of different types of weather with younger primary school children.

WEED

Put simply, a weed is an unwanted or uninvited **plant** growing where you do not want it to grow.

WEIGHT

It is very difficult for children to understand the difference between weight and

Table W.1   Activities for exploring the weather

Weather type	Resources	Possible activities
Rain	• Chalk • Wipeable pens • Rain-catchers • Powder paint • Fabric squares • Paper boats • Paper towel strips.	• Make different shaped rain-catchers from plastic bottles, and use them to collect rain. • Form a shelter from the rain using a plastic sheet. • Create pictures using powder paint and investigate what happens to them in the rain. • Investigate what happens to a range of both waterproof and non-waterproof fabrics in the rain. • Make a range of boats to play with in the puddles. • Draw patterns on paper towels using felt-tip pens and investigate what happens to them in the puddles.
Wind	• Pegs and washing line • Streamers • Plastic bag wind socks • Windmills • Paper kites • Balloons and pump • Bubble-making equipment • Parachute.	• Wash, wring out and peg out bits of cloth. • Play with the kites, windsocks and balloons investigating what makes them fly, turn and move. • Stand in a group around the edge of the parachute feeling the force of the wind. • Play with bubble-making equipment, watching the bubbles move in the air.
Snow	• Black card t-shapes • Paper cups • Gloves • Magnifiers • Scissors • White paper • Track-makers.	• Fill up cups with snow and place around the school in the sun and shade. • Catch snowflakes on the black card and observe them using a magnifier. • Make different tracks in the snow; make or follow a trail around the school. • Investigate which glove is the best; investigate which movements keep you warm outdoors.

(Continued)

Table W.1 Activities for exploring the weather *(Continued)*

Weather type	Resources	Possible activities
Sun	• Chalk • Collection of shapes • Brushes and buckets • Sand and trays • Sunglasses • Hat-making instructions • Paper.	• Trace chalk shadows of people and objects. • Observe the shadow created by a shape stuck to a sunny window over the course of the day. • Draw and write with water and brushes on walls and the playground, observing what happens to them after they are finished. • Feel the change in temperature of a sand tray placed in the sun. • Evaluate the effectiveness of a range of sunglasses (but **do not** look directly at the sun). • Make a range of paper hats and establish which is the best.

mass, particularly as the two concepts tend to be used interchangeably in everyday life. In scientific terms, weight is the **force** between an object and the Earth due to **gravity**. This gravitational **attraction** is dependent on the mass of the object: thus, as mass increases so does weight. Mass – the amount of 'stuff' in an object – is measured in grams (g), whilst weight – being a force – is measured in newtons (N). Scales can't measure mass, they can only measure weight, so strictly speaking should be graduated in newtons. However, since each kilogram (kg) of mass is attracted to the Earth with a force of about 9.8 N, so scales can work out our mass in kg by dividing our weight by about 9.8. Interestingly, we could change our weight by moving to a different **planet** with a different gravitational pull – for example, we would only weigh about one-sixth of our terrestrial weight on the **moon**.

Unfortunately, this would not affect the amount of mass in our bodies! If interplanetary travel becomes widespread in the future, the organisation Weightwatchers may need to change its name to 'Masswatchers' since weight is dependent on location, whilst mass of an adult human being is dependent on diet and exercise! What does a 1 N weight feel like? Well, it's about 100 g, roughly the weight of an average apple, which makes rather a nice link to the traditional story of Isaac Newton's sudden revelation concerning gravity.

WHEEL (D&T)

Wheels rotate about an **axle**. Usually this rotation is about the centre of the wheel but it can be off-centre, producing an 'eccentric' movement. Wheels can be fastened securely to axles in a number of ways: by Plasticine or Blu-Tack; by a drawing pin pushed through the end of the axle; or by wrapping a piece of card or tape around the end of the axle, thereby increasing its diameter until a tight fit is achieved. Toothed wheels are known as gears. Grooved wheels over which a cord can run are known as **pulleys**. Children's knowledge of wheels can be developed in projects that involve constructing vehicles. Wheels of different diameters and width, or made from different materials, can be investigated, linking technology work to the teaching of **forces**. For example, investigating what affect altering the diameter of the wheel has on the distance the vehicle travels will challenge children's understanding of **friction**.

X

X-RAY

X-rays are part of the electromagnetic spectrum, which includes **light**, radio waves, infra-red and ultra-violet radiation. X-rays have a very high frequency (the waves vibrate very rapidly) which gives them a very high **energy**. This means that they can pass through many materials which are **opaque** to the lower-energy waves of visible light. Such a material and the one which will be of most relevance to children is that of human soft tissue. Harder bones or teeth absorb or reflect the x-rays, providing a photographic image of what is normally hidden under our skin. Most children will have had x-ray images taken of their teeth at the dentist in order to find out where their adult teeth are coming through or to detect hidden cavities. Some may have been unlucky enough to break a bone, in which case they will have had x-rays taken of the fracture. Although data protection legislation makes it more difficult to obtain x-ray photographs from hospitals nowadays, some families may have old images which have been returned to them when their health records were computerised. Holding x-ray images up to the light or – even better – placing them on a light-box provides fascinating insights for children into the structure of the human skeleton (see **skeletal system**).

Y

YOGHURT

Yoghurt is a dairy product produced with the help of **micro-organisms** and is an ideal food to put into context the idea that bacteria can be helpful to humans (see **contexts for science**). To make yoghurt, milk is fermented, a perfect primary science activity: the process involves heating, measuring **temperature** carefully, cooling, adding a 'starter' culture of bacteria, incubating and refrigerating. By adding fruits and flavours to the yoghurt, making it can become a 'food technology' activity too. People have been making – and eating – yoghurt for at least 5,000 years. It is common around the world. It's nutritious too, with health benefits; it is rich in protein, calcium and vitamins (see **diet**).

Z

ZOO

Should we have zoos? It is important to allow children to gather and make sense of **evidence** so that they are informed as citizens and responsive to the needs of others and the world in which they live. By posing questions such as 'Are zoos a good thing?' children can be given the opportunity to gather evidence and opinions, make a case and present a position.

Zoos can be a great resource for teachers. Trips to zoos (see **visits**) can be very expensive but their websites can often offer an alternative. London Zoo (www. zls.org) offers a good selection of videos of its animals, with child-friendly commentary by education officers and keepers. San Diego Zoo (www.sandiegozoo. org) has a website which includes its 'pandacam', 'elephantcam' and entertaining zooblogs. Twycross, Bristol and Edinburgh zoos all have education material available online.

Who's Who of Some Important Current and Historical Figures in Science

AL HAZAN (PROBABLY AD 965–1039)

Like many primary-age children today, the Greek thinkers Plato and Euclid imagined that seeing was made possible by light rays coming out of the eye and falling on the object. It was the Arab scientist Al Hazan whose work challenged this and gave us our present-day understanding of seeing. His full name, Abū ʿAlī al-Ḥasan ibn al-Ḥasan ibn al-Haytham, has been westernised from the Arabic and he is often referred to as Alhazan or Al Hasen. He was born in Basra in Iraq, probably around AD 965.

Mathematics, particularly geometry, was well developed in Iraq, and as a skilled mathematician Al Hazan claimed he could apply this to regulate the floods of the Nile. When the caliph, the local ruler, ordered him to do so, he realised it was impossible, and to escape a possible death sentence he pretended to be mad and remained under house arrest. It was here that he carried out some important scientific work. He reasoned that because the sun had the power to damage our eyes and because sometimes after-images are left when we have looked at bright light, there must be something coming from the sun that affects our eyes. He worked out that the light must interact with objects in some way that distorts the light and that this distortion is held as information in the light that goes into our eyes.

Al Hazan has been described as the first scientist because he introduced careful experimentation and measurement, and so actively sought to produce empirical evidence for his ideas. Before Al Hazan, non-religious explanations for the natural world were based on logic of thought and on mathematics, but Al Hazan combined these with rigorous, controlled practical testing in his groundbreaking work in the field of optics. By carrying out various experiments with lenses and mirrors, he proved that rays of light travel in straight lines. He has been ranked alongside Newton in developing our modern understanding of physics.

The scientific method Al Hazan developed was this: first observation, then a statement of the problem. Next was a formulation of a hypothesis and testing of it by experimentation. Then there was analysis of experimental results followed by interpretation of data and the formulation of conclusions. Finally, there was publication of findings. Does this look familiar?

CARSON, RACHEL (1907–1964)

Can you recall a time when you were not concerned about 'environmental issues'? If you grew up in the last fifty years, then probably not. We now accept that our environment is fragile and can easily be damaged by humankind – for example, by the careless use of powerful chemical pesticides. One American woman is credited with bringing to our attention the dangerous consequences of our actions and sparking an environmental awareness which shows no signs of fading fifty years on. Rachel Carson should be celebrated as a scientist and a good citizen. Her book *Silent Spring* (Carson 2000, first published in 1962) is still considered a classic and drew attention to the damage pesticides were doing to our environment, particularly in relation to human health and to song birds – hence its title. She advocated more careful use of and better research into pesticides and, in spite of some rampant sexism within the science community of the day, took this campaign right to the top – to the president of the USA. Her biography shows what can be achieved by someone who has not only the scientific understanding but also the determination and skills to communicate her views to the general public. Her books are also considered very good literature – one is called *The Sense of Wonder* (Carson 1998, first published in 1965) and is described as 'words and pictures to keep your child's inborn sense of wonder alive'. Learning about Rachel Carson may inspire children to ensure influential adults hear their views. See www.rachelcarson.org for lots more information.

DARWIN, CHARLES (1809–1882)

The theory of evolution, developed by Darwin, is perhaps the most important scientific theory ever developed, but he was a slow worker. It took him more than twenty-five years to finish his book, *The Origin of Species*, published in 1859.

In 1831 Darwin's interest in natural history and geology led to him being invited to sail on the naval survey ship, HMS *Beagle*, as the ship's naturalist. The round-the-world expedition lasted five years, during which time Darwin visited many places, including South America, the Galapagos Islands and the Pacific oceanic islands, to name but a few. This was Darwin's

big break. His experiences on the voyage eventually led him to postulate that species evolve by natural selection. Others before him had proposed that one species can alter into another, but it was Darwin who explained what the reason might be for this happening. However, it wasn't until Darwin had read the works of Malthus on human population that he came up with the explanation. Malthus argued that human population, unless unchecked, would outstrip food production. Darwin took this idea and applied it to his work. He proposed that species are competing for resources. Those offspring with an advantage will prosper and pass on the advantage to their offspring.

One way to 'model' the concept of 'survival of the fittest' is by providing children with small balls of Plasticine and some matchsticks. Ask them to make a little creature. Then introduce the 'environmental factors' that will determine whether the creatures will survive. Food is available only 5 cm or more above the surface, and the planet is prone to earthquakes. Then give the table a bit of a shake. Wobbly animals will not 'survive', but neither will those who are too short to reach the food. Children can then make new 'generations' of creatures who are better suited to the environment.

DAWKINS, RICHARD (BORN 1941)

As well as being a scientist in the field of evolutionary biology, Richard Dawkins is a popular science author. His book *The Selfish Gene* (Dawkins 1976) presented a 'gene-centred' view of evolution. In his view, the organism – the ladybird, fern or shark – is just a vehicle to keep reproducing the gene, rather than seeing the gene as a way of reproducing the organism. This did not mean that the gene was actually selfish, but that it behaved in that way and might have effects that helped protect it.

In an interesting thought experiment he wondered what would happen if there was a gene that caused people with that gene both to develop a green beard and to be nice to other green-bearded individuals. The term 'green beard effect' has come to refer to situations in which a gene in one individual might have direct benefits for other individuals with the gene.

Dawkins is known for his outspoken opposition to religion and in particular to creationist theories. In his book *The Blind Watchmaker* (Dawkins 1986) he argues that rather than being the product of intelligent design – with God as the 'watchmaker' – the complexity of living things can be explained by the processes of natural selection, using the analogy of a non-intelligent, *blind* watchmaker. He promotes atheism as the rational scientific position to take and in his popular book *The God Delusion* (Dawkins 2006) he argues that it is almost certain that there is no supernatural creator and that faith in a god or gods can be understood as a delusion.

EINSTEIN, ALBERT (1879–1955)

Albert Einstein was a great scientist and a great thinker. Many of his ideas were developed by carrying out 'thought experiments' on topics that had puzzled scientists for many years. The series of 'Uncle Albert' books by Russell Stannard (e.g. *The Time and Space of Uncle Albert* – Stannard 2005) are an excellent introduction to his work for children aged 7–11. In them Einstein explores the amazing world of light-speed travel and black holes with his niece Gedanken (German for 'thought'). The reader is encouraged to conduct the same 'thought experiments' that led Einstein to his theories.

The year 1905 was a great one for Albert Einstein (aged 26 and looking very handsome in those old photos), for it was in this year that several of his papers were published in the journal *Annalen der Physik*. One of these explained the nature of light, another provided proof that atoms existed and a third outlined his Special Theory of Relativity. On light, Einstein reckoned that it must be made of particles (light-quanta), later renamed as photons, which in turn led to the notion of wave–particle duality so that light can behave like a wave or a particle depending on the experiment being performed. On atoms, he explained observations made in the previous century by Robert Brown. Brown had noticed that pollen grains move erratically in a fluid, and Einstein explained this as being the result of random buffeting of the grains by molecules in the fluid. Finally, in this momentous year for Einstein, his Special Theory of Relativity explained some of his ideas about space-time. He postulated that the speed of light remained the same for all observers however fast they are moving. Later this was developed as the famous equation $E = mc^2$ (E = energy, m = mass, c^2 = the speed of light squared). In 1915 Einstein developed the General Theory of Relativity which was his explanation of gravity. The attraction between two objects due to their mass was explained by warping of space-time. Objects warp space-time, and this 'tells' objects how to move, leading to their attraction. Einstein's explanations of light, the nature of materials and gravity are beyond the scope of primary school science, but as a critical thinker and someone who challenged ideas about how the world works he merits discussion.

FRANKLIN, ROSALIND (1920–1958)

Rosalind Franklin is best known for the controversy around her contribution to the 'discovery' of the structure of DNA, the molecule we now believe to be responsible for storing the genetic code that is passed from generation to generation. The shape of DNA – the double helix, like a twisted ladder – was very important evidence for its function as it might be 'unzipped' and then copied. This then could be how new cells replicated the old ones. Franklin took x-ray diffraction images of DNA that were important in prompting James Watson and Francis Crick to publish their hypothesis in 1953 that DNA took the shape of a double helix.

The controversy is that Watson and Crick did not fully acknowledge her contribution. Although accounts differ, it seems they were shown a key x-ray diffraction image by another member of the team working with Rosalind Franklin without her permission, though with the knowledge of the institution (King's College London). At this point she had left the college and went on to lead pioneering work on the tobacco mosaic and polio viruses. Acknowledgements of the work on x-ray diffraction focused on the contribution of Maurice Wilkins. Wilkins and Franklin were colleagues but did not have a good relationship. Franklin's PhD student Raymond Gosling acted as a go-between and also worked on developing the images.

The story was taken as evidence of a sexist culture that worked against female scientists, and sexism may have played a role in the story, along with the strong personalities of the scientists involved and professional and personal conflicts. Franklin herself died early at the age of 37 from ovarian cancer, so she was not able to present her own point of view. Wilkins went on to share a Nobel Prize with Watson and Crick, an award that is not made posthumously and so could not have included Rosalind Franklin.

It raises questions about whether individual scientists can ever be given the credit for developing an idea that actually emerges from the work of many different people, with ideas available

informally before being published. For primary science, rather than presenting scientists as lone geniuses making discoveries, it would be more realistic to talk about ideas in science as developing between groups of people, whether working together or in conflict!

HAWKING, STEPHEN (BORN 1942)

The two things most people know about the theoretical physicist Professor Stephen Hawking are that he has motor neurone disease – so is confined to a wheelchair and speaks through a speech synthesiser – and that he wrote the highly influential (though little-read!) book *A Brief History of Time* in 1988. His major contribution to physics and cosmology is uniting Einstein's General Theory of Relativity with the other great twentieth-century physics theory of quantum physics, to hypothesise that the universe began with a Big Bang and will end with a black hole. He is best known for his work on black holes – the super-dense 'singularities' (single points of infinite density) that we now believe to exist at the centre of every galaxy, including our own. One of Stephen's theories is that black holes are not actually quite 'black' – they actually emit radiation. Children greatly enjoy discussing black holes and what would happen if your spaceship disappeared over the 'event horizon' and got sucked into the middle of one, crushing it to zero dimension and possibly even spitting it out somewhere else in the universe through a 'wormhole' – one of Professor Hawking's more speculative theories. For more information see www.hawking.org.uk.

HUBBLE, EDWIN (1889–1953)

Many children will have heard of the Hubble Space Telescope, which continues to send back amazing images of unimaginably far-away galaxies and nebulae following its recent repair by astronauts from the space shuttle. However, they may not know anything about the scientist after whom the telescope was named. Edwin Hubble is regarded as the 'father of observational cosmology' and was the first person to observe galaxies outside the Milky Way, from the Mount Wilson Observatory in California during the 1930s. This was very significant, as up to that point we assumed that the Milky Way was the whole universe, rather than just one of hundreds of billions of galaxies. Hubble went on to classify different types of galaxy, and significantly noticed that the light coming from them was shifted towards the red end of the spectrum. This 'red shift', predicted by Einstein's Special Theory of Relativity, suggested that the other galaxies were moving away from us, very fast. The further away they were, the faster they seemed to be going. This remarkable finding led to the theory of the expanding universe, and ultimately to the Big Bang theory since, by inference, if all the galaxies are moving apart from each other, there must once have been a time when they were all in one place. This in turn led to a calculation for the age of the universe, currently believed to be around 13.7 billion years. So Edwin Hubble's astronomical observations led to some pretty mind-boggling ideas. See www.edwinhubble.com for further information.

MAATHAI, WANGARI (BORN 1940)

Professor Wangari Maathai received a Nobel Peace Prize in 2004. This is particularly notable as she is the first African woman to be awarded the prize. She received her prize 'for her contribution to sustainable development, democracy and peace'. She is a highly qualified scientist, a commissioner for the Earth Charter Initiative and a politician who, in 1976, initiated a massive tree-planting campaign through Kenyan women's groups in order to conserve the environment and improve their quality of life. Her campaign began when she planted trees in her own back yard and realised how trees could provide a family with shade, fuel, food and income. In spite of being frequently told that she should be at home looking after her husband, being harassed at public meetings and physically attacked by opponents, Professor Maathai has become internationally famous for her work. Her example may inspire children to do their own planting or to learn about how plants can be used to reclaim and stabilise soil.

NEWTON, SIR ISAAC (1643–1727)

Newton's explanations for the movement of objects are at the heart of teaching of forces in the primary school. So, for example, Newton's third law of motion states that every action has an equal and opposite reaction. When a child pushes a toy car, thanks to Newton we know that the car also pushes back against the child. Later, when that same toy car slows down as it travels across the classroom floor, remember Newton also stated that an object stays at rest or moves at a constant velocity unless a force acts upon the object. During PE, as a foam javelin traces a particular trajectory across the sky before hitting the ground, consider the force of attraction that pulls the javelin towards the Earth. It was Newton who first identified gravity. Newton became famous in his lifetime in particular for his work on gravity, becoming the first person in Britain to be knighted for scientific achievement. Perhaps the children in your class could decide who should get a 'knighthood' for their next piece of science work.

Children are fascinated by rainbows. It was Newton who first discovered that white light is made from a range of colours which can be split by raindrops or prisms. We learn in school that rainbows have seven colours. In fact, we can see many more hues – there isn't really a place where one ends and the next begins.

By all accounts Newton was a decidedly prickly character, flying off in a rage when his work was criticised, and he was something of an eccentric risk-taker too. On one occasion he wanted to find out what effect staring at the sun would have on his vision, so he looked at it for as long as he could stand. Fortunately for him, his eyes eventually recovered but only after he had rested in a dark room for several days.

POTTER, BEATRIX (1866–1943)

The children's author Beatrix Potter was a skilled artist and created a large portfolio of botanic drawings before turning to the telling of tales. The knowledge she gained from drawing can be seen in her children's books, for example where Jeremy Fisher and friends are seen sitting on very accurately portrayed mushrooms.

Beatrix never went to school but was influenced by family and friends with scientific interests. She was given a microscope, which opened a whole new world to her keen observational eye. At the time, drawing and painting was the only way to record images seen in the microscope. Potter applied her skills to produce numerous original drawings of fungi and lichens. As acknowledgement for her original contribution to this area of science, she became widely respected throughout England as an expert on fungi. However, she was subject to sexism and prejudices common at that time. Her uncle encouraged her to become a student at the Royal Botanic Gardens at Kew, but she was rejected because she was a woman. Although the author of a scientific paper 'On the germination of spores of agaricineae', she was not allowed to present it at the learned Linnean Society in London because women were not allowed to attend the meetings. It was presented instead by her uncle. In spite of these setbacks she continued her work and was later one of the first scientists to suggest that lichens were a symbiotic relationship between fungi and algae. In 1997, the Linnean Society issued to the author's estate an official apology for the way they had treated her.

Who's Who of Some Important Inventors

ANDERSON, MARY (1866–1953)

In 1903, the Alabama cattle rancher, vineyard operator and inventor Mary Anderson was a granted a patent for an automatic car window-cleaning device controlled from inside the car, called the 'windshield wiper.' The story goes that on a trip to New York during a winter she noticed that the drivers of street cars had to open their windows when it rained in order to see where they were going. Her invention was a lever that the driver could operate from inside the car, which moved a rubber blade on the windscreen outside. It took a while to catch on – she was first turned down by companies who thought it would be too distracting for the driver – but by 1916 windshield wipers were standard on most vehicles. Another woman inventor, Charlotte Bridgwood, went on to patent the automatic windshield wiper in 1917.

BABBAGE, CHARLES (1791–1871)

So much a part of everyday life, computers carry out a myriad of tasks, but how often do we stop to consider how they operate? One possible way to consider how a modern computer works is to study the machines from which they evolved. It is Charles Babbage who is credited with inventing the programmable computer, and it is from his ingenious Analytical Engine that modern-day computers have evolved. The difference between it and other calculating machines of the day was the way it could be programmed using punch cards. There was also a memory rather like the central processing unit in a modern computer that could store numbers as pegs in rotating drums for subsequent use in a program. For its day, the machine was capable of manipulating numbers at an impressive speed. The Analytical Engine was never fully built while Babbage was alive, through lack of funding, but its design went on to influence the work of others who developed electronic computers. But consider this: a 16 GB memory stick has nearly one million times the memory capacity of Babbage's vast machine. (See http://en.wikipedia.org/wiki/Charles_Babbage for more information.)

BRUNEL, ISAMBARD KINGDOM (1806–1859)

It is impossible to walk around the city of Bristol without encountering some of the engineering triumphs of I.K. Brunel, arguably the pre-eminent Victorian engineer and inventor. First there is the elegant Clifton Suspension Bridge across the Avon Gorge, which Brunel won a competition to design at the age of 25. Then there is the floating harbour and the SS *Great Britain*, one of three great ocean-going steamships he designed and built in the 1840s. Finally, there is the imposing building of Temple Meads station, once the terminus for the

Great Western Railway from London Paddington, which Brunel surveyed and built between 1833 and 1841. Nick-named 'God's Wonderful Railway', the GWR is a triumph of engineering and originally ran broad-gauge locomotives with wheels 2.1 m apart, enabling them to reach much higher speeds more comfortably than the standard gauge of 1.4 m. Eventually, however, Brunel was forced to standardise the gauge to fit in with the rest of the network – an example of how creative genius is sometimes thwarted by the need to 'fit in.'

It wasn't only Bristol that benefited from Brunel's vision, however; he started his career by surveying the Rotherhithe Tunnel at the age of only 20 and followed this with the 2.9 km railway tunnel at Box in Wiltshire. He went on to design innovative bridges at Maidenhead and Saltash, together with a range of docks, viaducts, buildings and a revolutionary prefabricated hospital for the Crimean War. Unfortunately overwork led to a stroke and early death at the age of 53, but Brunel's legacy, including the university named after him, continues to act as an inspiration to young engineers everywhere. For example, when children are asked to design bridges to span gaps as part of problem-solving activities, they could use Brunel's examples from Clifton and Saltash to give them ideas about structure and balanced forces. (See www. brunel.ac.uk/about/history/ikb for more information.)

COCHRAN, JOSEPHINE (1839–1913)

The oft-maligned chore of washing dirty dishes has undergone a revolution in the last thirty years or so thanks to more widespread ownership of dishwashers. Nowadays nearly 40 per cent of households own one, but it is a fact that the dishwasher was invented a long time before ownership of one became relatively commonplace. Josephine Cochran, an American, is credited

with inventing the first practical mechanical dishwasher back in the nineteenth century. Her motives for wanting a device to take over from handwashing of dirty dishes differ from account to account. Her invention may have been in response to the drudgery of the task and the way it made her hands shrivel up. Alternatively, so the story goes, Josephine was a rich woman who had servants to do the washing-up but she wanted a machine to do the job faster and without chipping her dishes. Her dishwasher worked by spraying streams of hot soapy water over the dishes by means of a hand-operated pump, after which hot rinsing water was simply poured over the dishes by hand. Other more elaborate versions of this basic model included one with a mechanical assembly which moved the dishes about under the streams of soapy water. Possibly a reason for studying Josephine is to show that a person with a problem and determination can find a solution through imaginative thinking – characteristics primary school teachers will no doubt wish to engender in children. You might ask your class to look closely at a dishwasher at home or in school, identifying the components and phases of the cycle it runs through to wash up the teachers' coffee cups. They could then come up with an improved design, perhaps by interviewing users and identifying their wants and needs.

COYLE, JOSEPH

Mr Coyle arguably came up with the greatest invention of all time – no, it isn't sliced bread (that was Otto Rohwedder). This invention is totally recyclable, made from recycled material, simple to make in one piece and works very well. We still use it all the time even though it was invented about eighty years ago. We are talking about the egg box, or more accurately the 'egg carton', as this is what Mr Coyle called it in his patent of 31 January 1933. All US patents are freely available on line – they are good examples of 'design' drawings. When children are drawing for design they might like to see how other inventors communicated their ideas. You can see Coyle's actual drawing of his design on line; search for United States Patent US1895974. Children could nominate their own 'greatest invention' and explain why they have nominated it. Perhaps they could also try to create their own, better egg box – plenty of people have lodged 'new, improved' designs with the Patent Office since 1933.

DONOVAN, MARION (1917–1998)

In these days of concern about household waste, it may be that disposable nappies are seen as a problem rather than a solution, but their convenience for many parents means they still sell in their millions. Marion Donovan grew up in a culture of invention and enterprise, with a father and uncle who were inventors and manufacturers in Indiana, USA, in the 1920s. After the Second World War she was a housewife and mother of two in Connecticut. Tired of changing and washing the cloth nappies, and bed sheets too, she designed a waterproof cover for the cloth nappy using her home sewing machine and an old shower curtain! She later added snap fasteners instead of safety pins. As no manufacturing companies were interested, Donovan set up her own business making and selling them. She then went on to develop a strong and absorbent paper for her nappies, so they became completely disposable. Again, no large manufacturer was interested in producing them, and it wasn't until 1961 that they went into production, as Pampers®.

DREW, CHARLES (1904–1950)

Charles Drew was an African-American surgeon and is notable for setting up large-scale blood banks for the Red Cross which saved many American and British lives

in the Second World War. However, the armed forces told the Red Cross that it did not want any 'coloured blood.' Under public protest, the Red Cross took the blood from black Americans but insisted that it was kept separately from 'white blood.' Drew argued that there was no scientific or medical basis for this segregation. He resigned from his post in protest at this racism. He continued his career in medicine and research and became the first black surgeon selected to serve as an examiner on the American board of surgery.

Charles Drew died as the result of a driving accident. A story developed around his death that he was denied treatment at the nearby 'whites only' hospital and died on the way to a 'black' hospital for the want of a blood transfusion. This story has been contradicted by the other doctors who were in the car at the time; they said he received the best possible treatment, and the kind of injury he had would not have been treated with a blood transfusion. However, this story has been perpetuated in primary science publications as a dramatic story with a black scientist as its hero. While the true story of the contribution of Charles Drew is less dramatic, he clearly deserves his place as a hero using scientific argument to challenge racism and for his role in establishing blood banks.

DUNLOP, JOHN (1840–1921)

It is Scotsman John Dunlop we should be thankful to for the smooth ride we get when riding our bicycles, for he is credited with inventing the bicycle tyre inner tube. It is said he developed the inner tube so that his son could ride on rough roads without getting headaches. His design went into commercial manufacture at the Dunlop Pneumatic Tyre Company, later to diversify its interests into sports gear, footwear and furniture as well as tyres. The bicycle is a good object to study to show how a series of improvements and

171

refinements have led to the design we have today, from the 'walking machine' to the mountain bike. There are a number of timelines showing the history of bicycles available online. The function of the various parts of a bicycle could be studied, with links made to the properties of the materials used in their manufacture. We might also ask: 'What are the characteristics of the individual parts that enable them to work? What difference did the inventors' work make to our comfort, safety and speed?'

EDISON, THOMAS (1847–1931) AND LATIMER, LEWIS (1848–1928)

Edison is widely known at the 'inventor' of the electric light bulb. However, such stories are rarely as straightforward as they first appear; Edison was in competition and collaboration with a number of other American-based inventors at the time, including Alexander Graham Bell (1847–1922) and Hiram Maxim (1840–1916), for several inventions including the phonograph and telephone. Edison gained the patent for the phonograph in 1877, but despite devising a means of amplifying the human voice he was very disappointed to lose out to Bell for the patent on the telephone in 1879. The drawings for Bell's telephone patent were made by a gifted African-American draftsman and inventor, Lewis Latimer, who has become celebrated as one of the earliest successful black scientists in the USA. He later joined Maxim's rival Electric Lighting Company and received his own patent for a process for manufacturing carbon filaments for the light bulbs. Latimer subsequently worked for Edison, who went on to devise a system for generating and distributing electrical power, together with over 1,000 patents for devices as seemingly 'modern' as the Dictaphone and storage battery. When studying electricity, children examining the filaments of light bulbs under a magnifying glass and using them to design circuits are building directly on Edison's and Latimer's achievements. For more information see www.thomasedison.com.

VAN LEEUWENHOEK, ANTONIE (1632–1723)

Science and technology often develop together, and this technologist and scientist provides us with a good example of this. Antonie didn't invent the first microscope but he was very good at making them, and made them better than anyone else – he had mastered the technology of making tiny glass lenses. He tried hard to keep his particular skills secret for a while because he realised his microscopes, which could magnify things at least 200 times, gave him an advantage. With his microscope he discovered a range of tiny things that people had never seen before. These included bacteria, blood cells, sperm and fibres in muscles. He examined the plaque from between people's teeth (it is said he collected some from old men who had never cleaned their teeth!). He reported seeing in the plaque 'very little living animalcules, very prettily a-moving.' At first, other scientists didn't believe him and he had to work quite hard to convince the scientific community that his discoveries were genuine.

Antonie's 'microscopes' were actually more like magnifying glasses as they had only one lens. Children could investigate with magnifying lenses or a digital microscope. They could be challenged to see something that none of their classmates had ever seen, or notice something no one else had noticed before. They might then need to think about the evidence they would need to present to their audience to convince them, without showing them the microscope. Antonie is still famous in the world of microbiology – there is a scientific journal published in his name. See http://lensonleeuwenhoek.net/index.html for more information.

Our Top 10 of Influential People in Primary Science Education

BELL, DEREK

Derek Bell has influenced science education in a variety of different ways. A former science teacher, he then moved into teacher education, and was researcher on the Nuffield Primary Science Processes and Concept Exploration (SPACE) Project. This involved finding out what ideas children held in different areas of primary science and developing strategies for helping them develop their concepts. He went on to co-ordinate the Nuffield Primary Science Project which developed from the SPACE research and led to the publication of a series of books for use by primary teachers. These publications made a significant contribution to the repertoire of teaching activities for science used in schools, and many teachers will use them without knowing where they began. He led the development of materials to support teachers in putting the SPACE Project approach into practice and, along with Ron Ritchie, he has written on effective subject leadership in the primary school. In a science education consultancy role he has offered guidance to many professional and government organisations in the UK and internationally. Chief Executive of the Association for Science Education (ASE) for over six years, he has been appointed as Head of Education at the Wellcome Trust, the UK's largest medical research charity, which also funds research in science education.

DRIVER, ROSALIND

Ros Driver (1941–97) was a highly influential science educator and researcher. During her career she contributed significantly to our understanding of how young people learn science. Driver showed us that students drew upon their own stable frameworks of concepts to explain simple events which were often radically different from 'correct' scientific knowledge. Rather than viewing students' knowledge as wrong, or 'misconceptions', Driver argued that learners' knowledge was internally coherent and useful and introduced the term 'alternate frameworks', suggesting we should respect and value all learners' ideas.

One of Driver's most influential publications was the 1985 book *Children's Ideas In Science*, an edited collection produced in collaboration with Edith Guesne and Andrée Tiberghien. In this book and others, Driver accounted for the development of conceptual understanding in science by referring to a constructivist view of learning, and her name became closely associated with work on constructivism in science education, particularly the pedagogy that emerges from a constructivist perspective.

During the 1980s, Ros Driver was the Director of the highly influential Children's Learning in Science Project (CLIS). One important aspect of the project was that it introduced a large group of science teachers to research and scholarship on teaching and learning science. Since then much work has been done around the concept of 'teacher as researcher.' Driver's work was focused on secondary school age children, so the reader may wonder why she is in our 'top 10' of primary educators. Driver didn't work in isolation, nor were her ideas only relevant to learners once they stepped foot in a secondary school. The CLIS Project laid the foundations for the science education community, some of whom had worked closely with Driver, to focus on primary school children for the Science Process and Concept Exploration (SPACE) Project discussed elsewhere in this book.

One of Driver's later interests involved developing notions about what might constitute an appropriate school science education for all future citizens, with the aim of promoting scientific literacy. It could be argued that the shape of the new primary curriculum owes a great deal to the work of this important and respected woman. For a much fuller account of her life's work, see *Rosalind Driver (1941–1997): A Tribute to Her Contribution to Research in Science Education* by John Leach (available at www.education.leeds.ac.uk/research/cssme/rosalind_driver.pdf).

FEASEY, ROSEMARY

Rosemary Feasey currently works as a private consultant for the Excellence in Primary Science Consultancy. Before this she worked at the University of Durham, where she undertook a wide range of research and CPD projects around investigative skills and creativity in science with beginning and serving primary teachers. After co-authoring the influential *Making Sense of Primary Science Investigations* with Anne Goldsworthy in 1997 – which introduced the 'Post-it'

method of planning fair tests – she was one of the three principal authors of the New Star Science scheme, which includes the explicit teaching of science enquiry skills within a carefully structured progression. More recently she has written *Creative Science – Achieving the Wow! Factor with 5–11 Year Olds* and *Jumpstart Science*, which focus on creative teaching approaches and children's questioning respectively. She is currently working with Lynne Bianchi on a pair of books to encourage primary teachers to make more use of the outdoor environment in their science teaching.

GOLDSWORTHY, ANNE

Many primary teachers, perhaps unknowingly, draw on the work of Anne Goldsworthy in their lessons. A former primary teacher herself, she has developed many strategies for supporting children in carrying out scientific enquiries. These have been disseminated through a range of publications including numerous ASE publications and the popular New Star Science scheme. Along with Rosemary Feasey, she popularised the 'Post-it' to planning an investigation that helps children identify the independent, dependent and control variables when they plan a fair test. As part of the influential AKSIS (ASE King's College Science Investigations in Schools) Project team from 1997 to 2000, she continued to identify aspects of scientific enquiry that children find difficult to understand, and developed teaching strategies to support their learning. She leads popular training courses for teachers and schools characterised by being interactive and with a sense of fun. Anyone who has taken part in these knows that Anne's hallmark is to enthuse and inspire, while her wry sense of humour shows she is very much in touch with the realities of classroom life.

She has had a long-standing involvement with the ASE, particularly the Welsh region, and acted as consultant on primary science to many professional and government organisations.

HARLEN, WYNNE

Throughout her long career, Wynne Harlen has been involved in teaching, research and policy in primary science education and assessment. In recognition of her achievements she was awarded the OBE for services to education in 1991. A description of her work reads like a definitive list of influential projects and ideas in primary science over the last fifty years. Her first forays into research began back in the 1960s at a time when Piaget's descriptions of children's ideas of scientific concepts were causing excitement. She wanted to discover the impact that children's experience of scientific activities had on their ideas. She concluded that the ideas held by those children who experience science were not markedly different from those 'untouched by science' but questioned the methodology of the type of research she had conducted. Using an appropriate methodology for her research was at the forefront of her mind then, and continued to be so in her subsequent work.

In the 1960s and early 1970s she was involved in evaluation of curriculum developments, including the Nuffield Junior Science Project and Science 5/13, the first large-scale attempt to introduce science into primary schools. In the late 1970s she identified what to assess in science at ages 11, 13 and 15 as part of her work for the Assessment of Performance Unit, and created a bank of test items. The science survey revealed children's strengths and weaknesses at the end of primary school and showed that subject-matter was important in the use

and development of processes – the content on which skills were used affected achievement. This work directly fed into two other notable research projects that further raised the status of primary school science: the Children's Learning in Science Project (CLIS) led by Rosalind Driver, and her own research with the Science Processes and Concepts Exploration Project (SPACE) team on children's ideas in science. At the same time in the late 1980s and early 1990s she worked on the Science Teachers' Action Research Project (STAR) which focused on development of scientific ideas by use of process skills.

In 1988, when the Education Reform Act created the National Curriculum, the profile of science at primary level had been raised by her efforts and others to such an extent that there was no question that science should be included in the new curriculum. Furthermore, working groups were established first in science along with English and mathematics, because these were considered to be at the centre of the curriculum, and these subjects were afforded special status by being singled out for national testing.

In the late 1990s and 2000s she led the Assessment and Learning Research Synthesis Group (ALRSG) and conducted four reviews of research relating to assessment. She directed, on behalf of Assessment Reform Group (she was a founder member), the Assessment Systems for the Future Project which sought to clarify the role that assessment by teachers can play in assessment systems. She was to question the effect that being a core subject had had on science teaching. The 'high stakes' nature of national tests had led to teaching to the tests, and their narrow focus provided a poor picture of pupils' achievement. However, the consequences for individuals and for society of marginalising primary school science justify its inclusion as a core subject. As an advocate of science education at primary level, she can lay claim to being one of its most influential figures over the last fifty years.

For her personal description of her research see the Sci-tutors website at www.scitutors.org.uk/, and for the history of science teaching in the primary school (a history which she played a major part in shaping) see the Wellcome Trust website at www.wellcome.ac.uk/.

JOHNSTON, JANE

If you are particularly interested in current developments in scientific learning in the early years, then you need take a look at the work of Jane Johnston. Jane has published a range of work that explores new research and thinking in early years and science education. Some key titles include: *Early Explorations in Science* (2005), 'Emergent science' (2008), 'What is creativity in science education?' (2009) and 'Science at Key Stage 1' (2009).

Jane's latest contribution is the development of thinking on 'emergent science', which focuses on the way children aged 0–8 years old develop their scientific ideas, skills and attitudes, and explores the factors that effect that development. There is an emergent science newsletter which can be subscribed to by contacting Jane on j.s.johnston@bishopg.ac.uk.

NAYLOR, STUART AND KEOGH, BRENDA

Stuart and Brenda are best known for inventing concept cartoons, a way to help children express their scientific ideas by identifying with cartoon characters discussing a phenomenon such as the melting of a snowman or falling of bungee-jumpers. The ideas expressed by these characters are based on research from the Science Processes and Concept Exploration (SPACE) Project about children's commonly held alternative frameworks, so there will usually be some debate and discussion about which character has 'got it right.' If, on subsequent investigation, the character whose ideas most closely matched a child's own turns out to be wrong, it is more likely to lead to conceptual change without losing face in front of classmates than if he or she had suggested the idea as their own. Concept cartoons are available in books and 'big books', posters and CD-ROMs, all published by Stuart and Brenda's own publishing company, Millgate House Education (www.millgatehouse.co.uk). Formerly working at Manchester Metropolitan University, Stuart and Brenda are now successful educational consultants, following up their concept cartoons with the use of puppets to discuss scientific ideas and the promotion of active assessment strategies in science.

PIAGET, JEAN

Jean Piaget (1896–1980) was a Swiss psychologist whose theories on cognitive development have had a profound influence on the teaching of primary science. His ideas on stages of cognitive development have been criticised by others such as Margaret Donaldson, but still particularly relevant to young children's scientific learning are Piaget's mechanisms for cognitive growth and change – assimilation and accommodation. Here he advocated that learners assimilate new items of learning by fitting them into their existing conceptual frameworks (schemata). However, sometimes the learner may have to accommodate his or her knowledge base by adapting schemata to take in some new information (Davies and Howe 2003). For example, a child may believe that a plant needs light to grow (schema). It may be easy for that child to assimilate into this framework the observation that as a water lily grows it sends out leaves to the surface of the pond. However, observations of a plant placed in the dark reveal it will grow rapidly as it seeks a source of light. This new information may challenge the child's thinking: the child's schema may need to be adapted. This adaptive model of learning proposed by Piaget is incorporated into the constructivist teaching sequence as the restructuring phase, when the learner is developing his or her viewpoint towards that of currently accepted scientific theory. Another Piagetian view, that learning is an active process whereby the learner constructs knowledge by testing his or her own theories of the world, has also influenced primary school practice. The constructivist view of learning values the importance of eliciting these ideas and theories. Indeed, the work of the Science Processes and Concepts Exploration (SPACE) Project revealed a range of ideas that children had worked out for themselves, and it was clear these should not be ignored but should be taken as a starting point for further development.

RITCHIE, RON

Ron has contributed to primary science and technology education in two particular respects. First, through his teaching at universities in the west of England he has enthused many undergraduates, trainee and in-service teachers to teach in creative and learner-centred ways. During his early career, Ron developed strong pedagogic principles informed by social-constructivist views of learning, building on the work of Ros Driver, Wynne Harlen and others. These principles have always informed his work and in particular his second contribution to the field, a key publication: *Primary Science – Making It Work* in 1997 (second edition, published by David Fulton). He and his co-author Chris Ollerenshaw explored reflective teaching and active forms of pupil learning through case studies that captured the richness and vitality of primary

science. The book has a significant influence on the authors of this encyclopedia in informing their own approach to primary science teaching. Ron is currently Assistant Vice-Chancellor and Dean of the School of Education at the University of the West of England and will probably be rather amused to find his name appearing in our list.

VYGOTSKY, LEV (1896–1934)

Lev Vygotsky was a Russian who wrote on education and psychological theory and has gone on to have a big impact on views of learning internationally. He was born at the same time as Piaget, but had very different cultural influences on his thinking; the Russian revolution had recently taken place and Marxist ideas dominated. In these Marxist ideas individuals were seen as secondary to the needs of the 'collective', of society as a whole. Individual success was seen as a reflection of the success of the wider culture. Vygotsky saw children's thinking as something they acquired from the surrounding culture. Children internalise the kinds of ideas and ways of thinking that are in the social environment around them and make their own use of them.

His main contribution to science education is that social interaction plays an important role in developing children's understanding of scientific concepts. Vygotsky (1978) states: 'Every function in the child's cultural development appears twice: first, on the social level, and later, on the individual level; first, between people (interpsychological) and then inside the child (intrapsychological).' He saw ideas as first being developed between people and then being taken on by the individual. He developed the concept which has been translated from Russian as the 'Zone of Proximal Development' (ZPD), which is the difference between what a learner can do alone and what he or she can do with the support of others or in collaboration with others. Vygotsky argued that providing this support within the ZPD was crucial in supporting learning. This was a challenge to the predominance of ideas in western education that focused on the individual, natural development and the role of hands-on experience in learning in science. Vygotsky's work suggested a more active role for teachers; identifying the ZPD for each child and using social interaction, particularly talk, to work within it.

Vygotsky himself valued collaborative dialogue with others, and after his death from tuberculosis in 1934 other members of his discussion groups took his ideas forward, sharing and developing them. For further information on the theories of Vygotsky, see the entries on social constructivism and sociocultural perspectives in the main body of this encyclopedia.

Bibliography

A full list of references can be found in the main body of the encyclopedia for each of the five boxed entries. These apart, a list for references and websites that have been cited directly in the text can be found below. In addition we have included a brief list of books for further reading, all of which we found useful in writing this encyclopedia.

REFERENCES

Adey, P., Robertson, A. and Venville G. (2001) *Let's Think: A Programme for Developing Thinking with Five and Six Year Olds.* London: nferNelson.

Adey, P., Nagy, F., Robertson, A., Serret, N. and Wadsworth, P. (2003) *Let's Think Through Science: Developing Thinking with Seven and Eight Year Olds.* London: nferNelson.

Association for Science Education (ASE) (2001) *Be Safe! Health and Safety in Primary School Science and Technology,* third edition. Hatfield: ASE.

Black, P. and Wiliam, D. (1998) *Inside the Black Box: Raising Standards through Classroom Assessment.* London: nferNelson.

Carson, R. (1998) *The Sense of Wonder.* London: HarperCollins.

Carson, R. (2000) *Silent Spring.* London: Penguin Books.

Cole, B. (1995) *Mummy Laid an Egg!* London: Red Fox.

DATA (Design and Technology Association) (1999) *DATA Helpsheets for Year 2000 and Beyond.* Wellesbourne: DATA.

Davies, D. and Howe, A. (2003) *Teaching Science and Design and Technology in the Early Years.* London: David Fulton.

Davies, N. (2004) *Poo.* London: Walker Books.

Dawkins, R. (1976) *The Selfish Gene.* Oxford: Oxford University Press.

Dawkins, R. (1986) *The Blind Watchmaker.* New York: W.W. Norton.

Dawkins, R. (2006) *The God Delusion.* New York: Bantam Books.

Department for Education and Employment (DfEE)/Qualifications and Curriculum Authority (QCA) (1998) *A Scheme of Work for Key Stages 1 and 2 Science.* London: QCA Publications.

Department for Education and Employment (DfEE)/Qualifications and Curriculum Authority (QCA) (1999) *The National Curriculum for Science.* London: DfEE/QCA.

Department for Education and Skills (DfES) (2004) *Drugs: Guidance for Schools.* Nottingham: DfES.

Driver, R. (1983) *The Pupil as Scientist.* Milton Keynes: Open University Press.

Goldsworthy, A. and Holmes, M. (1999) *Teach It, Do It, Let's Get To It.* Hatfield: ASE.

Goldsworthy, A., Watson, R. and Wood-Robinson, V. (2000) *Investigations: Developing Understanding.* Hatfield: ASE.

Harlen, W. (2006) *Teaching, Learning and Assessing Science 5–12,* fourth edition. London: Sage.

Harlen, W. and Qualter, A. (2009) *The Teaching of Science in Primary Schools*, fifth edition. London: David Fulton.

Hawking, S. (1988) *A Brief History of Time*. London: Bantam.

Howe, A., Davies, D., McMahon, K., Towler, L., Collier, C. and Scott, T. (2009) *Science 5–11: A Guide for Teachers*. London: Routledge.

Johnston, J. (2005) *Early Explorations in Science*, second edition. Maidenhead: Open University Press.

Johnston, J. (2008) 'Emergent science', *Education in Science*, 227: 26–8.

Johnston, J. (2009) 'What is creativity in science education?' in A. Wilson (ed.) *Creativity in Primary Education*, second edition. Exeter: Learning Matters.

Johnston, J. (2009) 'Science at Key Stage 1', in T. Bruce (ed.) *Early Childhood*, second edition. London: Sage.

Kuhn, T. (1970) *The Structure of Scientific Revolutions*, second edition. Chicago, IL: Chicago University Press.

Ollerenshaw, C. and Ritchie, R. (1997) *Primary Science – Making It Work*, second edition. London: David Fulton.

Osborne, J., Black, P., Smith, M. and Meadows, J. (1991) *SPACE Research Report: Electricity*. Liverpool: Liverpool University Press.

Palmer, J. and Suggate, J. (2005) 'Children's reasoning about global environmental issues: deforestation and global warming', *Primary Science Review*, 87: 12–16.

Rogoff, B. (1990) *Apprenticeship in Thinking: Cognitive Development in Social Context*. New York: Oxford University Press.

Russell, T. and Watt, D. (1990) *SPACE Research Report: Evaporation and Condensation*. Liverpool: Liverpool University Press.

Scott, P. (1987) *A Constructivist View of Teaching and Learning*. Leeds: Children's Learning in Science Project, University of Leeds.

Stannard, R. (2005) *The Time and Space of Uncle Albert*. London: Faber and Faber.

Vygotsky, L. (1978) *Mind in Society: The Development of Higher Psychological Process*. Cambridge, MA: Harvard University Press.

WEBSITES

Association for Science Education: www.ase.org.uk (last accessed 7 July 2010).

AstraZeneca Science Teaching Trust: www.azteachscience.co.uk (last accessed 7 July 2010).

BBC: www.bbc.co.uk (last accessed 7 July 2010).

British Nutrition Foundation: www.nutrition.org.uk (last accessed 7 July 2010).

Brunel University: www.brunel.ac.uk/about/history/ikb (last accessed 7 July 2010).

Buglife: www.buglife.org.uk (last accessed 7 July 2010).

Concept Cartoons: www.conceptcartoons.com (last accessed 7 July 2010).

Crocodile Clips: www.crocodile-clips.com (last accessed 7 July 2010).

Department for Children, Schools and Families (Publications): http://publications.dcsf.gov.uk (last accessed 7 July 2010).

Department for Children, Schools and Families (Standards Site): www.standards.dfes.gov.uk (last accessed 7 July 2010).

Drug Education Forum: www.drugeducationforum.com (last accessed 7 July 2010).

Edwin Hubble: www.edwinhubble.com (last accessed 7 July 2010).

Flowol: www.flowol.com (last accessed 7 July 2010).

Food Standards Agency: www.food.gov.uk (last accessed 7 July 2010).

Frog Life: http://froglife.org (last accessed 7 July 2010).

Leeds University: www.education.leeds.ac.uk/research/cssme/rosalind_driver.pdf (last accessed 7 July 2010).

Lens on Leeuwenhoek: http://lensonleeuwenhoek.net/index.html (last accessed 7 July 2010).

London Zoo: www.zls.org (last accessed 7 July 2010).
Millgate House Education: www.millgatehouse.co.uk (last accessed 7 July 2010).
NASA: www.nasa.gov (last accessed 7 July 2010).
Nuffield Curriculum Programme: www.nuffieldcurriculumcentre.org (last accessed 7 July 2010).
Rachel Carson: www.rachelcarson.org (last accessed 7 July 2010).
Royal Horticultural Society: www.rhs.org.uk (last accessed 7 July 2010).
Royal Society for Chemistry: www.rsc.org (last accessed 7 July 2010).
Royal Society for the Prevention of Accidents: www.rospa.com (last accessed 7 July 2010).
Royal Society for the Prevention of Cruelty to Animals: www.rspca.org.uk (last accessed 7 July 2010).
Royal Society for the Protection of Birds: www.rspb.org.uk (last accessed 7 July 2010).
San Diego Zoo: www.sandiegozoo.org (last accessed 7 July 2010).
Science Learning Centres: www.sciencelearningcentres.org.uk (last accessed 7 July 2010).
Sci-Tutors: www.scitutors.org.uk (last accessed 7 July 2010).
Stephen Hawking: www.hawking.org.uk (last accessed 7 July 2010).
Teachernet: www.teachernet.gov.uk (last accessed 7 July 2010).
Thomas Edison: www.thomasedison.com (last accessed 7 July 2010).
Wellcome Trust: www.wellcome.ac.uk (last accessed 7 July 2010).
West Point Bridge Design Contest: http://bridgecontest.usma.edu/ (last accessed 7 July 2010).
Wikipedia: http://en.wikipedia.org (last accessed 7 July 2010).
YouTube: www.youtube.com (last accessed 7 July 2010).

FURTHER READING

Davies, D. and Howe, A. (2003) *Teaching Science and Design and Technology in the Early Years.* London: David Fulton
    A book written by two of the authors of this encyclopedia which focuses on the contribution made by science and technology to young children's learning.

Harlen, W. (2006) *Teaching, Learning and Assessing Science 5–12*, fourth edition. London: Sage.
    We have referred to this book directly in the encyclopedia, but we would like to draw your attention to it as a very useful general text on primary science teaching and learning.

Harlen, W. and Qualter, A. (2009) *The Teaching of Science in Primary Schools*, fifth edition. London: David Fulton.
    This book is also referred to directly in the text, but we feel it deserves inclusion here as it is a book that discusses many aspects of teaching primary science with a strong emphasis on constructivist approaches to learning.

Howe, A., Davies, D., McMahon, K., Towler, L., Collier, C. and Scott, T. (2009) *Science 5–11: A Guide for Teachers.* London: Routledge.
    This book was written by four of the authors of this encyclopedia. Its outlines for teachers' subject knowledge and approaches to teaching science have informed our writing of the encyclopedia.

Wenham, M. and Ovens, P. (2010) *Understanding Primary Science*, third edition. London: Sage.
    This book provides clear and detailed explanations of the areas of subject knowledge primary school teachers need.